Success and Survival in the Family-Owned Business

Success and Survival in the Family-Owned Business

Pat B. Alcorn

McGraw-Hill Book Company

New York   St. Louis   San Francisco   Auckland   Bogotá   Hamburg
Johannesburg   London   Madrid   Mexico   Montreal   New Delhi
Panama   Paris   São Paulo   Singapore   Sydney   Tokyo   Toronto

Library of Congress Cataloging in Publication Data

Alcorn, Pat B.
  Success and survival in the family-owned business.

  Includes index.
  1. Family corporations—Management. I. Title.
HD62.25. A43   658'.045   80-28976
ISBN 0-07-000961-9

1234567890   DODO   8987654321

The editors for this book were William R. Newton and Esther
Gelatt, the designer was Mark E. Safran, and the production
supervisor was Thomas G. Kowalczyk. It was set in Garamond by
David E. Seham, Inc.

Printed and bound by R. R. Donnelley & Sons Company.

To my husband, Jay Lehr, without whose harassment this book would never have been written, and to my colleague, Edwin Cobb, for his invaluable assistance.

About the Author

Pat Alcorn was born and raised in Eden, North Carolina, a town with an economic base of small family-owned businesses. Throughout her youth, she was fascinated with the perpetuation of family operations, as peers were reared and educated to join the family firm.

After moving to Columbus, Ohio, she and her husband became the management team of a trade and professional society, the National Water Well Association, which in their 10-year tenure grew from a staff of 4 to one of 80 and became an internationally respected education, research, and publishing organization. Her interest and love of the family operation grew as she worked with the thousands of family-owned businesses in the water well industry. She developed business lectures and consulting services geared to focus on the special problems inherent in the family business, problems she had witnessed in her childhood and now experienced as a working adult. Few business difficulties and opportunities produced by the family operation are addressed in the normal educational process, so her special focus became much in demand. In 1974, she began interviewing family operations in a variety of professions to document the unique nature of the family business.

In her own company, she lived the problems, as she and her husband fostered the hiring of relatives in their business. Recognizing the trials, tribulations, and joys—and finding a void of literary material to assist in solving the problems and seizing the opportunities— she began writing *Success and Survival in the Family-Owned Business*.

The synergistic business relationship shared by Pat Alcorn and her husband, Dr. Jay Lehr, is the foundation for a broad spectrum of shared interests. The 70 hours they spend each week managing a business are well known to the family operator, and they attribute their successful marriage to the total sharing of work and play. Her energy is fortified by unusual athletic prowess which includes daily participation in such sports as running, biking, racket ball, or weight lifting.

Contents

Preface

There is little unique about our experiences as we follow our separate paths through life. Yet people involved in family business ventures believe the majority of the problems they encounter, as individuals and as families, to be unique to their special circumstances and interrelated personalities.

Few families have the opportunity to compare notes with others about their problems and the associated solutions. No broadly active groups have facilitated the cross-fertilization of information. Helpful literature on the subject is all but absent. Less than five major books have ever addressed the problems of family-owned business, and none exists with the personal approach I have attempted in this text.

My work as a writer, lecturer, and consultant on family-owned business problems has brought me into contact with literally thousands of families all across the United States. It does not take long to learn that the problems inherent in working for the entrepreneurial father—the rivalry of siblings, the complication of in-laws, and the countless other familial relationships—are the same from Maine to California.

Operating a successful business in our complicated society is tough. The job of operating a family-owned business is made tougher still by natural family rivalries. Unless all family members face up to their honest and natural emotions, the business suffers.

This book should make every reader aware that the problems plaguing his or her family business are not unusual. The entrepreneur is not alone with a problem: It has appeared before, will appear again, and can be solved through study of the experience of others.

The book will also attempt to record the rebirth and development of an organized and humanized approach to a special area of business management previously ignored by educators, writers, and consultants. While more than 90 percent of the one million American corporations are privately owned family businesses, their story is absent from the business literature and from the classrooms of our institutions of higher learning. Rather than being unified into a powerful, collective business population, these businesses have been maintained in isolation without a common knowledge or power base.

If the American family is truly the backbone of American life, so is the family-owned business an integral part of our nation's economy and prosperity. The family-owned business, however, is too often hidden in the back rooms and kitchens of its family leaders. Its personal and emotional problems escape the kind of intellectual inspection that can effectively separate real and imagined problems. Sound business management needs to be combined with psychological and sociological understanding of family-owned business problems; solutions must differ from those that apply to the less personal world of corporate business.

To make all this clear, I have included many real-life examples of families, in a variety of localities and businesses, who face remarkably similar problems. The solutions require far more than the ABC's of business management. They require a thorough understanding of interpersonal relationships in which blood is thicker than water and emotional desires are more important than the bottom lines of balance sheets.

Throughout the text the reader will note the preponderance of male-dominated businesses. This emphasis is not intended to deprecate the role of women; it merely reflects their previously subordinate role in the vast majority of family businesses. The emergence of the corporate female manager will undoubtedly result in more family businesses dominated by women.

This is a pioneering text in terms of the subject matter and its treatment. It is not to be considered a comprehensive treatise on the subject but rather the beginning of a literary foundation. This new literary tradition can help the family-owned business prosper in the future by clearing up the mystery of the complicated emotions which so strongly influence its passage through the seas of the business world.

Pat B. Alcorn

Success and Survival in the Family-Owned Business

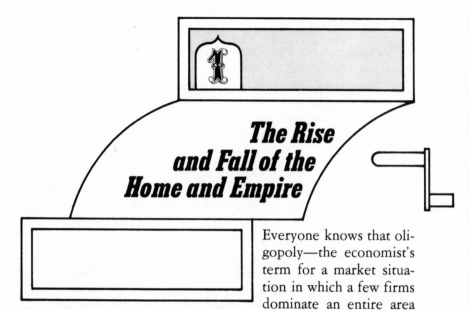

The Rise and Fall of the Home and Empire

Everyone knows that oligopoly—the economist's term for a market situation in which a few firms dominate an entire area of business—is the most notable feature of the American economy. The Fortune 500 and all that. Giant corporations owned by stockholders who cast proxy votes and scarcely know what business they are "in" except at dividend time. Colossal conglomerates ruled by faceless managers and technocrats with multimillion dollar salaries. So what else is there to know about American business? Quite a lot, actually.

Of Families and Business

The economic species known as small business—for the moment, firms with sales under $100 million a year—is not only surviving in the age of bigness, it is playing an important role. Small companies carry 58 percent of all American workers on their payrolls and account for 43 percent of the gross national product.[1]

Approximately 98 percent of the millions of corporations in the United States are not controlled by disembodied stockholders and managers and are not industry giants. Instead, they are privately owned and operated, and the majority of them are family-owned businesses. Add to this the thousands upon thousands of proprietorships and partnerships in which the work is done, the rewards are gained, and the losses are sustained by people who are related to each other by blood or marriage, and the family-owned business (FOB) becomes a significant part of the American economy. And

1

such businesses can lay claim to a goodly chunk of the human side of American capitalism, the joys as well as the sweat and tears.

The emphasis should probably be placed on the tears because family businesses, on the average, do not have long lives. They tend to rise suddenly from a burst of energy by hard-driving entrepreneurs who turn their homes into business empires if they can, and they fall just as suddenly, unable to carry on in the footsteps of the founding father. Family businesses usually fail in the first 10 years of operation; if they escape the grasp of this statistic, they are likely to be successful for an average of 24 years. It is more than a coincidence that the average time between the start of a family operation and the death of the founder is 24 years.

Despite the gloomy prospects for long-run success in family-owned business, millions of people continue to try. The desire to be one's own boss, to build something that bears one's name, and to see the magic phrase "and Son" added to that name is apparently a deep-seated drive amid the endless complexities of the human condition. (Perhaps the desire to add "and Daughter" to the company name will some day be an equally strong motivation.)

American filmdom, that great reflector and shaper of the nation's ways and means, treats the theme often, and the story has a sad ending in most cases. In *Twelve Angry Men,* Lee J. Cobb is ready to cast his jury vote to convict an innocent youth because he is down on young people in general. The reason emerges as he finally redeems himself with a "not guilty" vote: He had started a trucking business with one broken-down vehicle and built it into a significant business with a large fleet of trucks and hundreds of employees. His son, whom he dearly wanted to take over the business, had deserted trucks for more frivolous pursuits. In *The Long Hot Summer,* Orson Welles has lived by his wits, legally and not so legally, to build an empire in land and stores, but his only son, Tony Franciosa, is more interested in enjoying the pleasures of his beautiful young wife than in learning the tricks of storekeeping, farming, and horse trading, and so Welles gives up on him. "I put down a big footprint, boy, and said 'you will fit it' and you didn't. Go fishin', boy." In *Hud,* Paul Newman actually tries to have his father, Melvyn Douglas, declared insane so that he can take over the cattle ranch and put in some oil wells, which his father detests and has refused to do. ("You can't prowl amongst 'em.") Fortunately, the old man spares himself this indignity by dying first, and the loathsome Hud (Newman) gets the place anyway.

A Case of Rise and Fall

Most cases in real life, of course, are more complicated than those in the scripts that filmmakers must chop to 1 hour and 30 minutes. In some cases, success and failure come in the same scenario; the business fails, but the son tries to resurrect it. Perhaps the best way to illustrate this is with a case history from real life. The story speaks not only to the failure-success problem but also to some of the specifics of life in the family-owned business. (The actual names of people and places have been changed to avoid possible embarrassment to living persons, but the story is true.)

The Woodward Well Company had a very inauspicious beginning a few years before the United States entered World War I. Chester Woodward was a farmer in Illinois and, like many farmers unable to afford skilled artisans for every job, he became a sort of fix-it man himself. This involved fixing the pump that supplied water to the farm. Other farmers less skilled with their hands heard of Chester's prowess, and soon he was cleaning and repairing his neighbors' wells. As more and more people sought his advice and services, Chester thought more about business and less about farming. He hired a few people and began drilling wells and installing pumps, and the Woodward Well Company was formed.

At the time the business was founded, Chester's brother, Jacob, was the sales manager for a pump-manufacturing company in Chicago. Some 20 years later, during the mid-Depression years, Chester became physically unable to handle the well-drilling business, and Jacob took over the management of his brother's firm while still managing his own pump-sales organization. As the business grew, Jacob began to devote more and more of his time to the water well contracting business. It was after this time that the Woodward legend grew. Beginning with two locations, one in Chicago and one in Joliet, the entire operation was finally moved to Joliet, where it began to climb to a $6 million a year water well business.

Jacob Woodward was a driving entrepreneur. The familiar "business-is-life" syndrome took over and all social life faded into the background. He worked 7 days a week to expand his business to include all phases of the development of ground water, including the water and waste treatment fields. In fact, it was commonly said that Jacob Woodward could sell oil to the Arabs.

Many businesspeople climbing to the top leave a trail of bodies behind them. Not so with Jacob Woodward. Although he built an empire that towered above others in the industry, he managed to hold on to the friendship and respect of his competitors. On many occasions, competitors beat Woodward on contract bids but called on him for help when they found the jobs over their heads. He always sent crews and machinery to assist them.

The quintessential self-made man, Jacob ran the business in a patriarchal manner. If he needed machinery for a job, he ordered it and informed the "purchasing department" by memo. He made all decisions and interviewed all prospective employees, even down to the level of mechanics' assistants. The business was a "family" operation at all levels. Most company personnel came from the families of current employees. Many of the drill rigs were operated by father-and-son teams or at least by crew members who were related to each other. The employees were thus fiercely loyal to Jacob Woodward and he to them.

By this time, hard-driving-father-with-up-and-coming-son problems began to emerge. Jacob's son, Warren, studied business management in college, did a stint in the Air Force, and then came into his father's business, beginning as a helper on a drill rig. He was ultimately promoted to vice-president of the company; but with his father making all the decisions, Warren felt more like an office boy with a title than a responsible executive. Not feeling that he was sharing in the growth of the company, he thought often of seeking employment elsewhere, but this was far from easy to do. Prospective employers whose slots he would have loved to fill shied away because they felt he would ultimately return to his father's business. Thus, Warren devoted more time to his family than his father had ever devoted to his. But he still increased in stature in the water well industry. Although Jacob was proud of his son, there were frictions. Jacob was furious when he was introduced as "Warren Woodward's father"; he was accustomed to hearing Warren introduced as "Jacob Woodward's son."

By the 1960s, Woodward Well Company was the largest privately owned water well business in the industry. A staff of 60 at the Joliet headquarters supported 125 permanent employees and over 20 drill rigs in the field. In addition to its basic business of providing safe and efficient water systems for industrial and municipal users, the company was constantly involved in new and innovative ventures. Woodward pioneered the development of well water for air cooling; it installed a system of vertical and horizontal wells at beaches to provide crystal-clear water for swimming pools; it established a state-approved laboratory for biological and chemical testing of water, a laboratory staffed by three graduate chemists and assistants.

The mushrooming growth of Woodward Well Company had been a source of concern to its financial backers for some time, but things continued to work out, most people said, because of the genius of Jacob Woodward. But recession struck in the 1970s, and there was a general decline in business.

It was the beginning of the end for the company, but Jacob Woodward insisted that he had weathered many storms and could weather this one. He refused to lay off loyal employees and sent drillers earning over $9 an hour out to polish their equipment. Soon, payroll expenses and overhead were far outstripping revenue. Finally, sixty employees were laid off, but it was too late. The bank called in a loan. State and federal taxes were overdue, and the government tax collector seized the business assets. The remaining equipment was sold at auction. The combination home and business empire that Jacob Woodward built had fallen.

But life goes on, even when the business collapses, and Jacob did not admit defeat; he began a career as a consultant—in his eighties. His own man for the first time, Warren opened a new business, Warren Woodward Associates, and announced that he would continue to be an active participant in—what else?—the water well industry.

What does this saga tell us about the problems and prospects of the family-owned business? First, it suggests that there is still a place for small businesses, a great many of which will be family-owned, in the American economy and that such businesses are worthy of further study as social phenomena with a view to their long-run preservation. After all, there is a great deal to be said in favor of the indomitable spirit of people like Jacob Woodward, who built a major business, saw it crumble, and still could say, as he was reported to have said, "You can't drown in your sorrow," and Warren Woodward, who vowed that the Woodward name and reputation would grow again as they had for the past 60 years.

In the days of assembly line workers who are known only by number, there is much to be said for having the boss know and care about the employees. Also, there is something very laudable about being able to climb to the top of one's ladder and get there with reputation and friendships still intact. When the Woodward Well Company put up its equipment at auction, drillers from all over the country were shocked, and a typical comment was, "Why didn't you call me? I would have helped." And surely there is more to life than balance sheets. Is it an inexorable law that people should prefer reaping dividends from oil wells to prowling among cattle?

Even hard-boiled economists who are more comfortable talking in terms of cost-benefit ratios rather than indomitable spirits and the joys of cattle should still be able to recognize the practical virtue of small businesses. Small companies are an important source of business innovation—witness Woodward's pioneering efforts—and new jobs. Two-thirds of all the new jobs created in the American economy between 1960 and 1976 were generated by companies with twenty or fewer employees.[2] A great many of these are family affairs.

If there is a place for the family-owned business, however, the FOB should probably be kept in its place. It is probable that the close relationships—friendly or hostile—between the people and the informal procedures involved in a family-owned business will not prevent the business from functioning successfully in a clearly defined area of work. When expansion sets in, however, the old methods become a handicap. When the company has nearly 200 employees, for example, it is not really efficient for the boss to interview every job applicant and order every piece of equipment personally. With bigness, experience tells us, comes the need for delegation of authority, formal procedures, and impersonal decisions. When the Woodward Well Company expanded wildly, it lacked a sound managerial base and was unable to cope realistically with recession and a sharp business decline. Of course, many family businesses are certainly big (Ford, for example), but they succeeded by shedding many of the attributes of the classic family-owned business. The entrepreneur who founds the business must realize that, at some point, he must face this choice—and make a choice.

It is nearly equally certain, however—our third lesson—that the entrepreneur will try to avoid this choice. The same personality that drove him to go out on his own in the first place is likely to convince him that he can continue to conquer new worlds while doing business in the same way that made him successful to start with. In Hegelian terms, the entrepreneur is driven to create the means of his own destruction.

The fourth lesson to be learned from the Woodward story is that once the business becomes the entrepreneur's whole life, he is headed for trouble. His business becomes his wife (or at least his mistress), and the employees become his children. His duty is to correct their foibles but to stand by them in any case. Had Jacob Woodward begun to cut his payroll and overhead as soon as they

could not be justified by revenues, he might have escaped the ultimate disaster. But to the patriarch in the family-owned business, this
is unthinkable. Do you send your children away from home just because you are having trouble feeding them? Even in good times, if
the relative of an employee needs a job, should he not be given
preference? Thus, the business ceases to be a business and becomes
an extended family; when forced by adversity to react like a business,
it cannot.

The Woodward story also gives some insights into the father-son
problem in the family-owned business. The problem could be characterized as how to let the son shine in without having to dodge a
chip off the old block. Probably, Jacob Woodward should have given
his son a greater measure of responsibility sooner. However, not all
sons are above shoving the old man aside as soon as they get the
chance. Those movies again. In *Broken Lance,* to avoid having his
property taken in a lawsuit, Spencer Tracy divides the ranch among
his sons. Now legal owners, the unscrupulous sons, led by Richard
Widmark, promptly shove the ailing Tracy aside, selling off land to
copper mines, opening offices in town, and generally destroying the
business. As might be expected, Widmark comes to a bad end, but
by then the damage has been done and the father is dead.

The trick, obviously, is to teach the son the business—only if he
wants to learn it—bring him along gradually—if he wants to come
along—and then let him take over—when he's ready. Dream on. As
with all Aristotelianisms, if people really could follow such advice,
they wouldn't have to be given it. Having the father decide when the
son is ready to run the business is like having colonial rulers decide
when the native population is ready for self-government. The answer
is always "tomorrow"—and tomorrow never comes.

The Sarnoff Saga

The problem of father-son transitions is not limited to small businesses or to firms that are family-owned. When a family-*operated*
business is owned by outside stockholders, a new element enters the
equation. What can happen in such a situation when the son cannot
work his mentor's magic is illustrated by the Sarnoff saga, previously
chronicled in print media.

David Sarnoff came from Minsk to Manhattan at the turn of the
twentieth century and rose from the streets to become the ruler of

one of U.S. industry's greatest personal autocracies—Radio Corp. of America (RCA). After learning telegraphy as a teenager, he took a job as an operator with the Marconi Wireless Telegraph Co. of America. His big break came during one of America's most stunning tragedies, the sinking of the *Titanic* in 1912. For 72 hours at his post in New York, Sarnoff tapped the news to the world. Radio communication became the talk of the town—and Sarnoff became commercial manager of American Marconi. General Electric bought the company after World War I, changed its name to Radio Corp. of America, and installed Sarnoff as general manager.

David Sarnoff was a salesman who compelled others to share his dreams and make them come true by sheer force of personality. Not a scientist, he could induce scientists to invest their brainpower; not personally rich, he could induce capitalists to invest their money; not the company's majority stockholder—he owned only one-third of 1 percent of RCA stock in 1930—he became its president the same year. By that time, RCA was mass-producing home radio sets, had established a broadcasting network (NBC), and was beginning to move into the chancy field of television. He predicted correctly that color TV would be a commercial success, although his concomitant prediction that this would lead to a new era of art appreciation was far off the mark. By the time David Sarnoff stepped down as company head in 1968, RCA had become a $3.3 billion a year company. His own small slice of stock was worth in excess of $7 million. Sarnoff had some spectacular failures—most notably, a misadventure with computers—and probably had too much faith in technology as a means of social advancement, but his driving, even messianic, leadership had taken "his" company to the top.

Robert Sarnoff, age 51, succeeded his father as president of RCA in 1968 and as chairman in 1970, and it appeared that family domination of the giant corporation would continue as before. But in 1975, the RCA board suddenly handed Robert his walking papers and RCA was left without a Sarnoff at the top for the first time in 45 years. What had happened?

In the first place, nothing in Robert's training seemed suitable to prepare him to lead a major communications and electronics corporation. He was a Harvard graduate who had had brief stays in law school, the Navy, and the publishing business before coming to work for his father in 1948. He started as a time salesman for the National Broadcasting Company, an RCA subsidiary, and became NBC president in 1955. But like most self-made men, David Sarnoff had created a tough act for his son to follow. In his years with RCA, Robert could not escape his role as the "general's boy" (David was made a brigadier general during World War II). He could not even shake the nickname Bobby, which further symbolized his position as the kid who could never be quite the man his father was.

Indeed, this seemed to be the case. While his father's risky ventures had, by and large, led to company gold, Robert's similar efforts brought only company woe. He did abandon the computer business, into which his father had invested millions, because profits seemed a long way off, but he began to acquire a hodgepodge of companies that had to be merged somehow with an old-line electronics company. In short order, RCA was into car rentals (Hertz), publishing (Random House), real estate (Cushman and Wakefield), and carpets (Coronet Industries). Even David Sarnoff might have had difficulty turning this conglomeration into a unified business, and Robert had no success at all.

Although RCA's board of directors went along with the acquisitions, there was grumbling and there were even a few suggestions that Bobby was spending too much time attending to his wife, Metropolitan Opera Singer Anna Moffo, and not enough time tending to business. RCA profits declined 38 percent in 1974 and continued to slide in 1975. At this point the ax fell.

David Sarnoff had left office with a handpicked board that could be counted on to do Robert's bidding. By 1975, however, there were many new faces on the board, faces that did not view RCA as a family matter. Robert's demand for a salary increase—his salary was already at a level that would make most people blush—proved to be the final step toward his undoing. After making his wishes regarding a pay increase known, Robert left New York and toured the Far East and Australia with his wife. With the cat away, the mice met in conclave, but they were not in a playful mood. When Robert returned, he was told bluntly: "No salary hike." He promptly resigned, though according to one story, he had no difficulty being prompt because the board had already drawn up his letter of resignation. Anthony Conrad, RCA president, replaced Robert as chairman.

Clearly, Robert had misjudged the situation, assuming that Sarnoff and RCA were synonymous and ignoring the fact that trouble was brewing. The power base left by his father had eroded. Because of Robert's frequent journeys, Conrad had already assumed many of the chairman's duties, and the directors called upon by David Sarnoff to elect his son chief executive were gone. To demand a pay increase at such a time was plainly injudicious, and Robert compounded the error by leaving the country. David Sarnoff did not live to see the end of the empire he had built and bequeathed to his son; he died in 1971.

The Sarnoff story sounds a theme that is familiar in the world of family-owned business: When company positions are handed out on the basis of family ties rather than abilities, the business is likely to suffer.

A Shake-Up at Shaklee

Some businesses get to the problem in time. An example is the Shaklee Corp. of Emeryville, California, a real company that recently underwent a much-publicized shake-up. The company was founded in 1965 by Forrest C. Shaklee and his two sons, Forrest, Jr., and Raleigh. The elder Shaklee, usually referred to as "the doctor," foresaw that profits could be made from the back-to-nature trend that was developing. The company sells organic products, natural food supplements, and health-care items to a population that has become increasingly turned off by food products doused with chemicals and colorings. The term "sell" hardly does justice to the Shaklee marketing method, which consists of a direct-sales pitch delivered with a fervor bordering on the religious. The products are sold by some 100,000 "distributors," often married couples, who are highly motivated. Although a 35 percent commission on selling prices and big bonuses no doubt have much to do with the motivation, Shaklee sales conventions should not be overlooked. At these affairs, distributors stand together in a spirit of fellowship, singing company songs such as "I Can, You Can, We Can, the Shaklee Way." Shaklee began as a family operation and spread the family feeling throughout the company.

Family ties have also been influential at the management level. For many years, "the doctor" and his sons ran the business and filled other management spots on the basis of family considerations. Not surprisingly, the Peter Principle became an unwelcome adjunct to the Shaklee method. Managers were promoted until they had positions they could not fill competently. Although this is a problem in the smallest company, it becomes a very painful problem when a family company outgrows the family, and that is what happened to

Shaklee. By 1974, company sales reached nearly $80 million but profits had begun to slide.

For better or worse, the Shaklees saw the danger and brought in fresh management from outside. J. Gray Shansby, a management specialist with experience in several well-known firms (Clorox and Colgate-Palmolive), was brought into the Shaklee Corp. in 1976 and was made president and chief executive a year later. Shansby recruited six new vice-presidents from outside the company and also added six outsiders to the board of directors. Raleigh Shaklee is no longer a vice-chairman, and "the doctor," who is 82, is now chairman emeritus and is not active in company matters.

The challenge for Shansby was to consummate a marriage between modern management practices and the evangelistic style that had been an important factor in the company's success. Long known as an able game planner, Shansby had to become a cheerleader as well in the direct-sales operation. So far, the new management team has been successful. Manufacturing and marketing operations are now better coordinated, and the company is expanding its national market while withdrawing from many unprofitable foreign operations.

All concerned seem to agree that Shaklee Corp. is now a better-managed business than it was in the old days, when decisions were made from the heart and not the head. But it is no longer a family-managed business. Raleigh Shaklee has taken the transition gracefully and proclaims that company spirit is higher than ever before. The sales leaders still march and sing company songs at conventions. But can the family spirit long survive when the family is not in control? In any case, the growth of the company and the success of the new management approach must represent something of a Pyrrhic victory for the Shaklees; they have had to relinquish their power over the company. Is relinquishing family power the price that must inevitably be paid when the family-owned business grows?

A Brand Named Stuart McGuire

Apparently not. The Stuart McGuire Company, based in Salem, Virginia, has been selling shoes for about 75 years, and three generations of the Brand family have owned and managed the company all that time. The Stuart McGuire story is a happy one, and it seems appropriate to conclude this overview of the family-owned business with such a story. Problems and failures are certainly common enough in the FOB world, but there are plenty of successes too; they probably do not get enough press.

E. Cabell Brand's Virginia patrician demeanor and speech do not seem consistent with the restless business drive he possesses. In 30 years, he has built the Stuart McGuire Company, which he heads, into a major firm, although it would still be classified as a small business.

The roots of the Brand family stretch far back in Virginia history. Like his father and grandfather, Cabell was born in Salem, a small, middle-class city adjacent to Roanoke, which Salemites are apt to regard as a suburb of Salem rather than vice versa. (Salem was settled long before Roanoke.) The huge and well-appointed Brand house sits on Main Street; without its homey atmosphere, it could probably be called a mansion. Many of the rooms are empty now because Cabell and his wife, Shirley, have only two children at home. Once there were eight because it is a second marriage for both and each has three children by previous marriages. The house is just down the street from Stuart McGuire headquarters.

The company was started in 1904 by Cabell's grandfather. The Brand Shoe Company, as the firm was then called, was a direct-sales, door-to-door operation like the Shaklee Corp. The name was later changed to Ortho-Vent Shoe Company. About 10 years ago, when the decision was made to branch out into the clothing line, a new name seemed called for. It is a mark of Cabell Brand's businesslike approach that he put marketing ahead of vanity in choosing a name. Stuart McGuire was the name of a great-uncle, but he was in no way connected with the business. However, the name sounded good and scored well in market tests, and so the Stuart McGuire Company was born.

Cabell brought no real business background to the firm. He attended Virginia Military Institute, just up the road in Lexington (as his father and older brother had), and received a degree in electrical engineering, although his schooling was interrupted by a tour of military duty during World War II. He left the Army as a captain and after leaving VMI entered the foreign service, being posted to West Germany. He was in Berlin during the blockade of 1948.

In 1949, Cabell decided that he did not want to remain in government service but would go into business instead. His father was then in the process of liquidating the shoe business since it appeared that none of his children was interested in carrying it on. The liquidation stopped when Cabell returned home and assumed control of the firm, which then had five employees and gross sales of less than $155,000.

Today, Stuart McGuire has some 400 employees, several hundred thousand local distributors, and sales of nearly $50 million. In addition to the shoe-selling operation, which accounts for 80 percent of the business, the company now owns an ad agency, a travel agency, and a jewelry business. It also has five or six mail-order divisions that are responsible for an increasingly large part of the shoe sales. Although the company does import shoes, all shoe sales are in the United States.

Cabell is modest in assessing the reasons for the growth of the company under his leadership. He attributes it primarily to hard work, some luck, and a good product—a cushion-sole shoe that has been marketed in innovative ways, including the "Avon calling" approach with which the company began. He further notes that in 30 years others have been able to put together such vast conglomerates as Litton and Gulf & Western. Still, there is no denying that good family leadership has been an important factor in Stuart McGuire's march upward.

In 1970, the decision was made to go public with the corporation for the first time. The Brand family, including all eight of Cabell and Shirley's children, retained about 55 percent of the stock; 15 percent was made available to those in the top management positions of Stuart McGuire, and the remaining 30 percent was sold publicly. It is Cabell's intention that the business remain in family hands. One of Shirley's sons, John, seems the most interested and is being groomed for the succession, though it is not clear when this time will come; Cabell is in his mid-fifties and is in robust good health.

Stuart McGuire has grown and prospered but seems so far to have avoided the problems that crop up repeatedly in family businesses. Except for Cabell, for example, Brand family members do not hold top management positions. On occasion, family members have been hired (Cabell's brother is now in purchasing), but these have been exceptions rather than the rule. Thus the kind of housecleaning by outsiders that the Shaklee Corp. has undergone has not been necessary at Stuart McGuire.

Also, the company has made acquisitions carefully and integrated them into the firm's basic operations successfully. With the acquisi-

tion of the jewelry business, Shirley has become the company gemol-
ogist, taking courses and the like so that Stuart McGuire will have
the necessary expertise at the top to accommodate a new line of work.

Robert Sarnoff got into trouble by traveling too frequently; Cabell
Brand travels often but has had no problems with his board of directors, which includes a number of outside directors. Cabell and Shirley both firmly believe that travel is primarily an educational opportunity and that they need as much education as possible to make the
business successful in the long run.

Cabell still finds time for community involvement, and there is
one involvement in particular that is not common for successful businesspeople. For the past 14 years, he has been chairman of the
board of directors of the Roanoke-area community-action agency,
Total Action Against Poverty (TAP), an antipoverty agency established with Office of Economic Opportunity funding in 1965. Typically, the business community regards poverty warriors with grave
suspicion, viewing their programs as giveaways to the undeserving.
Cabell takes the view that it is in the self-interest of businesspeople
to help people out of poverty, and he has thrown himself wholeheartedly into the fight. With his support, TAP has become one of
the most effective community-action agencies in the country.

Despite Cabell's frequent absences, there have been no marital
strains. Although she holds no formal company position, Shirley is
deeply involved in all aspects of the business, functioning as a sounding board for new ideas and, as she puts it, a "consumer representative." Cabell's father. W. Lee Brand, was very much of the "woman's-
place-is-in-the-home" school and found it difficult to accept this as an
appropriate role for Shirley, but Cabell holds the opposite opinion
and would like her to participate in business matters even more than
she does now.

Like Cabell, Shirley has largely taught herself the ways of business. She grew up in Christiansburg, Virginia, but completed her
formal schooling at Marjorie Webster School in Washington, D.C.
(Ironically, this was also a small family business that could not survive the death of its founder.) She studied radio and hoped to attend
Northwestern University, but marriage and children intervened. She
and Cabell have thus learned the business together. Son John, if he
eventually heads the firm, will have more formal training; he is now
working on a master's degree in business administration.

The problems that arise when family meets business—when
home, as it were, meets empire—suggested in the detailed case his-

tories here will be elaborated in greater detail in the ensuing pages. The reader should be alerted by now to the fact that stories are not always heartwarming and wholesome. In fact, one perceptive analyst has noted that if the typical family-owned business were a movie, it would be X-rated. That is probably too harsh. Make it PG. After all, it is good parental guidance that the family-owned business needs most.

Notes

[1]"Small Business Blues," *Newsweek,* November 26, 1979, p. 84.
[2]Ibid.

Putting the Family-Owned Business in Its Place

The case histories of the Woodwards, Sarnoffs, Shaklees, and Brands are mosaics of men and motives, methods and maxims. The theme is that family plus business is a volatile mixture, an economic form not easily accommodated in modern American society. It is easy to leap to the conclusion that small family-owned firms as vehicles for doing business are beset by troubles within and without while large corporations glide placidly along without internal and external friction. A moment's reflection should dispel that notion, and should the reflection not suffice, there are always the movies to remind us.

In the motion picture *Executive Suite,* Avery Bullard, the dictatorial president (whose face is never actually seen) of a large furniture-manufacturing business, dies suddenly with no successor designated for his job. There is no end to the skullduggery and intricate scheming that takes place on the board of directors before design and development specialist William Holden, the good guy who actually works and gets his hands dirty, is finally awarded the job. There is even a quasi-family complication. Major stockholder Barbara Stanwick, who was in love with president Bullard, wants to use her vote to punish him—albeit posthumously—for not having returned her affection. In *From the Terrace,* Paul Newman shoves aside the boss's son-in-law and manages to rise to the top echelons of a large, prestigious investment firm. However, Newman refuses to make up with his two-timing wife just in order to preserve the image of the company, and so he gives up his rolltop desk, divorces his wife, and rides off into the sunset with his new love.

The Jeffersonian Social Ideal

The point is that matters of the heart, which is really what the family is all about, intrude in all businesses. So why the special concern for small family-owned business? The reasons are deeply planted in American history and tradition. This type of business, defined for the moment as one in which a family survives and prospers economically by working for itself rather than others, is widely seen as a form of socioeconomic organization that is good for the country. Consider the following sonorous declaration by Don DeBolt, chairman of the Small Business Legislative Council:

> And that is why small business is important. These are the people whose entire lives are spent building a business to serve their communities.
> These are the people whose lifetime savings are built by the unheard-of-manhour investments they have given to their business and their community. These are the people who believe the human spirit must be nurtured through religious and civic groups.
> And these are the people who make their communities great and America invincible.
> Without the small businessmen and women of America, we will become a Nation of computers, profit-and-loss decision-makers, automated robots who cannot give proper attention to the essence of living—the human spirit of our society and Nation.[1]

That prominent and specialized form of family-owned business, the family farm, has been especially celebrated for its alleged impact on the soul. In the seventeenth century, the poet Abraham Cowley penned these words in an essay on agriculture: "We may talk what we please of lilies, and lions rampant, and spread eagles, in fields d'or or d'argent; but if heraldry were guided by reason, a plough in a field arable would be the most noble and ancient arms."[2]

The rise of capitalism made the family-owned business possible. Basic to capitalist theory is the notion that not only individuals but society as well benefit when there are many firms competing with each other for the customer's money. Free enterprise means better products, lower prices, and a sounder economic base than other types of enterprise. And the hard work involved in prospering in the free marketplace creates the thrifty and industrious citizenry that is necessary for the survival of a free nation. This vision is often called the Jeffersonian ideal—small self-sufficient proprietors as the mainstay of the American political and economic democracy. It was a reality in the 1820s, when an estimated 80 percent of the people owned their own means of livelihood.

Whether self-sufficient proprietors are still the mainstay is a matter of debate, but this continues to be the ideal. The virtues of large corporate enterprise are extolled by very few—mean-minded drudges all, most feel—and Congress has passed a steady stream of laws—e.g., the Homestead Act of 1862 and the Small Business Act of 1953—intended to keep the family and business alive in as many places as possible, even as large corporations have come to dominate major segments of American manufacturing. The latter piece of legislation restates the Jeffersonian ideal flatly:

> The essence of the American economic system of private enterprise is free competition. . . . The preservation and expansion of such competition is basic not only to the economic well-being but to the security of this Nation.[3]

A government agency, the Small Business Administration, has been set up to carry out this congressional mandate. But clearly, there is a desire to preserve something more than smallness. It is undemonstrable that a small business, however defined (more on that later, unfortunately), owned by several unrelated persons, dedicates itself to serving its community whereas a large business does not. In fact, most large firms make it a point to do their corporate giving in places where they have plants or offices, not in outside communities. And it is not only small business people who believe that the "human spirit must be nurtured through religious and civic groups," as maintained in the earlier quote from a small business spokesman. Nor is big business necessarily incompatible with free competition. There is little agreement about the number of firms that must be competing to prevent free competition from turning into oligopoly, but given the size of the American gross national product, there can be pretty free competition among some rather large firms.

If these things are true—and they are at least defensible—it is evident that there is more to the Jeffersonian business ideal than smallness, and that something is probably covered adequately by the phrase "family-owned and operated." Americans believe that people work harder when they work for themselves than when they work for others. They believe that when a number of family members are involved in a business, a family closeness of spirit which is of social value is created. They believe that it is good for men and women to build their own means of livelihood and pass it on to their children because this brings continuity and stability to society.

Thus it is not small business *rather than* big business of which so many people are solicitous; it is, in a sense, family business rather than nonfamily business. To be sure, size is an intersecting variable. The good things believed to flow from family business seem to flow more easily when the business is small. Family togetherness and direct work involvement by family members are more difficult to achieve when a business becomes very large. But they are not impossibilities, and all small family businesses therefore do not choose to remain small; many are small businesses working very hard to become at least bigger businesses if not big business. A majority of American adults could probably fill in the following blanks: "It's just as good as a _____"; "Get the One-Step from _____." Both these companies began as small businesses. (Readers who cannot fill in the blanks will find the answers at the end of the chapter. No peeking.)

The point need not be belabored, but it is worth stressing. Otherwise, those who exert themselves to preserve this good thing called small business are likely to be misled when they try to assess where small business is in the economy today and where the dangers to it lie.

The Economic Challenge

It may seem strange to refer to the economic position of small family business when its principal virtues have been judged to be social, but there is no inconsistency. Americans are schizoid in their attitudes toward work and business. They believe that self-reliance and community responsibility are key items to preserve, but they are also extremely devoted to the concept of economic efficiency, both in the hardware sense of technology and the software sense of management systems and the like. In a clash between the two—the social and the economic—it is usually the economic that wins. Whatever the contributions small business makes to the preservation of the American way of life, it is not likely to survive as a business form unless it exhibits some economic efficiencies.

Luckily, the defenders of small business as the way for America to go can point to such efficiencies, although not all can be quantified or stated in dollars-and-cents terms. Probably the strongest economic claim for small businesses is that they are an important source of business innovation and new jobs. Some studies estimate that small business innovations per research-and-development dollar are as much as 4 times greater than in medium-sized firms and 24 times greater than in the largest firms. Companies with sales under $100 million a year carry 58 percent of all American workers on their payrolls and account for 43 percent of the gross national product. Two-thirds of all the new jobs created in the American economy between 1960 and 1976 were generated by companies with twenty or fewer employees.[4] A U.S. Chamber of Commerce spokesman told a House of Representatives subcommittee in 1978:

> Historically, small business has created the bulk of new jobs. If problems of unemployment are to be resolved, it is likely that we must depend on small business as a principal factor in the solution.[5]

Thus informed, the subcommittee concluded in its report that the effect of small business on unemployment was almost 66 times as great as the effect of big business and that small business was the "one sector of our economy capable of resolving the unemployment problem and providing benefits rather than additional tax burdens to the consumer."[6]

Speaking more generally, the same report opined that "small business people today are the leaders of tomorrow," noting that many members of Congress and a certain peanut farmer occupying the White House "got where they are" because of their small business ties.[7]

Even the well-known "economies of scale" principle, long the key argument for big business superiority, has come under critical scrutiny recently. In his widely cited *Small is Beautiful*, E. F. Schumacher denies the proposition that with firms as with nations, there is an irresistible trend dictated by modern technology for units to become larger and larger. On the contrary, he notes that as soon as organizations become very large, their leaders cast about for ways to attain smallness within bigness. (General Motors, in fact, is characterized as a federation of reasonably sized firms.)[8] Decrying the "idolatry of giantism," Schumacher contends that people need order—the virtue of large-scale organization—but also the freedom that comes with many small autonomous units. He may have the family-owned business in mind when he says:

... it is true that all men are brothers, but it is also true that in our active personal relationships we can, in fact, be brothers to only a few of them, and we are called upon to show more brotherliness to them than we could possibly show to all of mankind.[9]

A spectacular example of the virtues of smallness is provided by the Republic Hose Manufacturing Corp. of Youngstown, Ohio. This was a failing business when it was owned by Aeroquip, a large firm that is part of the Libby-Owens-Ford conglomerate, and the parent company decided to close the plant. With the unemployment line close at hand, the former company manager and many of the employees, with full union support, worked to reopen the plant as a smaller, more streamlined business with quite different attitudes. Of the 5000 shares of stock, 3200 were made available to the employees. The business, now a small independent corporation, is booming. Same manager, same employees, different structure. And productivity and quality of work have improved dramatically. The firm reports that its reject rate is just 1 percent. Under Aeroquip, the reject rate ranged from 5 to 9 percent, and the industry norm is 4 percent. Small can be bountiful as well as beautiful.[10]

After making all due allowances for the considerable amount of bombast that shows up in discussions of the role of small business, it does appear that the family business is an institution worth preserving. It outperforms big business in a number of important economic areas; it serves as a transmitter of certain basic values that society holds dear; and its theoretical underpinning has not really been destroyed by modern developments.

Small Is Not Large

If the act of preservation is accepted as a laudable objective, the question to answer is where America stands in terms of achieving it. Some take the view that the small business is an endangered species. One gentleman states the matter so gloomily that his remarks are worth quoting:

Starved of capital, deprived of incentives, submerged in bureaucratic red tape and surrounded by the burgeoning bigness of the corporate giants, the small business sector has become a victim of the upheavals and recessions of the 1970s. It is a matter of national urgency that the small entrepreneur, while not yet extinct, has become an endangered species.[11]

Is this true? To attempt to answer this question is, regretfully, to launch a battle of definitions leading to a war of statistics. We will try to make it as painless as possible.

Substantial agreement could probably be obtained regarding what a family business is. It is a profit-making concern that is either a proprietorship, a partnership, or a corporation. In a corporation, the stock is either privately owned by a family or, if part of the stock is publicly owned, the family owns a controlling interest. For our purposes, however, the family must also operate the business. Typically, the owner selects the employees, maintains direct contact with them, works in their behalf, and expects a relationship of mutual loyalty. One problem with these lines of demarcation is that they exclude some businesses that are relevant to the general subject, i.e., the family in business. Some companies—for example, RCA for 45 years—are run almost as family businesses, even though the family does not have a controlling stock interest. But this definition probably covers the subject better than any other.

Trying to define the word "small" when applied to business is like trying to agree on the meaning of "valuable" in the sports phrase "most valuable player." A search of the literature, as they say, reveals that about the only thing everyone agrees on is that small is not as large as big.

Obviously, businesses in the United States come in all shapes and sizes and any attempt to define them on a common basis is difficult. Small is a relative term, but the development of a set of rational, objective criteria for defining it requires an adequate data base that portrays all business and that can be used as the benchmark for measurement. No usable benchmark exists. What does exist is either ambiguous, incomplete, inconsistent, contradictory, misleading, or any combination of the above.

Some observers like to define small business in essentially qualitative terms. For example, a business can be considered small if the owner is involved directly in the work and is not merely a supervisor. This concept has been used here as a typical hallmark of family business, but it is far too ambiguous to be used in separating the small from the big. More commonly, measures of smallness are stated in quantifiable terms such as annual gross sales, annual net sales, total assets, number of employees, and so on. The problem here is that a business may be small under one measure, such as gross sales, and large under another, such as number of employees. It all depends on the kind of business it is.

The Small Business Administration cannot treat the matter as academic since it must, as a matter of law, determine whether a business is small for the purpose of receiving government loans, obtaining government contracts or subcontracts, and so on. But SBA standards only show how complicated and arbitrary the whole matter is. For example, for *loan* purposes, a *service* company's annual gross receipts cannot exceed $8 million; for contracting purposes, they cannot exceed $9 million. Manufacturing concerns are limited by number of employees rather than by gross receipts. For loan purposes, the average employment maximum is 250 to 1500 people; for contracting purposes, the figure is 500 to 1500.

Suffice it to say that there *is* no simple and fixed definition of a small business; in using statistics to determine how such firms are faring in the economy, one is advised to move cautiously, lest there emerge propositions such as "A pig is fatter than a giraffe is tall."

Security in the Industrial State

Many people do not take this advice, however, and it is easy to understand why. The careful use of terms is no fun at all; in fact, it is downright tedious. Take this sentence: "Firms with manufacturing as their principal activity and with an employee work force in excess of 250 persons account for 71.5 percent of the total employment by companies in the manufacturing sector of the American economy." No punch at all. Substitute this: "Big business dominates American manufacturing." Has a much better ring. Note, however, that the latter sentence, while it would be considered an accurate statement of a *major* economic theme, has the unfortunate effect of grossly downplaying the *minor* theme, i.e., that nearly 30 percent of manufacturing employment is not covered by big business. The major theme thus becomes implanted in the public mind as the *only* theme, especially when it can be expressed in a catchy way.

A prime offender, if that is the word, in the literature of business is John Kenneth Galbraith, who has become to economics roughly what Dr. Joyce Brothers is to psychology. Galbraith, who was trained as an agricultural economist in Canada, first told us that contrary to free enterprise theory, competition on one side of the marketplace, e.g., between businesspeople, did not serve as a check on their tendency to buy cheap and sell dear, whether products or labor were involved. Instead, the only checks had come from the other side of the market. In other words, labor unions and collective bargaining, not business competition, determined wages. The analysis actually fit well only in regard to the large manufacturing sector of the economy, but this fact was often overlooked. Then, in proclaiming a "new industrial state,"[12] Galbraith treated small business as if it did not exist. The entrepreneur who both owned the capital and controlled the other factors of production, argued Galbraith, had been replaced by the modern corporation, in which ownership and control are divorced. That this has occurred in many instances is undeniable, but it is doubtful that this is the most important thing to know about American business.

In the first place, the kind of modern corporation that Galbraith is describing represents about 2 percent of the total number of corporations in the United States. Around 5000 corporations are listed on Wall Street, and perhaps another 25,000 firms offer stock for sale to the public; a lot of the latter stock is rarely traded. Thus diffusion of ownership and management by technocrats—Galbraith's model—is not characteristic of some 98 percent of American corporations.[13]

Many of these are small corporations, of course, but even among large corporations the disappearance of the entrepreneur is hard to validate. Robert Shuhan took a look at the Fortune 500 in 1967 and found that in approximately 150 of them, controlling ownership rested in the hands of an individual or a single family. Many of these owners were newcomers in the business world, not the remnants of robber-baron dynasties.[14] Philip H. Burch, Jr., reached a similar conclusion in 1972, calculating that over 40 percent of the nation's largest publicly held corporations were probably under family control, with another 17 percent possibly in the same category.[15] It would seem that the new industrial state is not so new after all; certainly it is not completely new. But the phrase has a nice ring to it.

Even in terms of economic impact rather than sheer numbers, the entrepreneurless modern corporation does not dominate. As noted earlier, small firms accounted for nearly 60 percent of the national business employment and over 40 percent of the gross national product in 1979.

In addition, employment in small business is increasing. Total civilian employment in the United States exceeded 91 million in 1977, and small business contributed substantially to the rise; employment in this area increased 5.7 percent between 1974 and 1977. Other 1977 figures covering new business formations and failures also pointed to continued improvement in the state of small enterprises. The number of business incorporations, nearly all of which are small, increased by 17 percent from the second quarter of 1976 to the second quarter of 1977. At the same time, the number of business failures declined. According to Dun and Bradstreet, the rate of business failures declined to about 31 per 10,000 concerns for the second quarter of 1977.[16]

The presence of large businesses is felt most strongly in the manufacturing and service industries that require major capital investment or in which limited competition seems more productive (often stated as "more in the public interest") than unrestricted competition. Thus Detroit, big steel, the major oil companies, railroads, and television networks loom large in the public eye as big business. But there are huge sectors of the American economy in which big business played a minor role and small business dominates.

An example is retail trade, perhaps the citadel of small business. This is likely to be the easiest way for the family entrepreneur to enter business. Large numbers of employees and heavy capital investment are not required. Business risk in this type of enterprise is reduced by the fact that stock turnover is relatively rapid and inventory requirements are low. The technical knowledge required to operate a retail business is not extensive, and assistance in this area is readily available from large distributors, trade associations, and even neighbors and friends.

For these reasons, family-owned businesses abound in the world of retail trade: gasoline stations, car dealerships, hardware stores, specialty shops, lumberyards, jewelry stores, building-material suppliers—the list goes on and on. If the present is pleasant for retail trade, the future is even brighter. Rising personal incomes, increased consumption, and constantly changing tastes offer an expanding market.

Selected service businesses are another prime area for small entrepreneurs. The continued increase in the number of businesses in the United Streets has a ripple effect. It creates opportunities for business services that small businesses can easily provide, such as advertising, credit reporting, collection, and mailing. Small businesses can also prosper by servicing other small businesses. Frequently, managerial competence in a family-owned business calls for a wider range of skills than the owner possesses. Family-owned business can provide specialized services such as planning, production, and assistance with financial analysis.

The construction industry, which is localized in nature, also offers many small business opportunities, as do many other related trade areas such as plumbing, electrical, and water well drilling contracting. Wholesaling appears to be another area of small business concentration, although information to support this is scanty. Until recently, the Federal Trade Commission did not maintain data on wholesaling, and the only information published dealt with assets. That information indicates that firms with below $10 million in assets maintain over 50 percent of wholesaling assets; the billion dollar firms control 18 percent.[17]

The only reasonable conclusion to draw from the facts and figures cited is that nonfarm family-owned business is secure in its place in the modern industrial state. Small business is not being gobbled up by big business; the entrepreneur is not being replaced across the board by bloodless managers. In sum, the species does not seem endangered, at least not by any irresistible ecological trends.

Fear for the Family Farm

There is one traditional area of family-owned business that must be examined separately, not only because it is a very special kind of business but because it has always had a special place in American hearts and because the optimistic prediction regarding small business may not apply to it. This is the family farm.

We have characterized family-owned business as more a question of operating style than size. The family both owns and operates the business; the entrepreneur is as much worker as supervisor; and employer-employee relations are personal. The family-owned farm producing crops and livestock typifies this style better than any other business. Our noble essayist Abraham Cowley expressed it this way:

> I shall only instance in one delight more, the most natural and best-natured of all others, a perpetual companion of the husbandman; and that is, the satisfaction of looking round about him, and seeing nothing but the effects and improvements of his own art and diligence; to be always gathering of some fruits of it, and at the same time to behold others ripening, and others budding; to see all his fields and gardens covered with the beauteous creatures of his own industry.[18]

The vision rarely fails to stir American hearts. Senator Hubert Humphrey of Minnesota, campaigning for the Democratic presidential nomination in 1960, noted ruefully that the small family farm might not be economically efficient but, doggone it, it was good for the country.

And what is happening to the family farm and the family farmer? In numbers, both increased greatly in about the first 150 years of the nation's history and then began a precipitate decline. If this were the whole story, it could easily be deduced that the family farm as a family-owned business type was definitely on the way out, but that is not the whole story. First, however, the number.[19]

When the First Census was taken in 1790, four of every five people gained their livelihood from farming, but it was backbreaking labor at the mercy of nature's caprice. The hoe tilled the soil, the sickle felled the grain, scarred hands harvested the crops, and all were propelled by the human arm. The mule, the horse, the ox, and the tillage instruments to which they were harnessed lightened the farmer's load. But with unpredictable weather, ravenous insects, and runaway weeds, the fear of hunger was always about. Still, there were 1.4 million farms in 1850, most of them family-owned and operated. Between 1850 and 1910, a period coinciding roughly with the coming of the industrial revolution, American agriculture experienced a sharp upswing. During this time, the slavery that supported the large plantations was abolished, the Homestead Act opened up the West, and the Plains Indians who had plagued the homesteaders (or bravely resisted their encroachments, as Native Americans would say) were confined to reservations. The number of farms increased to 6.4 million. The trend continued, and the number of farm units reached a peak of 6.8 million in 1935.

Since that year, the number of farm units has been dropping sharply. The number was down to 3.7 million in 1961 and has now declined to about the 1850 level of 1.4 million. The number of people living on and working the soil has likewise declined. A hundred years ago, when the nation had about 32 million people, nearly two-thirds of them lived on farms. Now, the United States has a population of about 250 million, but only 5 percent live on farms if we count only those who actually produce food and fiber and exclude those who use farming largely as a tax shelter. In 1910, it took 35 percent of the population to produce food for the nation.

Improved technology is the explanation. The invention of the cotton gin by Eli Whitney revolutionized cotton farming once, and the mechanical cotton picker, which can gather as much cotton as forty pairs of human hands, did it again. The invention of the reaper by Cyrus McCormick in 1847 had the same effect on grain farming. The early reaper combined wheels, blades, knives, and mechanical fingers on a horse-drawn platform, allowing two workers to harvest in a day what it took five to do by hand. Today's combines can do much better. (McCormick's company, incidentally, has always been family-owned; today it is a multimillion dollar operation known as _____. Those who cannot fill in the blank will be given a sickle and 56 hours to harvest an acre of wheat, which is how long it took in 1800.)

The tractor and other fuel-fed machines (hay balers, corn pullers) have simply replaced the human effort once necessary to plant and harvest crops. In addition, chemical means have been devised to control insects and weeds; fertilizers to make crops grow better have been developed; and irrigation techniques have turned dust bowls such as the Midwest and California's Central Valley into garden spots.

There is very little in farming today that cannot be done by machine, and it is not only the vast cotton, wheat, and corn fields that evidence mechanization. Orchards are trimmed by saws mounted on hydraulic beams moved by tractors; there are many devices for pruning the trees and picking the fruit. Henry Fonda and family *(The Grapes of Wrath)* worked all day picking oranges to earn enough money to buy supper in the 1930s.

The lettuce fields of California offer some of the most impressive (some would say depressing) images of modern agriculture. Remember when James Dean's father *(East of Eden)* failed in a pioneering effort to ship refrigerated lettuce back east? Today, motorized packing plants followed by trucks move through the fields. One crew of workers wraps each head of lettuce in a plastic bag and another crew packs them for the trucks that carry the cartons to rail sidings with cooling plants; within a few hours, iceberg lettuce is being distributed throughout the nation. Iceberg lettuce may not be a gourmet's delight, but it is available in the coldest climes of America throughout the year. Machines have made it possible for the same thing to be said about radishes, tomatoes, and other vegetables and fruits. (The "same thing" refers to both availability and taste. Supermarket tomatoes have almost no juice and skins that are $\frac{1}{4}$ inch thick, but they are virtually indestructible.)

All this has certainly lifted the load from the farmer's back. One farmer can bale and load 10 tons of hay in an hour while sitting down. And today's tractor seat is likely to be in an enclosed cab equipped with heating and air conditioning, carpeting, and a CB radio. But is it the same farmer? The answer is no, but one should not, as many do, leap from this fact to the conclusion that today's typical farmer is the Jolly Green Giant rather than Old MacDonald.

For various purposes, the Department of Agriculture must specifically delineate what a farm is, but we will not bore you with the details because the definitions change frequently. Suffice it to say that if a farm enjoys more than a few thousand dollars a year in sales, it is classified as a commercial firm. Such farms, which are the only ones that concern us, are then classified by size in terms of annual sales volume.

In these terms, it cannot truly be said that big farms are taking over American agriculture. The fact is that the average size of *all* size classes of farms has been increasing. If all farms are ordered by size and divided into quintiles, the top two-fifths account for 80 percent of total farm output, the bottom two-fifths are responsible for 10 percent, and the middle quintile covers the remaining 10 percent. These proportions have changed little for decades. Although farms have become fewer and larger, the relative size distribution among farms has remained about the same. The typical small farm is simply larger today than it used to be.[20]

It does not appear, however, that the trend to larger farms is being caused by corporations moving into the farming business at the expense of family farms. Instead, more family farms are being incorporated. A 1971 study of corporate farming in the United States showed that 66 percent of all corporation farms were family-owned and another 14 percent were individually owned; only 20 percent were owned by a group larger than the family. The incorporation of existing family farms, not entry into farming by new "outside" corporations, seems to be the trend in American agriculture, with greater flexibility in estate planning and various tax benefits as the principal incentives.[21]

There is no clear trend that enables us to predict with any degree of certainty the future of the family farm in America. The number of farm units may continue to decline and the number of nonfamily corporate farmers may increase. The small farm may become as obsolete as the small automobile-manufacturing company. Should this occur, it does not mean the end of family-owned business. Agriculture, after all, is only one segment of business. Americans have perhaps been too prone to endow the soil with magical powers for human enrichment. Cowley's "husbandman" is too frequently seen as the best, even the only, repository of thrift and virtue. Perhaps it is natural for a nation that has become so urbanized to yearn for a pristine past when rivers were not polluted and subdivisions did not dot the landscape, forgetting that the good old days were a time of hardship.

The technological revolution in agriculture has unquestionably brought tremendous material benefit to the American people. If the fruits of that revolution can be enjoyed only by sacrificing a certain type of business operation—the small family farm—entrepreneurs of the future will have to seek their opportunities elsewhere. Indeed, many believe that the decline in the number of farm units over the last 40 years is partially explained by the fact that business opportunities have been better off the farm than on it. In other words, the decline of the family farm, if it is in decline, can be seen simply as a rearrangement in the composition of the small business world. No doubt the traditionalists will never be convinced that the family farm is not essential to civilization, but there is little historical basis for this belief.

In any event, there is no need to argue the worst case. In all probability, the family farm will survive by making the necessary accommodations to the new order of things. Four hundred acres and a modern tractor may not seem as romantic as 40 acres and a mule, but it can still be a small family business.

A Farm Family Portrait

Bob and Brenda Hobart can stand as a real-life example of today's small farmer and as an example of the Jeffersonian tradition itself. They are wheat farmers in Oklahoma, a flat and nearly treeless land with blazing summers and harsh winters, though the fields of waving wheat at harvest time present a beautiful sight.

The Hobart home is comfortable but plain and somewhat rambling because it was built by joining together two houses, formerly those of Bob and Brenda separately. They have been married only since 1970 and have one child, daughter Karen, 9. The house is surrounded by outbuildings, and the barn has a telephone. A tall windmill looms over the homesite.

Bob Hobart is tall, lean, and handsome with a face and hands made leathery by years of outdoor work. When he talks, which is not a lot, it is in a deep Oklahoma drawl, but he puts a lot of thought into what he says. He is 51. Brenda, who is younger than Bob, *does* talk, and she is a whirling dervish of activity. A licensed practical nurse working toward registered nurse status, Brenda is heavily involved in community affairs and has been named the county's woman of the year. She and Bob met in a hospital where he was visiting a patient and she was working as an aide. They discovered that they had both been at Oklahoma State University ("down 't Stilwater") at the same time. Bob studied agricultural economics but never got around to completing the degree.

The Hobarts are basically conservative, churchgoing people, but they are not prudish. They laugh easily at themselves and each other and have been known to enjoy bourbon with friends.

The Hobarts love farming their own land because it keeps them independent and self-reliant. But they always believe in being good neighbors and are members of the local wheat-production cooperative. Bob's farm was owned by his father before him and will pass on to the children when Bob and Brenda are gone. Bob has been living on the farm since 1941.

Although the Hobarts definitely consider themselves small farmers, this is no "40-acres-and-a-mule" operation. Bob owns 160 acres in one spot (the "quarter" where the house is located), another 80 acres "a few miles north," and another 40 acres "up the road." In addition, he rents 100 acres of cropland and 60 acres of grassland. On this acreage, both wheat and cattle are produced, but wheat is the principal cash commodity. (Bob also grows a little hay for his cattle, and daughter Karen has nine sheep.) With land in that part of the country selling for roughly $1000 an acre, the Hobarts have about $280,000 tied up in land. Farm assets also include about $89,000 in machinery and equipment—two tractors, two combines, two trucks, disks, cultivators, and drills. When the value of the crop and stock inventory at any given time is added to the other assets, the Hobart farm ends up being worth between $400,000 and $500,000, depending on the current prices of land, cattle, and wheat.

In terms of cash, however, the Hobarts, while comfortably middle-class, are certainly not rich. Bob estimates that his annual cash income is between $50,000 and $60,000. It is hard to tell because he pays himself no regular salary (the farm is not incorporated). When he needs to pay bills or buy things, he gets the money from his bank account. If the money is not there, he sells off something: cattle, or wheat that is stored in nearby grain elevators.

Bob feels that his biggest problem is fluctuation in wheat prices. Most wheat produced locally is shipped out through Galveston. As of December 1979, wheat on the Gulf Exchange was selling for just over $4 a bushel; it costs just over $3 for the farmer to produce each bushel.

The Hobarts hire no labor at all. Instead, Bob and Brenda do all the sowing and reaping and livestock feeding. This, says Bob, often means "working your butt off," but on the whole he does not feel overworked. During the summer harvest, work is from daylight to dark (and sometimes after dark), but there is slack time in winter when the wheat has been planted. Bob sometimes takes a part-time job to make a little extra money.

Although he is not very active politically (he never drove his tractor in Washington), Bob believes firmly that the federal government should have gotten out of wheat farming in the 1950s rather than continuing price-support programs. "Wheat prices would be higher if they had," says Bob. "Sure it would have been tough at first and some of the real small farms might have gone under, but they're going under anyway." He is sounding a theme that is echoed by many small farmers.

Do the Hobarts really own a *small* family farm? By today's standards, yes. They own and operate the business and do all the work themselves. The farm has a lot of assets, but many of them are not liquid and the cash flow is modest. They are happy with what they have and are determined to pass it on to future generations. If that is not a family farm, nothing is.

The Problem of Government

Despite rather reassuring statistics, many small businesspeople—farm and nonfarm—still feel threatened. Is this all paranoia? Not really. Small businesses do have some legitimate causes for worry, but the real bogeyman (bogeyperson?) is probably not big business but big government.

Small and large businesses have, by and large, learned to coexist peacefully in the same economy. To be sure, the banks give better interest breaks to large firms, and sometimes when a small entrepreneur comes up with a bright product idea, a big firm will buy out the bidding competition; but there is no real effort being made by big business to eliminate small business. The two are usually not even competitors. There is room for the small fry in all sectors of the economy, and some sectors are dominated by the little guys. The government—federal, state, and local—purports to be a friend to all business, but especially to small business. However, government also exercises tax and regulatory functions, and therein lies the problem. Allow us to cite a specific illustration as an entry to this subject.

A recent study at the University of Chicago looked at changes in the American mattress industry following imposition of flammability standards by the Consumer Products Safety Commission in 1973. The findings: Small business's share of the pretax net income from industrywide sales declined by 15 percent while large manufacturers increased their share by 12 percent. The researcher, Peter Linneman, whose work was funded by the university's Center for the Study of the Economy and the State, gives the following reason for this redistribution of wealth:

> A large portion of the compliance costs are relatively fixed, such as the expense associated with learning and implementing the testing and record-keeping requirements of the standard. The large firms are much better able to deal with those expenses because they can amortize them over a large number of units.[22]

Linneman intends to follow the mattress industry research with similar studies looking into the impact of Occupational Safety and Health Act regulations on small businesses. He suspects that "similar redistribution of income effects will hold across all types of industries and regulations and that small businesses will come out the loser in every case.[23]

This is depressing news for the family-owned business. Government regulation of business and economic life has been increasing for about 100 years in the United States and seems to be at its height today. Some of the regulations, such as the antitrust and fair trade laws, have been directed toward protecting small business and promoting free competition. More recently, government has interceded on behalf of other interests such as environment, energy conservation, consumer protection, and advancement of women and racial and ethnic minorities. However laudable these efforts in their own right, they have imposed burdens on American business, large and small.

As indicated by Linneman's research, however, the smaller the business, the heavier the burden tends to be. Large corporations can hire people who do nothing but fill out government forms; the small businessperson must usually do it alone. A large corporation can absorb the cost that inevitably accompanies compliance with a government regulation; a family-owned business operating at the margin feels the pinch when costs go up even a few dollars. Large corporations, especially those in essentially oligopolistic sectors of the economy, such as automobile manufacturing, can pass increased costs on to the consumer and lose little if any business. A small retail business cannot be so cavalier in its treatment of consumers, not because it will lose customers to other businesses in the same trade (all businesses must meet the regulations and pay taxes) but because customers may make alternative purchases. If a toy costs too much because of the safety standards it had to meet, Christmas shoppers may simply buy clothes instead. Besides, rising costs to consumers usually have only a monetary impact at the manufacturing level. The retailer is likely to be personally affected. The person who has suffered the most abuse as gasoline costs have skyrocketed is not the president of the large oil company but the operator of the local filling station. Of course, the retailer can suffer monetary loss too. In periods when there have been gasoline shortages and the lines at the pump have grown long, filling station operators claim they lose money despite the great increase in gasoline prices. Customers hesitate to come in for repairs or tires—real money-makers for the station—because station employees have no time for them; they are busy pumping gas.

It is difficult to find a clear solution to this problem. Certainly no responsible small businessperson is likely to assert that highly flammable mattresses or unsafe toys are good things to have around. In today's complicated market, "buyer beware" cannot be the sole principle applied. Regulation is here to stay and small business will have to adjust. There are some things that can be done, however, to ease this adjustment.

In the first place, the full burden of proof that a given regulation is necessary in order to promote a legitimate interest should fall on those who are proposing regulations. There has been a tendency in the recent past at all levels of government to regulate on suspicion. The Peking Restaurant is famous for its Peking duck dish, the preparation of which requires that the duck be hung in the open air for a period of time. D.C. health authorities decided that this practice violated health codes and ordered it stopped; no evidence was produced that harm to anyone's health had ever resulted from a hanging duck. The proprietor made the obvious comment: "No hang up, no Peking duck." In the end, a compromise of sorts was reached on the matter, and the restaurant still offers Peking duck on its menu. However, a good business could have been harmed by the ill-considered application of a regulation.

Second, no regulation should be applied until its impact on small business is assessed and every step has been taken to minimize the likely adverse effects. The U.S. Environmental Protection Agency showed us how *not* to do it. In its fight against pollution in the early 1970s, EPA was very big on "watershed planning" and regional sewer systems with massive treatment plants. The enormous cost of such facilities was not given enough attention. Thousands of small utilities, many of them privately owned, had to go out of business. In 1977, EPA changed its mind and began putting the stress on "alternate and innovative technologies" and on-site waste treatment. Someone was finally able to convince the agency that there were environmentally acceptable solutions for pollution problems other than the costly ones imposed by its regulations. Of course, EPA and other agencies go through elaborate procedures before regulations are issued; they publish preliminary proposed regulations, call for comments, hold hearings, and so forth. But apparently this does not work. EPA's emphasis went from areawide to on-site sewage treatment in the space of 5 years, while the problem they were trying to deal with had not changed at all.

Particular attention should be paid at government levels to the amount of paperwork that a regulation will create for small businesses so as to keep that amount to an absolute minimum. Bureaucrats, for whom paperwork is the staff of life, pay far too little attention to this. Congress might consider a law requiring any government official preparing a form to fill it out 100 times before forcing it on someone else. (Well, someone did once introduce a bill requiring that the number of employees in the Department of Agriculture not exceed the number of farmers in the United States.)

Third, government could provide additional assistance to small business beyond what is provided now. The federal Small Business Administration provides loans to businesses covered by its mandate, reports to Congress annually on the "state of small business," tries to identify and deal with small business problems, and so on. (The Farmers Home Administration in the U.S. Department of Agriculture does the same thing for small farms, though on a less extensive basis; farm loans are only one of numerous FHA rural programs.)

The experience of government assistance to agriculture suggests, however, that small business cannot be saved by all-out government assistance. In order that farms might remain small and still be able to compete economically, the federal government, working with the states, constructed a college grant for agricultural experimentation to serve the farmers. To this was added a complicated price-support system, the essential feature of which is direct government subsidies. Despite all this, the number of farm units has declined drastically. The technology developed through the land-grant college system can be applied more easily by large farmers than small ones, and the large landowners also benefit the most from farm subsidies.

Perhaps we can get a sharper perspective on the problems that government can cause for family-owned business by listening to Harry Stedman, a man in his early forties whose family has been operating a car dealership in a major city for nearly 60 years. (The names are fictitious, but the story is true.)

"My father started in the auto business in 1921 with a small, one-room 10 x 10 location. He would buy one car, sell it, and then buy another. He would get up at 4:00 A.M. to get the early paper and would knock on a person's door who was selling a used car. By 9:00 A.M., he would have two or three cars and would try to sell them that day after polishing them, tuning them, and putting on new tires or retreads. This was the business that I eventually entered, working with my father.

"Most people couldn't pay the full price, so if Dad got his cost out, he would personally finance them with small weekly payments, and he would buy another car with their down payment. These same people couldn't get car insurance, so we went into the insurance business. The same was true with repairs and small household appliances, so we soon found ourselves in the used car, auto repair, auto insurance, home appliance, and loan business. The company was originally called Stedman's Automobile and Home Appliance Company. Eventually, though, the laws changed and financing insurance was declared a usury business, so we got out of that. However, we added motorcycle insurance, so we went into that field too. In 1958, we had twenty-five employees and gross sales of about half a million dollars.

"In 1968, we had race riots like most major cities and the block where our business was located was wiped out—except for us. We were the only operating business in a four-block area. We had always treated the people in the area right and were not touched by the rioters.

"The citizens may have left us alone, but the city destroyed us. We were to receive fair market value for our ground or replacement ground in another area. Prior to the riots, our property was valued at $2,500,000; we received $460,000 by condemnation. After this, we relocated to the suburbs in 1971, using all our surplus cash and the money given us by the city government. My father died before we could move into the new building.

"Now Uncle Sam stepped in and taxed my father's estate as a private person, so we had to pay the taxes in 1 year instead of 10. At the time Dad died, the company assets were in his name rather than in the business name because the business had not opened up yet in the new location. Again, the government took what cash we had.

"Well, I wouldn't quit. I pooled all the money any of us had left, mortgaged homes, sold jewelry, and borrowed as much as I could. I had a dream, and I wasn't going to let the government crush me. Banks and private citizens believed in me, and we pulled it off. At the end of 1977, we had the largest dealership for our particular car in the United States—125 employees and about $10 million in gross sales.

"We bought more land and were ready to expand when some street construction took so much of our property that we were almost put out of business again. This time I decided to fight the government, but I lost. The government appraiser lied or at least misrepresented the facts. We found out that the government appraiser had done work for banks that had turned us down for loans; they had given him phony information to use against us.

"The bottom line is that without capital, the small family business can't make it. Banks give if you already have, and government takes if you can't afford to fight. But I'm still here. The business now has annual sales of $15 million.

"In the end, the small business will have to survive by helping itself. Even if the process of government regulation is cleaned up to perfection—absolutely necessary, clearly understandable regulations that are easy to comply with—there will still be regulations and they are likely to involve costs and require capital.

"There are ways that small businesses could help each other. They could make an alliance to compare ideas, pool resources in things like buying, advertising, computer time, legal help. The problem is that most small business people don't trust each other. They're reluctant to give out information to people in the same field because of the fear of competition. Some ideas and business facts are being shared in areas where direct competition is not a threat. Maybe this will become a trend."

In addition to working with others, the small business must make sure that its operation is tight and that money is not leaking away through the crevices of poor management systems, incompetent personnel, and family discord. This is a tall order because the family-owned business, virtually by definition, is a creature prone to contracting all these diseases. To continue the medical analogy, no vaccine to eradicate these diseases has been developed, but there are preventive and corrective measures that may be taken. That is what this book is really about. The family-owned business has a firm place in the American economy, but it will have to work harder than ever before to keep it.

By the way, those three companies are Xerox, Polaroid, and International Harvester.

Notes

[1] *Future of Small Business in America.* A Report of the Subcommittee on Antitrust, Consumers, and Employment of the Committee on Small Business, 95th Cong., 2d Sess., 1978, pp. 8–9.

[2] Abraham Cowley, "Of Agriculture," *The Harvard Classics,* Charles W. Eliot, ed., reproduced by permission, Grolier Incorporated, Danbury, Conn., p. 61.

[3] Pub. L., Title II, Section 202, 163–83.

[4] "Small Business Blues," *Newsweek,* November 26, 1979, p. 84.

[5] *Future Of Small Business in America,* p. 8.

[6] Ibid.

[7] Ibid.

[8] E. F. Schumacher, *Small Is Beautiful,* Harper & Row, New York, 1973.

[9] Ibid.

[10] "We Broke Out of Business," *Inc.,* November 1979, pp. 91–94.

[11] *Future of Small Business in America,* p. 9.

[12] John Kenneth Galbraith, *The New Industrial State,* Houghton Mifflin Company, Boston, 1972.

[13] John H. Carson, "Family Companies—A Mixed Bag," *Industry Week,* March 1, 1971, p. 32.

[14]Robert Shuhan, "Proprietors in the World of Big Business," *Fortune,* vol. 75, June 1967, p. 179.

[15]Philip H. Burch, Jr., *The Managerial Revolution Reassessed,* Lexington Books, Lexington, Mass., 1972, pp. 101–102.

[16]U.S. Internal Revenue Service, *Statistics of Income,* 1977, p. 4.

[17]*Future of Small Business in America,* p. 14.

[18]Abraham Cowley, op. cit., p. 64.

[19]Edward Higbee, *Farms and Farmers in an Urban Age,* Krauss Reprint Co., by Twentieth Century Fund, New York, 1963, pp. 8–11.

[20]Walter Wilcox, *Economics of American Agriculture,* Prentice-Hall, Inc., Englewood Cliffs, N.J., 1974, pp. 10–12.

[21]Ibid.

[22]"Standards Shift Profits to Larger Corporations," *Inc.,* August 1979, p. 26.

[23]Ibid.

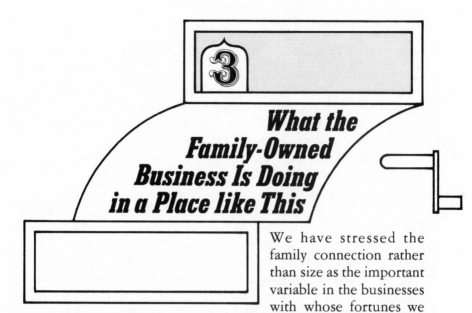

What the Family-Owned Business Is Doing in a Place like This

We have stressed the family connection rather than size as the important variable in the businesses with whose fortunes we are concerned. Most family businesses are small businesses, but many are very large indeed, and both types make a substantial contribution to American society. Some family businesses begin as small operations and become corporate; others begin small and remain that way; still others rise to a position of some prominence and then fail. Each and every business has its own story to tell about what it is doing "in a place like this," whether that place is a major metropolis or Middle City, America, a fictional place that we shall visit.

Of Rags and Riches

Stories of those who started poor and became rich seem to be the most heartwarming to American ears because this is the American dream. With hard work and a little luck, it is said, the lowliest born among us can become rich, or become President of the United States, or perhaps both. The person who said this most often and most convincingly was Horatio Alger. Alger became a crusading preacher of the gospel of success in 1864, and his heroes have lived for over a century. He wrote 100 enormously popular dime novels for young boys, and his rags to riches theme gained him immortality. Three stories—*Raggedy Dick, The Luck and Pluck,* and *The Tattered Tom*—were especially successful.

These heroes were not mere figments of the author's imagination at the time he was writing; the arrival of Raggedy Dick and Tattered

Tom coincided roughly with the rise of such industrial giants as Henry Ford, John D. Rockefeller, and Cyrus McCormick. These men acted out Alger's fantasies in real life. Ford wanted only one thing in life—to see his dream of the automobile realized; he did. Rockefeller fought poverty as a child and wanted very much to amass a fortune to pass on to his heirs; he did. Cyrus McCormick, of whose reaper we have spoken, wanted his invention to be the basis for a major family business; it was. Alger could not have written better rags to riches scenarios.

These men wanted more than riches, however; they wanted the personal satisfaction that comes from creating a new thing, from seeing dreams come true, from building institutions that would last. And in this way they not only achieved personal power and fortunes, they also made social contributions, not just by serving as Algerian examples or by making philanthropic contributions but by giving the nation tangible things that would help it achieve prosperity.

The road to the top is not always a happy one because people with tremendous drive are frequently misunderstood, or, to be fair to the detractors of such people, the same quality can be seen in two ways. Courage may appear to be stubbornness; firm control may come across as despotism; ambition may be seen as a lust for power. Thus understanding from family members may or may not be forthcoming. Let us look at some of these giants.

Ford Had a Better Idea

The Ford Motor Company is one of the best known industrial giants both in the United States and throughout the world. Americans were told there was a Ford in their future, and for many millions of Americans there has been. The familiar clicking light bulb signifies that "Ford has a better idea"; it often does. It all began on a farm.

Henry Ford was born on a farm, which he grew to hate more and more each year he was there. The death of his mother at the early age of 37 was a tremendous shock to Henry; he blamed his father and the grueling farm life. The seeds of Henry's outrageous ambition germinated when he met a man with a steam engine, who convinced him that he had the instinct of an engineer and the ambition and drive to do anything he chose in life. What he chose was to develop a machine that would make horses obsolete and ease the drudgery of the farm life that had killed his mother.

After completing school, Henry deserted the farm and began work as a press engineer, but success in this field required 4 years of pittance wages, and Henry was in too great a hurry to wait that long. He switched jobs and lodgings several times a year on the theory that he could learn more by sojourning in different places. His loving and devoted wife, Clara, stood behind him in his job transfers and waited patiently as he worked all through the night at home on his inventions.

Ultimately, with many different financial backers, Henry would go into business as the Ford Motor Company, producing the "Tin Lizzy." His only son, Edsel, after completing boarding school, was an obvious employee, making the Ford Company family-owned and family-operated. Edsel faced great difficulties as heir apparent to his father's business. Many of the employees and surrounding neighbors commented that he never appeared happy. As head of the purchasing department, he recognized that his father's company functioned as an autocracy, and any employees offering assistance or standing up for Edsel would soon be fired. Henry appeared to be so jealous of his son that anyone complimenting or defending him risked losing his or her job.

It was said that Henry still looked upon Edsel softheartedly as a lad in knickerbockers and not as an adult working in the company. Henry was insulated by his ego from his staff, his money, and the things that were happening around him. "He loaded his son like a willing camel, with one straw after another, in what could be interpreted as a plan to either test his mettle or break his back."[1] When Henry was 74, Edsel's forebearance toward his father was wearing thin. He resented Henry's brutal attempts to avoid unionization and his lack of human compassion. The situation worsened even further when the old man suffered a stroke. To prove that he was left unimpaired, Ford increased his interference in every detail of the company operation until it reached unmanageable proportions.

Edsel Ford died at age 49 of what was said to be inoperable cancer, but sentimentalists included heartbreak among the sicknesses that had killed him. The millions of dollars in gross revenue and the hundreds of employees at Ford Motor Company did not buffer or alter the conflict between Edsel and his father. It is cruel fate that Edsel Ford is remembered by the American public primarily because of the automobile that was Ford's greatest failure; it was, of course, named the Edsel.

Meanwhile, Henry Ford II, the third generation, had joined the company, although "join" is possibly not the right word since he had little choice in the matter. At his wedding, he received a present of 25,000 shares of Ford stock and an accompanying letter that said: "In recognition that after being married you will join the Ford Motor Company as your future business and also because of the fact that you are at the present time a director of the company."[2]

Perceptions of Henry II were rather negative. It was said that he had inherited a billion dollar organization to which he had contributed nothing. His playboy reputation, including the ownership of a 187-ton yacht, did nothing to improve his image, but possibly he had learned a lesson from his father's experiences. Said Eleanor, wife of Edsel: "The company killed my husband and it is not going to kill my son."[13]

Despite its inner turmoil, the Ford Motor Company has survived and prospered. The elder Henry saw a dream come true, but even though it became something of a nightmare for his heirs, the dream became a fixture for Americans.

The Robber Baron

The name of Rockefeller has also found a permanent place in the world of family business, but the Rockefeller dream was somewhat different from the vision that motivated Ford. John Rockefeller's entire goal in life was to make money. In his semiautobiographical *Random Reminiscences,* published in 1908, he said: "I determined to make money work for me." A schoolmate once asked him what he was going to do when he grew up. Said the young Rockefeller without hesitation, "I want to be worth a hundred thousand dollars, and I'm going to be."[4]

Whether or not a disadvantaged and poverty-stricken background is a psychological prerequisite for successful entrepreneurship, it was certainly a factor for Rockefeller. William Rockefeller was known as a poor dirt farmer, but somehow he had amassed fairly large sums of money. John D. Rockefeller would later discover his father's primary occupation was that of pitchman and con artist, cut from the same mold as P. T. Barnum.

Rockefeller achieved his goal of wealth in the Standard Oil Company. Much of the public considered him a monopolistic robber baron, and his life was threatened routinely, but he achieved his goal. By 1890, there was little doubt that he was a rich man who had come a long way from his youthful days, when the thought of great wealth would make him click his heels together in delight. His accumulated fortune in 1890 was estimated at more than $100 million. It would take him the rest of his life to orchestrate his income and expenses, and if his business career had ended, he could have spent the remaining lavish years clipping coupons.

The Rockefellers who followed him would probably have been no different from the other descendants of the great robber-baron industrialist had John not directed his effort at yet another creation—a philanthropic institution that would find a more receptive place in the public's heart and direct their attention from robber barons to great donors. He had made his money, and now he would put it to work to ensure that his heirs would not face the same hatred that he had faced.

The Rockefellers to follow were benefactors of humankind involved with power, prestige, and humanitarian goals. The generations to follow John Davidson Rockefeller I would go off in their own way to create foundations and funds and to take jobs that were meaningful to them as individuals. They never experienced the frustration their father felt with a poverty-stricken childhood that he spent the rest of his life overcoming.

The Newhouse Jack Built

A look at large family-dominated corporations as they exist today confirms the fact that these operations make a significant contribution to the gross national product. Family-managed Newhouse Publishing owns twenty-two newspapers, six TV stations, five magazines, twenty cable TV systems, and four radio systems. In 1976, *Business Week* commented: "The vast publishing and broadcasting empire of Samuel I. Newhouse seems to run with all the managerial finesse of a family operated grocery store."[5] Newhouse frowns on systems planning and budgeting and takes a dim view of titles and elaborate management schemes. He manages to run his business without the organizational structure of most modern large companies with employees exceeding 15,000. He is a careful operator and reacts quickly. All his businesses function as small company projects, though they are under one large corporate framework.

Newhouse, now 80 years old, was born on Manhattan's Lower East Side, the eldest of eight sons of impoverished Jewish immigrants. His father was an invalid who worked intermittently but was unable to support the family. Newhouse finished school at 14, enrolled in evening high school, and went to work as an office boy.

The business he created remains a foundation for relatives; at one time the company had sixty-four brothers, cousins, sons, and sons-in-law on the payroll. Currently, there are only fourteen relatives around, but a platoon of younger sons is coming along. Newhouse's two sons have been carefully groomed for taking over the business for the past 25 years.

Samuel I. Newhouse, Jr., is chairman of Condé Nast Publishing, which includes *Vogue, Mademoiselle, House and Garden, Glamour,* and *Bridge,* and, with his Uncle Norman, oversees the Cleveland *Plain Dealer.* Donald, age 46, the younger son, runs the Newark *Star-Ledger,* oversees newspapers in Syracuse and Jersey City, and runs the radio and TV operations, which are based in Syracuse. Neither son will be designated a chief officer under normal corporate circumstances.

A situation such as this could breed competition between the two brothers for the role of president, but the family regards such rivalry as unthinkable. Newhouse, Sr., describes the operation as nonbureaucratic, decentralized, and highly autonomous, with strong individual companies that act as small family-owned businesses in each of the communities. They do not believe in budgets or profit goals and, more important, have not allowed themselves to be limited and confined in an overpowering corporate structure.

No other major magazine chain is as well positioned mechanically and financially as Newhouse, and its strong financial position has left little need for outside stockholders. The Newhouse business is indicative of an entrepreneur's drive for freedom.

A Lust for Longevity: McCormick

Small business as a whole is faced with a high failure rate, and family-owned operations particularly fall victim to the grim business reaper. But there is one company that used the reaper to establish a record of longevity that few can match. International Harvester, formerly known as McCormick Reaper Works, has been in business for 148 years, building its success on Cyrus McCormick's invention and sustaining it with family control.

This is not easy to do. With death and taxes, families tend to sell off their stock in the family company and lose control of its affairs; public ownership and nepotism are not really compatible. There is another factor: The younger generation of wealthy families frequently has a sense of guilt about inheriting great wealth. Many of them feel a need to demonstrate their competencies to themselves, and this often leads them away from the family company. Brooks McCormick, age 62, does not express these feelings; if anything, he feels that it is the family ties that have *kept* him at International Harvester rather than simply getting him to the top. He attributes his involvement in the corporation mainly to his admiration for his cousin, Fowler McCormick, who headed International Harvester during the 1940s and who hired Brooks, a latter-day relative who came to the company by marriage. Despite the longevity record, death and taxes have taken their toll on International Harvester, and before Brooks McCormick took control, the vast majority of family-owned stock had dwindled away. No other McCormick owns a significant amount of the stock, and, indeed, Brooks may be the last reigning McCormick of International Harvester. None of his four children (two sons and two daughters) is in the company.

The Master Builders: Bechtell

For three decades, Bechtell has been one of the construction world's most famous and respected names. The organization is not known to the public, and that is the way the Bechtell family prefers it. The San Francisco family-owned business has worked in some two dozen countries on 116 major projects with jobs costing from $25 million to more than $1 billion each. *Fortune* estimates the company's growth as approaching $2 billion a year, and calculated profits, although more difficult to predict, may well top $40 million. The firm has more than 25,000 full-time employees, nearly 10,000 of them engineers, and some 35,000 temporary workers at different construction sites. It has twenty-five permanent offices scattered from New York to Los Angeles and from Jakarta to Beirut. About 40 percent of the firm's current undertakings are outside the United States.

The relative obscurity, like many other characteristics of the company, is reflected in the attitude of the owner and founder. Warren Bechtell first settled on building as his life's work in 1898, when as a young rancher he hired himself out with his mules in an Indian territory known as Oklahoma. For 30 years, the company did little more than railroad work, but in 1931, "Dad" Bechtell helped organize six companies. Today, actually, there are eight companies besides Bechtell: Henry J. Kaiser, Utah Construction, McDonald & Kahn, J. F. Shean, Pacific Bridge, Morrison, Knudsen, and Warren Brothers.

In 1933, at Warren Bechtell's death, the command passed to the second of his three sons, Steve Bechtell, Sr. In the early fifties, Steve, Sr., helped pioneer the building of nuclear power plants, and today the company has a commanding position in this difficult but fast-growing field. In 1961, Steve Bechtell, Sr., released the reins of the company to his 35-year-old son. This decision surprised many because the father was a healthy 60-year-old man enjoying an exhilarating way of life. The Bechtells denied that they ever had family disputes. This release of the company that he had built to such mammoth proportions was a tribute to the senior Bechtell's self-discipline; once he released the chief executive's spot, he avoided second-guessing his son's decisions, although he remained on the board of directors.[6]

Men from Mars

Like Bechtell, Mars, Inc., a large multinational manufacturer of candy and other food products, enjoys the privacy of family operation in one of the nation's largest privately held corporations. Its exact sales and earnings are deep secrets to outsiders, but based on *Business Week*'s estimates, sales range from $1.5 billion to $2 billion.[7] The company continues to preserve its privacy because all its stock is owned by Forrest Mars, his two sons, other family members, and the tax-exempt Mars Foundation.

Few companies preserve their privacy with the zeal of Mars. Its headquarters is located in McLean, Virginia, near the headquarters of the Central Intelligence Agency, and some people think Mars *is* the CIA. Outsiders are strictly barred from the premises, as if the company were manufacturing atom bombs rather than Snickers and Milky Way bars.

Mars formed the corporation in 1964 by merging his own British company with his late father's U.S. Candy Company. The merger was preceded by a prolonged dispute pitting Mars against his half sister and his stepmother's family for control of his father's company.

The overseas operation was centered in Britain, where Forrest Mars, Sr., began making Milky Way for the local market during the 1930s.

As a hot-tempered young man, Mars, Sr., quarreled with his father, the owner of a Chicago candy company, for whom he was working. According to gossip and folklore, the father, whose personality traits were not unlike the son's, gave the son several thousand dollars and the recipe for Milky Way bars and told him to start his own business abroad.

Today, the elder Mars, who is in good health, has relinquished the day-to-day corporate operations to the control of his sons, Forrest, Jr., and John. Mars, Sr., is said to be one of the nation's richest men, with a personal fortune estimated to be in the billion dollar range. The sons apparently share the president's title, though Forrest, Jr., is generally regarded as the chief executive. It is hard to establish who is really responsible for the company, but it is assumed that the brothers have divided the corporate responsibility.

Most family-owned businesses, of course, do not involve well-known names like Ford and Rockefeller. They are run by families named Smith and Jones and Brown; they are not multimillion dollar operations, and they do not all go from rags to riches. Some remain in rags, and some that rise to riches fall back to rags. To hear some of these stories, let us go to Middle City, America. Instead of, as it were, looking over the owner's shoulder at the business, as we did with the corporate giants, we will let the owners tell their stories in their own words.

A Meal in Middle City

Middle City lies at the foot of a hill so that the highway leading into town from a northerly direction descends a long grade called Broadway. It is a town of 15,000 people, and a billboard at the city limits proclaims that 14,999 of these are friendly folks while 1 is an old grouch; the grouch is not named. Where Broadway intersects Main Street is the center of the town's business district. Downtown is still doing fairly well economically, though there is some pressure from two shopping centers that have cropped up to accommodate Middle City's small but growing suburban population. Main Street is narrow, and the city leaders had to put in a parking ban which the citizens protested bitterly, just as they continue to protest the parking meters that were installed some years back on side streets.

The post office, the courthouse (Middle City is the seat of Central County), and the First National Bank—all fine edifices—cover three corners of the Main-Broadway intersection. On the fourth corner is a variety store, although it is clear from the shape of the entrance that the building was once a movie house. The Palace Theater closed several years ago and Middle City now has no downtown movie, only a drive-in. (In *The Last Picture Show,* the woman who worked with Sam at the movie house sadly removes the letters from the marquee. "If Sam had lived, we might have been able to keep it going, but with him gone, I just can't do it by myself." Sam had no family.) Beside the variety store on Main Street sits the Middle City Hotel, the only building on the street over four stories high. The new motel outside the town has taken away a lot of the business, and many of the hotel's occupants are permanent residents, elderly people mostly. The barbershop in the lobby still thrives, however, and it still "cuts" hair as opposed to "styling" hair. Next door is Neal's Restaurant.

The restaurant is clean and gleams with Formica. To the right of the doorway is a long counter with stools on which a dozen midmorning coffee drinkers are perched. A row of booths runs down the left wall, and round tables are placed down the center of the room. The kitchen is in the rear. Mary Neal gives up her post at the counter cash register to sit at a booth at the back of the restaurant to talk about the family-owned business.

"Well you've really come to the right place. Just about every businessman—I guess I should say 'businessperson' these days, shouldn't I?—in town comes in here. The place is usually called 'Papa Neal's.' I guess it's sort of a meeting place. Why, I hear talk about everything from government regulations to lousy son-in-laws—sons-in-law?—every day. I guess maybe the other businessmen feel some kind of alliance to Papa Neal because they are all pretty much in the same boat—small family-owned businesses.

"Don—that's Papa—and I have run this same restaurant for 35 years. I guess you could call us prisoners of the business. We don't have any bars on the windows, but we are inmates just the same. I don't know whether it's loyalty or helplessness or plain old inertia. I know we do feel that the community kind of depends on us. It's a meeting place they feel comfortable with. And Don and I both enjoy the meetin' and greetin' that goes on every day.

"Now business has not always been that great and we have sure had our ups and downs in keeping this restaurant afloat—is that what you call 'mixing a metaphor'? Food costs keep going up, we've had some employee problems, and now a McDonald's is going to open up down the street!

"Don is a skilled tradesman, but he got tired of working for other people. He had this dream—I guess his one goal in life—of being an independent entrepreneur—is that the right word?—with some standing in the community. At first, I guess it was just his dream, but as I worked side by side with him, it gradually became my dream too. I like being independent, being my own boss. I'm not sure how independent we really are, but we have certainly put in a lot of long, hard hours. It's been a struggle, sure, but I think we do have good standing in the community now.

"Anyway, it's provided a means of livelihood for us, let us put our three children through school and get them started in careers of their own. None of them liked the restaurant business—I guess they spent too many years working behind the counter or back in the kitchen peeling potatoes—whatever, they all chose other professions, and now we have a family-owned business without a family to leave it to.

"I guess we'll sell the business when we retire. We'll need some kind of financial security when we're unable to work, and neither of us is getting any younger. I think we can get a good price because we have a good business at a good location. Over the years, we've had offers from people who wanted to buy us out. But, you know, selling this business would be like putting one of the children up for adoption. This business is our dream, and we built it with a lot of hard work. Every time Don and I talk about selling, we both practically break down and cry.

"I guess all dreams come to an end sometime, though. We've had a good life and we've run a good restaurant. I hope the next owner loves it as much as we do."

Going Out with Style

Up the street from Neal's Restaurant, at the corner of Main and Jefferson, is the cater-cornered entrance to Styles Unlimited. It is evident that this is a business that has kept up with modern trends. The shining mirrors, attractive displays, and generally "mod" decor would not be out of place in Chicago. The store beckons to the purchasing power of youth. The owner is Les West, a handsome man in his forties who appears to have studied Molloy's *Dress For Success*. He leans back in his chair in his private office at the back of the store and ponders the statement that according to Mary Neal, he should have quite a lot to say about family-owned business.

"Well, actually, this is not really a family-owned business, though the idea did originate with my father about 20 years ago. He operated a small clothing store in Jackson, which is about 40 miles from here. Man, did I put in some hours in that store—tagging merchandise, selling clothes, you name it. Dad used me as a kind of handyman. It was a good little business.

"But, you know, merchandising trends change, and as Dad got older, he didn't change with them. Dad was stubborn. *He* was the founder of the business, *he* knew what was good for it, and so on. So he refused to make any changes, and sales gradually shifted to shopping centers and other stores that were more modern and diverse. Now I had invested about 10 years of my life in merchandising, and I think I had learned a few things. I didn't think the business could last long. Certainly it couldn't support both my family and Dad's. I faced what I guess you could call an emotional crisis. I loved Dad but felt I had to go out on my own, pursue my own dreams. So I came to Middle City and started Styles Unlimited.

"Of course, it was natural that I would start a clothing business because that was what I knew. But look at the position I was in. I was competing with my own father! Talk about guilt feelings. It wasn't simply that Dad thought I had deserted him; *I* thought I had deserted him. So I spent many years 'on the couch,' you might say, discussing the problem with a psychologist. Meanwhile, Dad's business was being suffocated by the modern shopping centers; Jackson is full of them now.

"Keep in mind, I tried to help, but any advice I gave fell on the deafest pair of ears I ever saw. Dad not only resented me as a 'deserter,' he resented my advice. It never occurred to him that I might know more about merchandising than he did. By the time Styles Unlimited had been in operation 7 years, it was a successful business. Now, I'm no genius but I *can* recognize modern trends in merchandising. Dad never could.

"When I got the news that Dad had gone bankrupt, all the old guilt really came back. I kept asking myself, 'Would he have made it if I had stayed?' We'll never know the answer to that, but, what the heck, I had to live my own life anyway.

"Dad worked in a filling station about a year, and seeing him there—a man who had been so proud of his business—pumping someone else's gas was just too much for me. I asked Dad to come to work for Styles Unlimited. And it wasn't charity; I really could use him. Dad's strong suit was always customer relations. He was very outgoing; both young people and old people liked him. Many of his customers became lifelong friends. So I gave him the job of operations manager. His job was to see that all the salespeople in the store put forth some effort in the area of customer relations. He wouldn't take the job at first; knowing Dad, I didn't expect him to. He still saw me as a deserter. But after about 5 months, he swallowed his pride and came around.

"We're doing fine now. Maybe it would have been nicer if Dad had been able to hand his business down to me, but the ball didn't bounce that way. I guess you could say we're working in our second family business."

The Descent of Mann

Grand Avenue in Middle City is a tree-lined boulevard with a grass median strip that winds through the town's best residential section. On it sit the old and stately homes of most of the town's affluent citizens, but there is a sprinkling of middle-class and even lower-middle-class dwellings. There are no commercial establishments. Joe Mann's home is one of the newer, more middle-class houses. Joe works as a manufacturer's representative for a number of national companies, but it is not his work that he has agreed to talk about on his day off. In his well-appointed living room, Joe is clearly sad as he tells the story of the Mann Company.

"My father, John Mann, started the Mann Company back in the 1940s. It served as a manufacturer's rep and distributor for International Harvester. Dad had a very warm sort of personality; he was also a good salesman, and he built Mann into a very successful business. In addition to my mother, there were two sons and a daughter in the family, and Dad had built the firm for us. My older brother joined the company first, then I came in, and finally my sister's husband came on board. As family members became a part of the business, Dad kept the controlling stock interest but made gifts of stock to all of us. Eventually, as the business grew, the family members also had pretty liberal fringe benefits made available to them, and Dad was pretty liberal with the salary compensation too, not just for us but for the other thirty or so company employees who did the sales and service work for the heavy equipment.

"Then Dad died, and the family members started fighting among themselves. I guess I was as guilty as anyone else if you want to start placing blame for what happened to the business. Through all of it, my mother was naturally pretty upset because her modest source of income was at stake.

"Dad had a will that left the business to Mother, but she had not had any management role for 10 years, so it was up to us to run the company. We didn't do it very well. My brother and I began jockeying for position in the company, and we both wanted to control things. Well, my sister objected to that and thought that my brother-in-law should have an equal say in things and get the same money we got.

"Anyway, this kind of feuding went on for some time, and naturally the business was hurt by it. The company stopped growing, and the high salaries and bonuses put us in financial trouble. We were letting a profitable firm go to pot. I pulled out first and became a manufacturer's rep in my own right. Then my older brother went to work for another firm here in town. At some point I guess we all decided that the day of reckoning had arrived; we decided to liquidate the business.

"We're all doing okay on our own right now, but I think it is a shame that we let my father's business get away from us. Dad dreamed of a business that would one day be run by his children for the benefit of the family. Our feuding certainly made a mess of that dream.

"Of course, you might be able to fault Dad some for not having made more specific provision for what was to happen after his death, who was to control it, and so on. I guess he figured that we could work it out ourselves. Boy, was he wrong. When he died, the business, for all practical purposes, died with him. Dad's out there in Greenwood Cemetery now, and I guess the tombstone should read, 'Here lies John Mann and the Mann Company.'"

Their Brother's Keepers

Grand Avenue ends at the highway bypass going north around Middle City. Just off the bypass, and outside the city limits, is a sign that proclaims the neatly landscaped site to be the headquarters of Middle City Industries, the largest manufacturing operation in Middle

City. Inside the plant, over sixty employees are using assembly line production methods to produce window frames. Jim Samson, the owner and manager, who represents the second generation in the business, conducts the grand tour of the plant, talking as he points out the various operations.

"My father, Howard, started the business some 40 years ago with a few people and an idea of working closely with the construction industry. They started in a garage with five employees, but the business grew and they bought their own property and buildings. I was the only one of three sons who chose to work in my father's manufacturing plant; my older brother became an attorney, and my younger brother is an accountant.

"Growth was really small in the early years, and it was very hard management for both me and my father. We worked very closely together. We hired an outside consultant, who spent 6 months in the company, organizing the employees, running management seminars, outlining a growth pattern for our future years, and so on. A month before he left, he called Dad and me together and said, 'Look, Howard, you need to retire in 3 months; get out of the business and let your son take over.'

This was quite a shock to Dad and not easy for him to take. He finally did retire from the business a year later, but it was traumatic for the entire family. He probably wouldn't have retired, but we had already spent some $20,000 on the management team's supervising plans, and I guess he figured that he had to give it a chance. He appointed me president of the corporation and kept a small amount of the stock, which was to be turned over to me when he died.

Dad left the business and went home to try to make a new life for himself, but he failed. God, did he fail! He and Mom took a lot of vacations, he golfed, but there was always a look of misery in his eyes every time the families got together for dinner. I felt pretty guilty that I was now running the company, which he longed to be in every day of his life. Somehow, he managed to stay away, but 17 months after the day he retired, he suffered a heart attack. During his stay at the hospital, the doctors told us he had no will to live, and he died 1 month later.

"Dad had carefully planned his estate, and the stock he had kept in the corporation reverted to me, the owner; he left each of my brothers half the real estate. The company rents the building from them at a sizable amount of money each month. They don't have any interest in the business and never really cared anything about it, but they wait for their checks to come. The money they receive is really their share of the estate, and, of course, the majority of the estate is tied up in equity, with payments to my mother for life.

"This has created a problem for the company at the moment. My brothers wanted professional careers, but the opportunities in law and accounting did not pay as well as they expected, and they all have a pretty good idea of what *I* make. They probably resent the fact that the money they get from the land and the building is as little as it is in their eyes. They know it is peanuts compared to what I am taking out of the company, but, of course, they fail to realize that I am putting in 12 to 15 hours a day to keep the company going.

"I offered to purchase the building and property from them at a price over market value, but my brothers are convinced I am out to take advantage of them and won't even hear of selling. The company needs to expand the building, but my brothers are not willing to do this themselves and won't let me do it. The expansion is necessary to put in new machinery to make us competitive in the market.

"My managers warned me that without the new machinery we may lose our segment of the market, which means the business would go nowhere. For the past year, I have looked into buying my own plant and moving to another location, but all of this takes money and I'm not sure I can handle the capital outlay right now. Also, I face the problem that my mother and two brothers would probably never speak to me again if I pulled out on the business and the money they receive each month.

"I've attempted to be very professional about this and have brought my lawyer to meet with theirs in hopes of working out a relationship and a financial settlement that would prove beneficial to everyone. They are not receptive to the idea, and Mother constantly warns that I cannot split up the family by 'doing this reckless thing,' and so on. She thinks I should be satisfied to make the kind of money I'm making and keep the family unity. She's never been involved in the business and doesn't understand the need for expansion and new equipment, so I really can't have hard feelings about her desire to keep everything as calm as possible.

"In the next year, though, I've got to make a decision whether to sever the relationship with my brothers or stay in the business and face a slow suffocation. I have two sons training in the business at this very minute. Although I know Dad had no idea that what has happened could possibly happen to me, I am going to make sure that I plan properly for my two sons to handle the business and not be stifled by the relatives who are not working in the business.

"The plot thickens in this family as my wife, of course being on my side, tries to socialize with my brother's wife. The tension is even felt when our children try to play together at family affairs. It's such a mess that I've often considered scrapping the whole thing, shutting down the plant, and taking a job with someone else. But I know I'm only kidding myself because there is too much of my father in me. His need for independence and the joy of running his own successful company has been an overriding factor in my entire life.

"Well, at least I don't have the problems that Harvesty Building has, with his four sons and son-in-law working in the company."

A Bitter Harvesty

Middle City sits in a great bend of the Middle River. It was never a river-port town, however, because the sluggish yellow water barely conceals huge sandbars that only canoes and rowboats can navigate. The old wooden bridge that once carried traffic in the eastern part of town over the river still stands but is no longer open to traffic; it has been replaced by a new concrete bridge. The headquarters of Harvesty Building lies just beyond the bridge. In his spartan office, the son-in-law gives his version of the company story.

"Yes, indeed, this is quite a family business. Four sons and a son-in-law in addition to the old man. The sons range in age from 18 to 35; I'm 28. But Jay Harvesty, the old man, is the one who really counts because he runs the company with an iron hand. There is no organizational structure in the company at all, even though we will be working a fifty-worker crew in the city and surrounding counties this year. The four boys in the company are all paid the same salaries, although they certainly don't do the same amount of work. As you might expect, there is some bad blood between us. Some people say that we just barely tolerate each other's existence.

"Mr. Harvesty is a tyrant. He expects everyone to work 12 to 15 hours a day and live this business. He pits one son against another, thinking that this will make them work harder to win his approval. Sometimes it works, but frequently it fails. It has created an atmosphere among the brothers that is absolutely unbelievable. They are always trying to get the others in trouble, and they create problems for the crews the other brothers are working with.

"The older brother has found a lazy hiding place. As a matter of fact, the crew he is assigned to work with has turned over twice in the past year because, each day going out to a job, Doug will find a place to sit under a tree and sleep as he directs the crew to do the job he was sent out to do. The workers are not in a position to say much about what is happening, because obviously Mr. Harvesty wouldn't even begin to believe them, so they move on to other businesses, where they are not treated so unfairly. Doug takes 100 percent credit for everything done properly, and when anything is botched, he blames the inept workers under him.

"The second brother, Michael, works himself to death—eats, lives, and breathes this whole job. He's had two divorces because neither of his wives could bear to be alone all the hours that he spent on the job. He unfortunately has fallen victim to his father's games— that the hardest worker will win the company—and he may die trying to gain the presidency of the corporation. His crew pities him because they recognize the effort he puts forth. So they try to help him by playing practical jokes on the other brothers.

"Michael suffers greatly from being the second son because somehow his father fails to recognize that Doug is not a hard worker. Therefore Michael is constantly trying to gain praise from his father. Jay, the third son, in his early twenties, is working in between colleges; he has been in seven. His father touted higher education and even helped with some of the expenses, but Jay will work 6 months in the business, go back to college, flunk out, and return to the same position and pay the other brothers are making. This, of course, infuriates the brothers and the crew because they recognize that he is always in a holding pattern for something better.

"Three months ago, when Jay returned from another experience at college, the brothers gathered Dad together and threatened to resign if he allowed Jay to come back in the company, managing the crew. They were in favor of allowing him to work as a crewman with no management responsibilities. Their father promised that he would consider their recommendations, but on Monday morning after the Saturday meeting, Jay was back managing the crew and the other supervisor was placed under him.

"The younger son, Steve, just turned 18 and has been working in the business for many years. He appears to be a hard worker but becomes emotionally involved in all the family turmoil to the point that he is frequently visiting with a psychologist. He is a meek, mild-mannered person, unwilling to accept a lot of responsibility, but he will work from dawn to dusk if directed to do anything. His father still views him as the baby of the family and tries to give him the easiest job with the most pay. The other three brothers do not seem to have developed hostilities to their younger brother, probably because they are so busy putting out the internal fires among themselves.

"Mama Harvesty is a nervous wreck, and if you frown at her, she begins to weep and wonder what is wrong. Mr. Harvesty appears to love the conflict and the challenge of going to work and wondering which one of his fifty employees is going to resign or at least threaten resignation. While he is only 55 years old, he has had two heart attacks, and the mention of a will or estate sends him screaming out of his office, throwing papers. The board meetings, which he is forced to have because of his corporate structure, are little more than a joke and a 2-hour screaming session on everyone's incompetencies.

"My wife and friends frequently ask me why I am working in this hellhole, but if you stand back and objectively watch the circus, it is constantly exciting. My real purpose is my journalism career. Currently, I am writing a novel dealing with the problems in a family business with fathers and sons angry, hostile, and resentful of their life and the situation around them. What better place than Harvesty to serve as a basis for a very good novel?"

All Is Well

A short distance west of Middle City is a place called Broad Lake. There is one general store, a gas pump, and the office of Hunt Drilling. There is a birth announcement on the business front that says "Sam Hunt III arrives—the Fourth Generation water well driller." On a bench in front of the store, Sam Hunt, Jr., in his sixties, talks about the business his father established.

"My father, Sam, Sr., started the water well drilling business in 1930. There weren't many drillers in the area then and business was great. Becoming a driller myself was no passing fancy because it had been ingrained in me since childhood. I worked side by side with my father, learning the skills, learning the technology—all I could learn about water well construction. Since I was the only son and clearly the heir apparent, my father never discussed estate planning or anything with me. He died one day at a job site.

"I was left with the business, and it became my entire life, just as it had been for my father. Of course, we were small and had to struggle, but the whole family pitched in. Heck, we needed cheap labor. My wife, Susan, handled the books, did a lot of the sales work, and collected the accounts receivable. By the time they were 12, my two sons were working on the rig with me.

"The business grew, but it was truly a family operation. Most of our workers—thirty or so now—come from the families of present employees. There are a lot of father-son teams operating rigs for Hunt drilling.

"My oldest son, Dana, really threw himself into the business from the start. He really likes the mechanical end of it and was eager to work and learn the technology. But my other son, Sam III, had other ideas. He worked in the business during the summer but was bored with it and couldn't wait every fall to get back to school. He went on to college, saying that he could do better for himself than the water well business. Ha! He got his bachelor's degree and then an M.B.A. But, lo and behold, he looked around for jobs with the education he had and came back to Hunt Drilling. I was glad to get his business sense into the company. I guess I welcomed him back like the prodigal son.

"I'm really proud of this family operation. We have served many thousands of people around here. Our greatest sales tool is referral; we are drilling wells now for the grandchildren of people my father worked for.

"The boys and I get along fine, but I can't say the same thing for their wives. Each wife thinks her husband is better qualified than the other and should be president of the company. So our family gatherings are a little tense. I know one day I will have to make a choice about which one should be in charge when I'm gone, but it's sure a hard decision to make."

The First Black President

Like many American communities, Middle City was built on a railroad. When the tracks were finally laid late in the nineteenth century, this spot in the bend of the river was used as a place to take on coal and water. Houses were built for the people who serviced the train, retail businesses were developed to service the people who serviced the train; and a town was born. It grew back toward the hills, which provided a cooler location in summer, rather than toward the river. Of course, the train station had been built on the flat land because the locomotives of the day could not stop until they reached the foot of the hill.

Only freight trains rumble through Middle City today. Henry Ford's automobile gradually eliminated much of the need for passenger service, and what is left is accommodated by the Greyhound buses that come through town.

The area "across the tracks" is occupied mostly by warehouses, a few small retail establishments, and Peterson's Lumber Company. Grady Peterson, now in his forties, is a huge black man who reminds one of James Earl Jones. His smiles are broad and his laughs are booming, but his words are all business.

"My father started this business about 30 years ago, although, in a way, it was started by my grandfather. You see, my grandfather owned a little sawmill about 10 miles out of Middle City. They were called 'peckerwood sawmills' in those days, although my grandfather sure never used the word. He thought only white people could be peckerwoods. Anyway, he made a pretty good living at it, with my father helping him as soon as he was old enough. But there wasn't a lot of money in sawing boards. Granddaddy never even had a bank account, just an old iron safe that had a padlock on it. Didn't matter much; he never had more than a few hundred dollars at a time.

"My father was in World War II—all-black unit—and was wounded in action in Germany. Lost a finger. He got a medal for it. Used to say that he cut off his finger trying to open one of those K-ration cans. Actually, it was a piece of shrapnel. Anyway, he decided he didn't want to spend the rest of his life running saws, so in 1949 he talked Granddaddy into letting him open up a yard in town to see if they couldn't sell more lumber that way. Sort of a factory outlet, you could say. Granddaddy finally said okay, although he really didn't think much of the idea, and my father set up shop on this very spot.

"You see, Dad figured that with the war over and everything, the town would grow and people would need lumber and other building materials, and he didn't think they should have to go all the way to Jackson to get it. He was right. People started building those little houses you see over across the river and out toward Broad Lake and up on Graball Hill. Most of those houses were built with materials the people bought at Peterson's Lumber Company. Dad had set up a real business, you see, and he was really keeping books and everything.

"He even made enough money to send me off for 2 years of college. I was the first member of my family to even finish high school, mind you, let alone go to college. I sort of wanted to get that college degree, but Dad thought 2 years was enough. He used to say, 'My daddy never spent a day in a schoolroom and he made it, and you wanting to sit there all your life.'

"I came back and worked with Dad in the business, doing the books and things like that. Dad was always the salesman, and I learned what I know from him. Most of his customers were white people and most of mine are. He would say, 'Look those white people in the eye and talk dollars and cents to 'em. Let 'em know you don't cheat and won't be cheated. They understand business talk.' He didn't think black people were bad off because they were black but because they didn't have any money.

"I guess I agree with him. I have two teenage boys, and you can bet they're going to college, if they can make it. And not just to play football, although—guess I can brag a little—my oldest boy is quarterback on the Middle City High football team. Can you imagine that? Quarterback. There was a time when he couldn't have been the water boy.

"But times change, and I think black people making it in business has had a lot to do with times changing. There are a lot of black businesses in Middle City now.

"My son Donnie—he's the quarterback—will probably take over the business after me. That boy has got his whole life planned already. He's going to college on a football scholarship, get a degree in business administration, play pro football awhile, and then become a tycoon. He's not just talking either. You know, he's been trying to talk me—me!—into setting up a construction business, serving as our own supplier. Seventeen years old.

"Of course, I'm proud of my other son, Larry, too, but he's not much interested in the business. Wants to be pianist. But my grandfather—he's gone now, of course—would really be proud of Donnie. I know my dad, who's retired—he's 72—is. He said the other day, 'Son, we have never had a no-account in the Peterson family and I never figured you would father one either.' I told that to Donnie. He said, 'Look, old Pops, my kid is gonna be the first black President of the United States.' You know, he just could be right."

In The Final Analysis

The businesses of Middle City are not unlike the billion dollar operations of far more famous families. They were built on dreams, sustained by ambition, and sometimes torn by conflict. The struggles in the Harvesty family differ very little from those in the Ford family. Family-owned businesses may change form, and they may be larger and buffered by layers of management, but the characteristics remain basically the same.

Nearly half a century has passed since Adolf Berle and Gardiner Means published their famous *The Modern Corporation and the Private Company,* the forerunner of Galbraith's *New Industrial State.* In 1932, they observed, the American corporation had ceased to be private business as individual owners and founders moved toward professional management. Public ownership of large corporations was becoming the trend in business. Certainly Berle and Means underestimated the diversity of the American society and economy. Many good and large corporations insist on remaining privately owned and operated.

The big advantage of the private corporation, large or small, is its ability to react quickly to any management decision without endless committee, board, and stockholders' meetings. Public companies are torn between the desire to show earnings and to minimize taxes. The executive has lost the right to run his own show as he pleases. The $375 million Estée Lauder Co. is an example of how a privately owned company can work with products to make them pay off in the future. When Aramis and Clinique were launched, the two products depressed earnings for many years, but today they have paid off a hundredfold. If this had been a public corporation, management probably never would have been able to stick with the original products because the stockholders would have voted a change in management.

The highway going south out of Middle City passes a filling station. One of Mr. Ford's products is having its tank filled with one of Mr. Rockefeller's. The man from Mars has left his products in the nearby candy machine. In a distant field, one of McCormick's products is at work. The man pumping gas owns the station.

"Yeah, I've got the franchise. Same as my father. With these high gas prices, it's been tough keeping my customers happy, not to mention making a profit. But I'm stocking more spare parts now, and I just expanded my repair business. We can do a whole engine overhaul right here in the station. I have some people who come up from Jackson to get their repair work done. You know, in those great big repair shops, they never even see the man who's gonna do the work, much less talk to him. Here, they tell Harry—he's my top mechanic—that the engine is going bing or bong, and Harry jumps right on it. My son will probably go into the business too. Loves to work on cars, and Harry is teaching him. Why just the other day . . ."

Notes

[1] James Brough, *The Ford Dynasty: An American Story*, Doubleday & Company, Inc., New York, 1977, p. 155. Excerpt from *The Ford Dynasty: An American Story* by James Brough. Copyright © 1977 by James Brough. Reprinted by permission of Doubleday & Company, Inc.

[2] Ibid., p. 29.

[3] Ibid., p. 228.

[4] Peter Collier and David Horowitz, *The Rockefellers: An American Dynasty*, Holt, Rinehart and Winston, New York, 1976.

[5] William Shepard, Jr., "S. I. Newhouse and Sons," *Business Week*, January 26, 1976, p. 56.

[6] Dan Cordtz, "Bechtel Survives on Billion Dollar Jobs," *Fortune*, January 1975, p. 93.

[7] Alice Priest, "Mars," *Business Week*, August 14, 1978, pp. 52–56.

Evolution of the Entrepreneur

Entrepreneur. So far we have tossed this term around without providing much explanation, hoping that the context would make the meaning reasonably clear. It is such a key concept in family-owned business that we wanted to hold off in order to do a big number later. The time has arrived. Says Webster: "en·tre·pre·neur (äńtre·pre·nûŕ; F. ańtre-), *n*. [F. See ENTERPRISE.] One who assumes the risk and management of business. . . ."

Economists once described the "factors of production" in business enterprise as land, labor, and capital. It is now accepted that there is a fourth factor—management—that indeed involves work, but a different kind of work than what is meant by the term "labor." The manager makes the decisions, and the "laborer" carries them out. But first there must be a business to manage—someone to put the land, labor, and capital together in the first place. That someone is the entrepreneur. In the established family-owned and -operated business, the entrepreneur and management functions merge. Putting things together is hard work. It takes drive; it takes bright ideas. Thus entrepreneurs tend to be special people.

Now, all this can be pretty heavy stuff in economics and psychology textbooks. But we are not writing a textbook, and so we will lighten it a little while at the same time striving to preserve the accuracy of those distinguished disciplines. We certainly do not wish to make Dr. Galbraith and Dr. Brothers any angrier than they already are.

Good Guys and Bad Guys

The term "entrepreneur" has been around a long time, first appearing, according to one economic historian, in a dictionary of commerce written in 1723. Clearly, it was the rise of capitalism and the industrial revolution that facilitated the rise of entrepreneurship. Feudalism and mercantilism offered little room for maneuver for enterprising individuals who wanted to strike out on their own. Peasant economies with cottage industries offered them few places in which to maneuver.

In addition, popular attitudes toward those skilled in business matters were largely negative until perhaps the eighteenth century. In the Middle Ages, lending money at interest was regarded as usury, a sin. Merchants in Western Christendom were generally regarded as a low class of people.

The surge of capitalism in the West made the successful merchant a good guy for the first time. Adam Smith told the world that spirited competition—buying cheap and selling dear—was a commendable practice that benefited everybody in the end. At the same time, the rise of Protestantism encouraged people not only to engage in business but to do so with all their might, with their souls at peril. In Protestant doctrine, hard work had been divinely commanded. Those who worked hard would be rewarded by God with fame and fortune; the slackers would be justly punished. Intoned the preacher: "They that will not sweat on Earth will sweat in hell."[1]

With individualism, competition, and hard work installed as virtues, and with the industrial revolution expanding the business territories available for colonizing, the stage was set for some major successes by hard-driving entrepreneurs. And the colonizers came in the form of the Fords and Rockefellers and other Horatio Alger figures we have noted.

Public attitudes began to be characterized by second thoughts, however. Apparently, one was supposed to work hard and be thrifty and become financially successful, but if one became *too* successful it was probably not due to hard work and thrift alone but was accomplished through shady practices or even outright dishonesty. After all, good horse traders had been eyed with mixed emotions all along. (Glenn Ford, in *The Sheepman*, is the prototype. He offers to buy a horse from Edgar Buchanan, no mean trader himself. Gazing into a corral full of sorry-looking critters, Buchanan offers Ford "any horse on the premises" for $20 or so. Whereupon Ford marches into the barn and brings out Buchanan's own fine stallion as his choice. "I meant the corral," growls Buchanan. Says Ford, mounting: "But you said the premises, and the barn is on the premises.")

When the sharp horse traders became millionaires, they were as likely to be called robber barons as successful entrepreneurs. Surely they had exploited the public in amassing such great wealth, and they would have to be stopped. Hence, antitrust laws and regulatory commissions became a major feature of the late nineteenth and early twentieth centuries in America. No one knows how much robbing was actually going on, but some certainly was. The industrial nations decided that entrepreneurship was a fine progressive force, but it had to be kept in bounds.

To this day, public attitudes toward business success are schizoid. Witness the tendency for big business to pop out as the bad guy in economic discussions. Of course, American businesses, particularly big corporations, work very hard today to correct the "public be damned" image of the rags-to-riches era. On practically any Saturday afternoon, for example, corporate executives are likely to be on live sports telecasts, making contributions to colleges in the name of this or that skilled athlete. Or there is Xerox bringing us movies to remember with only one commercial interruption.

Still, entrepreneurs must face the fact that they probably will not be loved by all. They may not *want* to be loved (George Peppard, in *The Carpetbaggers,* portraying a character strongly resembling Howard Hughes: "I don't want love or children or home-baked cookies"), but if they do, they may be disappointed.

What Makes Them Run?

Mention of love and disappointment reminds us right away that there is likely to be a psychological side to this entrepreneurship thing. In the famous Bud Schulberg novel *What Makes Sammy Run?* (there are things to be learned from books as well as movies), Sammy Glick rises to prominence over the bodies of lots of people. One of his obsessions is shoes. He has hundreds of pairs at all times and rarely wears the same pair twice. Why? It turns out that when he was a poor lad, he never got a new pair of shoes. He always wore hand-me-downs from his older brother, and they were always several sizes too large and flopped around on his feet. Those flopping shoes became a major force in his life. Shoes and success or not, Sammy was very unloved. ("He said I was his best friend, and I thought, My God! I probably am.")[2]

Sammy's story suggests a major theme in the literature of entrepreneurship. Putting a business together and carrying it to the top calls for a forceful person. This life force probably consists of more than the desire to make a living; the skills are far more than a matter of technique. Genius, as Edison said, may be 99 percent perspiration, but successful entrepreneurship is not just a matter of genius. Indeed, "genius," defined purely as a matter of intellect, may be a drawback; ignorance and confidence, if we are to believe Mark Twain, are surer guides to success.

The entrepreneur, all would agree, must be ambitious, confident, extremely hardworking, and possessed of plenty of a certain kind of "smarts." That person must have some kind of dream and a great determination to fulfill it, even if it means cutting a few ethical corners, and a goal and a strategy for achieving the dream, even if it means putting the hammer down on a few people. The entrepreneur must have a knack for, and enjoy, mastering apparently insurmountable obstacles, overcoming life's setbacks, and dealing with the never-ending stream of difficulties that accompany the building of new things.

The question is, Why do some people have these talents and desires while others do not? Are the seeds of entrepreneurship found in the genes? Are they environmentally induced? Alas, we do not really know for certain. This is not from want of trying by the psychologist and the sociologist and the economist. And some plausible hypotheses can be put forth regarding the factors that produce entrepreneurs. We will talk here of poverty backgrounds, patterns of family life, and other environmental factors that are often associated with the entrepreneurial personality.

Before we get too carried away with Freudian analysis, however, we should put the matter in perspective. Probably the great majority of people who create, sustain, and pass on family-owned businesses have motivations that are simple to understand. They want a decent living for themselves and their families; they are independent-minded and willing to take risks, and so they go into business for themselves and, by hard work and some luck, do pretty well. No flopping shoes, like Sammy Glick, or grinding poverty, or fathers who do not love them. Sure, the business is a kind of dream and they have determination, but these things are not obsessions. The points about obsessions seem to apply most clearly to the minority of entrepreneurs who *did* go all the way to the top—the Rockefellers and Fords, not the Neals and Petersons. All of them *do* have some of the same motivations, but it is equally good to keep the differences in mind. In other words, we do not wish to leave the impression that one has to be a little bit crazy to be successful in a family-owned business. With this caveat, let us look at the early lives of entrepreneurs.

Up from Poverty

Ah, yes! Who can forget Scarlett O'Hara on a hilltop in Civil War-torn Georgia, tearing a turnip from the earth to quell her hunger and proclaiming to the heavens: "As God is my witness, I'll never be hungry again" *(Gone With the Wind)*. Presumably she was not. She marries her sister's beau, takes over his business, squeezes every dime she can out of the customers, marries Rhett Butler, and lives unhappily ever after. All self-made people are not men.

The theme of poverty, with the deprivation of body and spirit implied by that term, as a motivation for the entrepreneur shows up again and again. The escape from poverty becomes an obsession that drives people to become rich so that they will never be hungry again: Dickens's Oliver Twist and David Copperfield, hungry waifs bravely facing an unfriendly and uncaring world. The stories told by real people in the academic studies of the subject are often heartrending tales of childhood struggles. Would there be food on the table? Shoes could not be resoled for lack of money, and so cardboard was used to cover the holes. Newspapers were read and then used as wall-paper. Christmas gifts were apples or oranges. The entrepreneurs quite often see poverty backgrounds as being responsible for the strong characters they developed, even bragging about the hardships they endured. As children, they could not be dependent on others; as adults, they resent dependency. Here are some examples from interviews:

> My father did his very best, and we always had the necessary things in life. I knew that if I wanted to go to college like my friends, I would have to make the money. I never finished school because the idea of making money became more important than school. I work hard to make this business successful, so someday my children will have the educational opportunities I lacked.

Moral: Work hard so that your children will have it better than you did.

> Our food and existence was totally dependent on the farm surroundings. My mother and the eight children worked from dawn to

dusk to provide enough money and food to carry us through winter months. I respected my father's independence and hardworking approach to life, but at an early age, I decided I would not be a victim of a poverty-stricken background as an adult. I left home at 17 and worked two jobs to learn a trade and establish financial security for myself. My job as a helper on the drilling machine gave me the idea that I could buy my own machine and set out to conquer the world of poverty in which I had been surrounded.

Moral: You can conquer poverty if you put your mind to it.

At age 12, I had the awesome responsibility of running my father's plumbing business. He was paralyzed as a result of an accident, and since I was the oldest son, it was my responsibility to provide the livelihood for my mother and brothers. The entire family worked in the business as a means of survival, but as I grew older, I realized our efforts had provided not only an existence but a thriving business in the community. My two brothers and sister now work together daily with only minor problems because our early survival was based on our efforts as a team. I think we might experience business problems working together if the past were not so deeply embedded in our minds.

Moral: The family that survives together thrives together.

Many people clearly *believe* that their success in life is a response to the harsh challenges of poverty, and their testimony does stand as evidence that poverty and entrepreneurship are related. However, we are far from having proof that poverty is a major causal factor.

In the first place, the sad fact is that most people who are born poor remain so. The United States has struggled for generations without success to eliminate poverty. For every one person who escapes the welfare rolls, it seems that there are two others who see their children and grandchildren go onto the same rolls. Poverty tends to be self-perpetuating because it drains from people the energy they need to fight it. Thus, most people born with two strikes against them do not hit home runs. At best, they continue to foul off pitches, and many strike out. At most, we can say that *some* people with deprived childhoods use this as a springboard to success.

Rather, we should say, they *tell* us that they do. Finding out what motivates people is a very difficult matter, even for the psychologists and psychiatrists who make it their business. We can draw inferences from people's behavior, but if we accept these inferences as the most telling evidence, we must conclude that poverty backgrounds are a minor factor in success. As just noted, what we *observe* is that a majority of poor people remain poor.

Our best evidence that poverty is a factor comes from the success stories that people tell, and it is hard to determine whether they are telling the truth. We know that people have mixed feelings about poor childhoods, even if they relate their experiences with pride in how far they have come in life. Practically always, they say that they want to spare their children such hardships. Why spare them if the hardships are such a prominent reason for success? It is hard to imagine anyone saying, "I was very poor as a child and this gave me extra motivation to become successful, so I will make sure that my children are also very poor so that they will also become successful." Yet that is the logic of the rags-to-riches theory.

Besides, people commonly exaggerate when they talk about themselves. They sometimes make up outright lies and often come to believe the lies themselves. An outstanding example from literature is Fitzgerald's Great Gatsby. Perceived as a man of some wealth, with most of the gains ill-gotten, Jay Gatsby tells his friend:

> I am the son of some wealthy people in the Middle West—all dead now. I was brought up in America and educated at Oxford because all my ancestors have been educated there for many years. It is a family tradition. . . .
> My family all died and I came into a great deal of money. . . . After that, I lived like a young rajah in all the capitals of Europe—Paris, Venice, Rome—collecting jewels, chiefly rubies, hunting big game, painting a little, things for myself only, and trying to forget something very sad that happened to me long ago. . . .[3]

Gatsby's friend could hardly restrain his laughter. "The very phrases were so threadbare that they evoked no image except that of a turbaned 'character' leaking sawdust at every pore as he pursued a tiger through the Bois de Boulogne."[4] In fact, Gatsby had been born James Gatz and had changed his name at 17; he also changed his childhood rather dramatically. Fitzgerald gives us this interpretation:

> I suppose he'd had the name ready for a long time, even then. His parents were shiftless and unsuccessful farm people—his imagination had never really accepted them as his parents at all. The truth was that Jay Gatsby of West Egg, Long Island, sprang from his Platonic conception of himself. He was a son of God—a phrase which, if it means anything, means just that—and he must be about His Father's busi-

ness, the service of a vast, vulgar, and meretricious beauty. So he invented just the sort of Jay Gatsby that a seventeen-year-old boy would be likely to invent, and to this conception he was faithful to the end.[5]

Even if we accept as fact the notion that poverty has a psychological effect that often leads people into entrepreneurship, no one can predict when and where this effect is going to strike. After all, poverty, in an economic sense, is a relative thing. Even the most impoverished family in an inner-city ghetto today will almost certainly have running water, a bathroom, electricity, and so forth. The poor of the nineteenth century had none of these things. Thus we must be cautious in explaining today's entrepreneur on the basis of studies of the impoverished leaders of the past.

The People, Yes—and No

The role of the family in shaping the perceptions of children is generally recognized. As the tree is bent, and so forth. As with poverty, however, it is difficult to predict specific outcomes from specific family situations.

One notable attempt to give us a model for doing this was made by Anne Roe in 1957.[6] In Roe's formulation, people come from either warm or cold home environments. Warm environments are accepting and loving in nature; cold environments are characterized by neglect, avoidance, and excessive demands. Children from warm environments will have an orientation *toward* people and will be drawn into occupations that are people-oriented, such as the arts and entertainment, services, and business. Those from cold environments will be drawn *away* from people and into occupations that are not people-oriented, such as jobs involving scientific, organizational, or technical skills.

Roe's theory, which was based on research done with students, has been found by later studies to be of only limited usefulness as a predictive device. In a 1959 study, for example, it was predicted that a group of students determined by a questionnaire method to have been interested primarily in things, not people, as children would have come from cold home environments. They did not.[7]

In any case, it is not clear where our hero would fit in Roe's various occupational constructs. Being a successful entrepreneur involves far more than "business contact," which, of the occupational categories given by Roe, seems closest. Also, entrepreneurs may well be seen as both going *toward* and moving *away* from people. They must work with people, but they may manipulate or even abuse them.

Even if the warmth of the home environment were a clear guide to occupational choice, we would still be dependent on people's recollections as to the nature of their childhood homes, and these are far from reliable. For example, Henry Ford and his sister, Margaret, tell quite different stories about their father, William. According to Margaret, the home was warm. Her father, she said, was disappointed when Henry wanted to leave the farm, but would not hinder him if learning about machinery was what he really wanted to do. Henry, however, told a story of quarrels and frustrations that drove him to slip away without telling anyone and walk 9 miles to Detroit to find a place to sleep.[8] Sounds like a pretty cold home.

On the other hand, it must be recognized that child-rearing experts by no means agree on precisely what things make a home cold or warm. There are still plenty of "spare-the-rod-and-spoil-the-child" advocates in our society who feel that too much "permissiveness"— whatever that is—breeds wastrels. Others shrink in horror at the thought of corporal punishment for children. And exactly how much time does Dad have to spend with the kids in order for the home environment to cease being neglecting and start being loving? We do not wish to imply by these questions that society is in hopeless confusion about such matters. Inevitably, though, the experts tend to find their common ground in the middle; i.e., children should receive enough discipline to give them a sense of values and direction but not so much that their creativity is destroyed. Fine. Cattle baron Lionel Barrymore dishes out firm discipline to both his sons; one (Joseph Cotton) becomes a fine, humane adult, and the other (Gregory Peck) fully deserves what he gets when he is gunned down by his girl friend *(Duel in the Sun)*. Warm or cold, home life is remembered by entrepreneurs as a factor in their development, but there are many strands that emerge.

No Place like Home: Cold

One theme is the death of a parent, particularly the father, though the death of Henry Ford's mother was the telling blow for him. Parental deaths are often described as sudden, and dates are usually pinpointed in terms of how old the child was, not how old the parent was. For example: "He died when I was 7 years old." "I lost my father at the age of 12." The loss of the father when the child is young is remembered as a traumatic experience, a time when life took a turn for the worse, a time of loss. Sir Henry Deterding, the central figure in Royal Dutch Shell, and Don Johnson, a black entrepreneur who controls Johnson Publishing, experienced the death of their fathers when they were 6 years old; both felt the loss of a role model.

On the other hand, where the parents remain alive, they may withhold affection from the child or be casual in their attitudes, and these cold shoulders also have a psychological impact. Children in this situation may recall their fathers as malicious and worthless people who failed to provide economic support and moral leadership. "He was the laziest person I ever knew, in and out of business so many times but never made any money. We didn't starve to death, but we were very poor."

The withholding of affection, psychologists tell us, can leave an ugly scar. To humanists at least,[9] people are innately good and will tend toward self-actualization and development of the ability to manage their lives well if they are given the proper environment. A proper environment is one in which the person feels worthwhile because others are perceived as accepting and understanding him. When the person feels that there is no acceptance, this lowers self-esteem, and behavior is affected accordingly.

This does not mean that the behavior must be socially unproductive, which brings us back to the entrepreneur. When a child has suffered from an unaccepting family environment, the adult may become an entrepreneur as a way of establishing identity and building self-esteem. Such a person may go through many emotional agonies before achieving a feeling of real inner satisfaction.

If the entrepreneurial efforts are, in effect, a way of scoring victories over a hated father and getting even with a hostile world, the true feelings of love and hate are likely to remain buried for some time. All this time, the person fights harder and harder to find self-esteem and may achieve really great things. never being satisfied that enough has been done.

The inner drive that is an advantage for an entrepreneur may become a problem when there is something to manage. If the person continues to feel threatened, a type of paranoia may develop and others in the business may be seen as trying to seize control. Training of managers at all will be resisted, certainly of managers who might become successors.

This does not mean, of course, that all successful entrepreneurs are pursued by the Furies or hated their fathers. But modern psychiatry has certainly revealed that people often do things for reasons quite different from the ones they state to the outside world. There have been cases where people revealed that although they were perhaps 40 years old, they never felt they could vote as they wanted until their fathers finally died. If fear of the father can do *this,* it can certainly turn one into an entrepreneur.

Another pattern that emerges in studies and interviews examining life with father is that authoritarian households produce entrepreneurs. In this type of household, the father and mother demand too much and give too little. Not infrequently, authoritarianism develops around strong religious beliefs according to which superiors decide the rightness or wrongness of things and children are seen but not heard. The problem often becomes greater when children become adults and venture to suggest that they dare to think themselves equal to the parents and entitled to make their own decisions. Of course, Lizzie Borden had a mother and father like this, and she gave them forty and forty-one whacks, respectively. More often, the offspring just leave home to make a new place for themselves.

The business of entrepreneurship gives people an opportunity to be themselves for the first time. This sometimes means rejecting everything the parents liked, but it can also mean that adult entrepreneurs engage in some authoritarian behavior too. They do not take orders well and must go into business for themselves. Here is an example of the rejection approach:

> My father, a dentist, decided when I was very young that I would also be a dentist. I never had an opportunity to disagree with him because it was not allowed in our household, but as I approached adolescence, I became very friendly with an oil well driller living in my block. His type of profession became so attractive to me that I rejected all my father's instruction and graduated from high school with an intense desire to work in the oil industry as a skilled craftsman—everything my father rejected. My brothers and sisters took similar routes in that they did not elect the professional career my father picked out for them. We are all happy doing the things that interest us the most, but, to this day, Dad never fails to remind us that we have failed as individuals.

And the going-my-way school:

> Being from a strict Catholic home, and the eldest of six boys, I found satisfaction in my dreams to some day control a company and a lot of employees. My family didn't allow me to engage in extracurricular activities, so I quit school and left. It was a world of uncertainty, but at least I could control my own thoughts, convictions, and actions. The apprenticeships in business were tough, and my most meaningful job was in the carpentry business. The owner was an independent businessman who could take off days or weeks at a time and do exactly as he chose.
>
> The first 6 months of my employment were exciting because I was learning a trade that some day would be my profession. The longer I was employed, the more I resented the supervisors' actions. They never knew what to do and were always making bad decisions on the job. When I took this information to the owner, he was unreceptive. He said: 'Son, you are just learning. You have to have other people tell you what to do. They know what is right and you don't.' At this point, I decided I would not take orders from anyone else; I started my own construction company

In both cases, the people felt forced outside the family framework in order to find a territory in which they could feel secure, a piece of turf that they could control.

No Place like Home: Warm

So far we have talked mostly of family situations that create negative motivations for entrepreneurship. Having lost at home, as it were, such people are determined to win on the road. But not all homes are cold, and life with father is not always bad. Many entrepreneurs come from warm homes with positive role models to copy. Instead of recalling insecure childhoods and authoritarian parents, the budding entrepreneur remembers values like thrift and individualism learned at home and taught by the father. Rather than rebelling against the father's line of work, the entrepreneur looks forward eagerly to being in the same line, often actually in the father's business.

The following case study indicates the pattern.

> In school I was terrible in English and history and even flunked math. I tolerated the classroom situations because at three o'clock I could be in my father's shop visiting with the customers and selling

those candies. My father never had a lot of money, but I do recall never going without what I needed. I remember my father eager to open the store every day and visit with his friends, and he took great pride in the quality of the candy and baked goods he sold to the neighborhood. He even had a policy that if they found the product undesirable, they could come back for a full refund. He was so proud that in his many years of business this situation rarely presented itself.

I never considered any option other than going into the family business. It was exciting, and I thought I could help Dad do things a better way. I had dreamed of expanding with a chain of stores throughout the state, of becoming a business conglomerate, managing a lot of people, and making the community happy.

It will immediately be noted that this story is not particularly dramatic. The guy liked his father and the business and wanted to work with his father and expand the business. So what's the big deal? There is no big deal, and that is precisely the point. The warm home life as a launching pad for entrepreneurs is not a very exciting place. Dad does not fall victim to untimely death, nor does he rant and rave and throw out edicts regarding what the children will do with their lives. And the children do not grow up rebelling left and right, struggling against imaginary images. No one is going to write a book about that. Fitzgerald's Gatsby and Schulberg's Glick make far more interesting reading, than Joe Blow, who knows that he *is* Joe Blow and knows *who* Joe Blow is. Thus the stories of positive family reinforcement do not get into print very often, and the stories about families that produce tormented people do.

There is nothing to be done about it except caution again that when entrepreneurial motivations are discussed, the obvious should not be overlooked—that happiness tends to breed happiness.

Educating the Entrepreneur

The role of education in successful entrepreneurship, like economic status and family life, tends to be a mixed bag of "maybes" and "yes, buts." The self-made folks, i.e., those with little formal education, are probably the best known people on the entrepreneurial front. An awful lot of the real biggies like Ford and Rockefeller did bootstrap their way to success, and so did a lot of the little people.

The attitude that most of these people assume, however, seems to be that they made it *in spite of* the lack of education, not because of it. Partly this is self-glorification; success is so much sweeter and the accomplishment seems so much greater if they are obtained over great obstacles. However, those who did it the hard way tend not to recommend this way to others. Almost uniformly, as we have noted, fathers see themselves working hard so that their children can start out in life without bearing any burdens such as a lack of education. (In *Splendor in the Grass,* Pat Hingle, a self-made man who made it in the stock market, wants son Warren Beatty to go to Yale. Beatty only wants to work on a farm, and so he flunks out of college as quickly as possible. He does not have to worry about whether to enter his father's business; it has disappeared in the stock market crash.) Clearly, there is *some* conviction in the frequent assertions of the self-made that education is good to have, even though they themselves lacked it. National income and education figures tend to bear this out; as a general proposition, the greater the amount of education an individual has, the higher the income.

In any case, it is pretty hard to be totally self-made these days, what with the society in the grip of truancy laws, child labor laws, and "social promotions" policies. It is getting harder and harder for anyone who is not retarded or a hardened criminal to escape life in these United States without a high school diploma. This does not mean that people are educated, only that they have been exposed to some things they would have missed were they not in school. Another factor that links education to success is technology, soft and hard. Society has become so complex that some technical skills are necessary, whatever the field of work, and school is a reasonable place to get them. This is particularly true for those who use mastery over a machine as an entry to entrepreneurship. For example:

> The first job I started after school was with the Briggs Motor Company. Within 6 months, I had learned to run every machine in the shops. Then I went to Rockingham Community College, and within a few months I was ahead of everyone in the shop courses. I did so well in my job at the technical school that, at 22, I was promoted to supervisor in charge of all maintenance of equipment used at a local dam site. With my knowledge, I realized that I could operate more efficiently by developing a business of my own.

Despite the increasing acceptance in our society of education as a necessity for entrepreneurs, there is still some feeling among the business-minded among us that *too much* education is not only unnecessary but probably not good for you, especially if it is not on practical matters. Few entrepreneurs are true eggheads. Learning on the job rather than in the classroom is a practice that is endorsed in many quarters. Consider the following case:

> I went to night classes in Michigan and took courses toward a bachelor's degree in geology. My father, who had not received a formal education, insisted that I receive the book training he had never gotten. I knew that I would come back into the family water well business, and I continued my studies, but I never graduated because I could not take the twenty to thirty college credits in the required liberal arts electives. I did very well in college, but I did not see the importance of the classes that were not practical because these topics were unconcerned with the real world.
>
> I continued to work in the water well business and every day was convinced of my career directions. I wouldn't get more money or make a bigger profit based on this degree in geology, so I dropped out of school and poured myself into the long, hard hours needed to run the water well business. My father had always told me that he wanted me to do better than he had done in life, but he was never very specific, and I always felt his reference to "better" meant a bigger water well business which could support my brothers and myself coming into the firm.

The father in a family-owned business is thus in something of a dilemma when the question of the education of the children arises. He feels that it is right, and possibly necessary, that they receive good educations, but he wants to keep them in the business if he can. Thus he sends them off to college with his fingers crossed, hoping their studies will not lead them astray into some other type of business. Whether they do go astray, as we have seen, turns to a large extent upon whether the children perceive the family in a positive or negative way.

Of course, the children in a family-owned business also have some hard decisions to make. They may be reluctant to go to college, preferring to get into the business right away; they may choose college as a means of deferring the decision as to whether they will go into business at all; or they may be anxious to face the halls of ivy because they think it will be very helpful to them, not only because of what they learn but because of the contacts they make in fraternities, sororities, and the like. Here is an example of the latter type.

Actually, I was very active in high school. I hope I don't sound egotistical, but I was president of my class for 3 years, a member of the national honor society, a member of the drama group and the debate team, and a 3-year varsity athlete. I enrolled at Princeton when I was 17 and found my college years to be probably the most exciting time of my life. I was involved in many political activities and campus projects because I felt that these things would help me advance in the business world when I finished college.

I feel my high school and college experiences added to my abilities as a manager and owner of a business. My desire for my children is that they attend a good college; hopefully, one of them will be interested in returning to the business I've created.

The most defensible conclusion to draw from this excursion into education is that yesterday's entrepreneur was often lacking in formal education and tomorrow's entrepreneur probably will not be. Whether Cayuga's waters are a better place to learn the tricks of the trade than the streets of New York remains to be seen.

Gambling Fever

In *Beyond Survival*,[10] Leon Danco argues that most businesses are formed when the entrepreneur is 30 to 40 years of age. By this time, the person has had experience, obtained self-confidence, and established enough savings and sources of credit to get a business venture off the ground. In addition, says Danco, most people over 40 simply lose the energy it takes to leave a safe harbor for unchartered waters.

On the other hand, Gail Sheehy, in *Passages*,[11] believes that new business lives may begin at 40. The reasoning is that people frequently face a vocational crisis in their forties, they take stock of where they are and where they may be 15 to 20 years later, and they often do not like what they see. If they are in a profession they regard as boring with only the prospect of a lot more boredom, they will tend to venture into a different profession.

A glance at some of the great entrepreneurs of the past and when they established the businesses that made them rich and famous shows a range of ages from 19 to 40.[12] Daniel K. Ludwig started his own business at 19, Rockefeller at 20. Cornelius Vanderbilt entered the steamboat business in which he would make a fortune at age 35. Henry was 40 when the Ford Motor Company was established. All these men, however, had shown their entrepreneurial tendencies very early on, whenever they had actually set up a business. An example is Ludwig, said to be the richest man in the United States and possibly the world. Son of a Michigan real estate agent, he revealed a money-making instinct at age 9. He raised a sunken boat for which he had paid $75, repaired it, chartered it out the following summer, and wound up with a 100 percent return on his investment. He quit school after the eighth grade, worked in a marine-engine plant, and went into business for himself at 19.

Of course, Danco's theory would probably describe more accurately those entrepreneurs whose businesses do not become so large and well known because Danco's entrepreneur considers things like savings accounts and credit ratings—the marks of cautious people. The big tycoons have usually been plungers. Vanderbilt bought a small boat with money borrowed from his parents and began his rise to the top by ferrying passengers from Staten Island to New York City. H. L. Hunt lost his modest estate in the agricultural depression of the early 1920s, rushed to an oil strike in El Dorado, Arkansas, and is said to have won his first oil well in a game of five-card stud.

The willingness to take risks, rather than the prompting of age, appears to be the common theme for the entrepreneur, whether they are small risks—starting a business with some money in the bank and good credit—or let-it-all-hang-out ventures. The entrepreneurs have gambling fever. They actually *enjoy* the uncertainties of innovation, the pressures associated with the possibility of catastrophic failure, and the perils of pursuing dreams.

Many would regard the gambling instinct as an undesirable trait for successful businesspeople to have, feeling that gamblers do not control their destiny and businesspeople should. So that we do not appear to be telling dear old Dad that he should start rolling dice as a way of making business decisions, let us make a few distinctions. The talents that make for a successful entrepreneur are not the same ones that make for a successful manager. However he got into the business, Dad may find it advisable to become more cautious in managing it, relying on solid market information rather than hunches. Many entrepreneurs do not heed this advice, continuing to fly by the seat of their pants. Sometimes small businesses are built into family empires this way; most of the time the business fails.

Another distinction. Entrepreneurs are likely to know that they are gamblers—and be proud of it. But they do *not* feel that they are not in control of their destinies. Entrepreneurs tend to like being in situations in which the results depend on their skills and achievements, *including* the ability to make the odds work in their favor. A *real* gambler, true to the Kenny Rogers song, knows "when to hold 'em and when to fold 'em." When gamblers win, they do not regard it as a matter of luck but of personal skill in manipulating conditions of uncertainty to their advantage. Every gambler knows that the secret to survival is knowing what to throw away and knowing what to keep. For every hand's a winner and every hand's a loser.

Many years ago, Daniel Defoe was intrigued by the changes he observed in English social and economic affairs. People in every walk of life were leaving their traditional roles for new profit ventures, for innovative enterprises where the work had previously been performed indifferently by established institutions. Defoe predicted in *An Essay On Projects,*[13] that these people, these "projectors," would bring about fundamental changes in English life. And so they did.

In America, the same willingness to take risks was a factor of prime importance in the building of the cities and the winning of the West. The Great American Pioneer, after all, was an entrepreneur and a gambler. Gregory Peck, we are told in *How the West Was Won,* made several fortunes and lost them all; but in the process San Francisco had come into being and Arizona was being settled.

It must be noted sadly that many people are forced into entrepreneurship by circumstances, just as the pioneers went west because they had fewer opportunities in the East. And frequently ventures made in desperation end in tragedy. A bankrupt carpenter:

> My job was relatively secure until the 1974 recession, when I woke up one morning to find myself among the ranks of the unemployed. No matter how hard I tried to get a job, I always got the "don't-call-us-we'll-call-you" routine. I knew carpentry and I started my own business; it was a matter of eating or not eating. For a while, I did well because my prices were lower than other people charged, but after about a year, a lot more was going out than was coming in. So I decided life would be simpler if I let somebody else worry about business and I started looking for a job again.

Many people recognize early in life that they cannot measure up to the demands of entrepreneurship, that their economic future will consist of playing committee to someone else's organization. As Studs Terkel so aptly describes in *Working,*[14] many people have dead-end jobs and become prisoners of routine, their futures determined by the decisions of others. But they receive financial compensation on a daily basis, and so they sit tight while others go out and take their chances. (The two types are depicted in *The Misfits.* Eli Wallach has taken a job in a garage while his old range-riding buddy, Clark Gable, continues to hunt wild horses from a pick-up truck. "You got the smell of wages all over you," says Gable.)

A Vanishing Breed?

Over 10 years ago, W. J. Baumol mourned the departure of our hero:

> The Entrepreneur has been written out of today's model. There is no room for enterprise or initiative. . . . one no longer hears of clever ruses, ingenious schemes, brilliant innovations, or of the charisma of which the outstanding entrepreneur is made. One does not hear of them because they do not fit into a mold.[15]

Is this true? Has the entrepreneur gone the way of the swashbuckler, the conquistador, and the cowboy?

There is no question that social molds do have an effect on the restless entrepreneur. The type flourishes where the search for profits has general approval as a motivation, where job patterns facilitate movement from place to place, and where business organization shows cracks and seams and gaps that the entrepreneur can fill directly. Thus entrepreneurship as we have described it is more likely to be a recognizable function in America than it is in, say, Japan. In the United States, making a profit is the primary objective of business; in Japan, national interest plays a great role. A lot of American business is decentralized, and job-hopping is common. Both are less common in Japan.

Even in the United States, however, seen by many as the last bastion of rugged individualism, the maturing of the economy has closed some doors for entrepreneurs. Certainly entrepreneurship as we knew it in the late nineteenth and early twentieth centuries represents a style that is not common today; the robber barons are unlikely to return. They made their mark when the country was younger and had not quite decided what to do about the industrial revolution. Today, government intervention is seen everywhere, large public corporations play a significant role in the economy, labor unions are a fact of life, and—except perhaps in Alaska—there is no frontier left.

Despite these developments, it seems hasty to predict the demise of the entrepreneur. In the middle of the nineteenth century, it was recommended to Congress that the U.S. Patent Office be abolished on the grounds that everything had already been invented. Well, a couple of things have been thought up since then, and it is a good bet—and they love to bet—that the entrepreneurs still have a few cards up their sleeves. New business incorporations have increased in recent years, and whole new industries—such as data and word processing—have boomed. True, the time when business belonged to entrepreneurs and their families are gone, but we have a new entrepreneurial atmosphere, one that is more socially conscious and more aware of the world outside the United States, one that even tempts people beyond the planet itself. There will be new family-owned businesses.

And still the evolution of entrepreneurs is a process that is a little murky to us. Like Datsun, they are driven, but by a whole array of forces. Some, like Ford and Rockefeller, were born poor and made themselves and their families rich. Some, like J. Paul Getty and Howard Hughes, inherited wealth but expanded it greatly. Some come from happy homes, some from broken homes. Most have gambling fever and a variety of other addictions that researchers have noted.[16] They tend to shun the common vices like liquor and cigarettes and even the common pleasures like TV or fishing. They have little time for diversions, even adultery. Their single-mindedness of purpose reaches the point of boredom—for others. But they are not quitters, as long as the social mold leaves any room for maneuver at all.

Star Warriors

Whatever compels the entrepreneur to a certain destiny, it does not appear to be the planets, though the amateur hesitates to discuss this matter at all; people devoted to their signs are easily offended. Reading a typical description of sun sign characteristics alleged to be related to the way people make a living, one might well conclude that the entrepreneur must be either an Aries, a Scorpio, or a Leo. Aries's "fine sense of organization will usually allow you to rise quickly to positions of responsibility." Scorpio's "intensity can combine with an organizational ability that will enable you to step into many executive positions." Leo's "talents are generally of an executive nature." You Lions "have a great capacity for hard work and are not likely to throw up your hands when faced with a difficult and complex job." Perhaps we are not reading these somewhat ambiguous pronouncements correctly, of course, but a quick and admittedly not definitive bit of research into the signs of notable entrepreneurs reveals nary an Aries or Scorpio and only one Leo.

Among the fifteen persons (fourteen men) said to be the richest of all time—a good mark of successful entrepreneurship—for whom specific birthdates can easily be determined, we find the following signs:

Entrepreneur	Birthdate	Sign
Cornelius Vanderbilt	May 27, 1794	Gemini
John D. Rockefeller	July 8, 1839	Cancer
Henry Ford	July 30, 1863	Leo
H. L. Hunt	February 17, 1889	Aquarius
Jean Paul Getty	December 15, 1892	Sagitarrius
Howard Hughes	December 24, 1905	Capricorn
John D. MacArthur	March 6, 1897	Pisces
Daniel K. Ludwig	June 24, 1897	Cancer

Only Cancer appears twice. These people, it is said, "want a job that provides both security and a chance for advancement." Entrepreneurs are gamblers. "You are ambitious, but very self-protective." The model entrepreneur is only ambitious.

But Cancer is plausible. Ludwig's best scheme, developed in the 1930s, was to have oil companies charter unbuilt tankers from him for future delivery, whereupon he took the charter agreements to the bank as collateral on loans to build the ships. It could be said that, like all Cancers, he is self-protective. He never risks his own money when he can risk someone else's.

Notes

[1] Max Weber, *The Protestant Ethic and the Spirit of Capitalism,* Charles Scribner's Sons, New York, 1977.

[2] Bud Schulberg, *What Makes Sammy Run?,* Penguin Books, New York, 1978.

[3] F. Scott Fitzgerald, *The Great Gatsby,* Charles Scribner's Sons, New York, 1925, pp. 42–43.

[4] Ibid., p. 43.

[5] Ibid., pp. 64–65.

[6] Anne Roe, *The Journal of Counseling Psychology,* vol. 4, pp. 212–217.

[7]John Grigg, *Lloyd George: The People's Champion,* University of California Press, California, 1978.

[8]Excerpt from *The Ford Dynasty: An American Story,* by James Brough. Copyright 1977 by James Brough. Reprinted by permission of Doubleday & Company, Inc.

[9]Carl Rogers and Rosalind Dymond, *Psychotherapy and Personality Change,* University of Chicago Press, Chicago, 1978. Reprinted by permission of the University of Chicago Press.

[10]Leon A. Danco, *Beyond Survival: A Business Owner's Guide For Success,* The University Press, Inc., Cleveland, 1975.

[11]Gail Sheehy, *Passages,* E. P. Dutton & Co., New York, 1974, pp. 331–334.

[12]David Wallechinsky and Irving Wallace, "Money—It's a Living: The Richest People of All Time," *The People's Almanac #2,* William Morrow and Company, New York, 1978, pp. 213–220.

[13]Daniel Defoe, "An Essay on Projects," The Harvard Classics. Reproduced by permission, Grolier Incorporated, Danbury, Conn., 1910, p. 14.

[14]Studs Terkel, *Working People Talk about What They Do All Day and How They Feel about What They Do,* Pantheon Books, New York, 1975, paperback edition.

[15]W. J. Baumol, "Entrepreneurship Economic Theory," *American Economic Review,* vol. 58, May 1968, p. 67.

[16]William Copulsky, *Entrepreneurship and the Corporation,* American Management Association Incorporated, New York, 1974, p. 24.

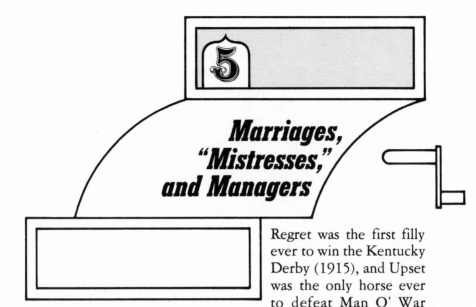

5

Marriages, "Mistresses," and Managers

Regret was the first filly ever to win the Kentucky Derby (1915), and Upset was the only horse ever to defeat Man O' War (1921); both 3 year olds were bred by Whitney Stud, founded by William Collins Whitney. Could this be the same William Collins Whitney whose forebears arrived on the *Mayflower?* Close; it was the *Arabella.* The same man who made more money during his tenure as Secretary of the Navy than any other person in Grover Cleveland's cabinet? Close again; Andrew Mellon made more. Not the guy who made stupendous fortunes in rails, tobacco, utilities, banking, steamships, mining, and practically everything else? You've got it; he also backed the Metropolitan Opera Company. So what is he doing breeding racehorses?

William Collins Whitney could not stop entrepreneuring. But he had so much money by 1898 that he had run out of Keenes and Dukes to vanquish in the business world, and so he took his competitive instincts to the racetrack. And he still could not stop entrepreneuring. Starting with bought or rented horses, he discovered that the *real* way to win was to breed your own. Thus, Whitney set up his own stable and passed it on to his heirs, along with the other gold mines he found.[1]

Otis Towne (his wife added the "e") came to the sprawling Mississippi Delta when it was a water moccasin-infested floodplain. He stomped the cottonseed into the mud; and when he sold his first meager crop, he used the proceeds to clear more land and plant more seed. When he was able to build a house, he brought a schoolteacher from the hills of Tennessee to be his wife, although he had already fathered a mulatto child.

As the price of cotton rose, Otis Towne continued to expand the plantation, buying land with mortgaged cotton and adding to his holdings and his debts. His family grew to include two daughters and another son, all by his wife, for whom he built a house in town. He invested in anything new, including an automobile when Ford's future became the present. But he never learned about cars, letting his mulatto son drive; when they had their first flat tire, he chopped off the rubber and rode home on four rims. Nor did he learn to manage a family business. His legitimate son could never be trained to work and was killed, drunk, in a car wreck. A man practically a stranger was paid to marry, also while drunk, Towne's youngest, and pregnant, daughter. The mother and oldest daughter became virtual recluses behind drawn blinds. But cotton was a dollar a pound.

When the stock market crashed, the price of cotton dropped under a dime, and Towne was so overextended that he was wiped out quickly, his creditors being forced to sell "dollar cotton" for pennies to recoup anything at all from their investments. Otis Towne died without ever understanding what had happened. He knew about hard work, but he knew nothing of markets, banking, management, or technology—or of fitting a family into his work. His mulatto son was shot and burned by a mob.[2]

The Rights of Passage

The passage from entrepreneur to manager is not an easy one. Some people never make the passage but continue on a perpetual journey which may end in great success but which also may terminate in tragedy. Whitney made indescribable fortunes with overcapitalized holding companies and watered stock, but Towne could not do the same with cotton futures.

The person who succeeds in business by really trying is well advised to pause and reflect upon appropriate courses of action. Shall he pursue a bigger dream or shall he settle down to manage a business and watch it grow gradually and successfully? For those who choose the latter course, we have a few things to say about right ways and wrong ways to make the passage.

We have used the pronoun "he" in posing the question, not because no women have ever faced the dilemma—remember Scarlett—but because until recently American society prescribed roles for men and women that put men at the head of successful businesses most of the time. This same society has not necessarily done the male sex a favor in the process. The male child has typically had notions put in his head that launch him on a success trip that leaves successful men in a dilemma as to their future.

A young boy is taught to evaluate himself in terms of achievements, successes, victories. Despite having suffered through the process themselves, fathers—often egged on by mothers—are prone to making "that's-my-boy" statements that let the son know precisely what pleases Dad—his being number 1. (Did Vince Lombardi really say, "Winning's not everything, it's the only thing"?) The sentences begin with "My boy," and you fill in the blanks. Learned to talk at 2 months. Learned to read at 4 months. Got straight A's on his report card. Got the lead in the senior play. Got the game-winning hit, touchdown, basket. Married the prettiest, richest, sweetest (rarely smartest) girl in town. Really has a great business. Really takes after his old man.

Now it can be a bothersome thing to a man, a worm that eats at the core of the apple of his father's, mother's, wife's, friend's eye. He never seems to be able to prove himself enough. Instead of feeling good about what has been accomplished (that's a no-no called "resting on your laurels"), he is primarily concerned with looking for new challenges and worrying whether he will be able to meet them. Like Alexander, he cries if there are no new worlds to conquer because conquering new worlds is what it's all about. Everybody says so. He owns a successful business and has a family. Should he start working in the little world he has created or should he look for new worlds right away?

Now, it would be easy to be glib and say that a person in this situation should forget about all the bad old achieving stuff, ignore the urgings of acquisitive society, and be content. Giving such advice has become almost fashionable. Think happy, we are told. Losing is not good, but it is not death, as George Allen says, and ties are okay. Wonderful; a man who has been an achiever all his life is told to become another person. Some people do, but don't count on it. Besides, if people decide too quickly that they have already achieved enough of their potential, they are not being fair to themselves and need not be applauded. Let's face it, people who quit too easily *are* slackers.

We think that there are guidelines that the owner of a family-owned business can follow in deciding, rightly, whether to entrepreneur or manage. The first thing he must do, of course, is recognize that there is a problem and a decision that must be made. If he is demented and sees no dilemma, he should put down the book and go see a psychiatrist. For those who see the dilemma, we offer the secure sector theory.

The world of the owner of a family-owned business consists of four sectors that divide him into four parts. He is, first of all, an owner, and this part of him is the chunk that urges him to expand. He is also the manager, and this part tells him to make plans, establish procedures, and run the things that he has. Between these two sectors is, first, the worker with real work to do; he is not at the point where he can only *make* decisions, he must also implement some of them. Second, there is the human who must eat, sleep, relate to his wife, children, and friends, and otherwise tend to psychological and social needs.

Before the owner assumes an expansionist posture, he should look closely and satisfy himself that things in all four sectors of his present world are in good shape. If the business is in a very shaky capital position, the owner sector is not secure. If there are foul-ups between the production and marketing departments, the manager sector needs some work. If he must constantly rush his paperwork and is doing a sloppy job, the worker needs improvement. If he has insomnia and his marriage is falling apart, there is trouble in the human sector.

Cynics will immediately say that if people could follow this advice, they would not need it. That is true for some people, but those who are all gut feeling and no logic in their approach to decision making are not reading this book anyway. Other people will line up on a predictive continuum ranging from the eternal optimists who never see trouble anywhere and plunge ahead to the extreme pessimists who always see gloom and doom and never think the time is right for a move.

A family of our acquaintance in a Midwestern city typifies the extremes. The father had a substantial hardware business downtown; as the suburbs grew, opportunities for branch stores at new locations appeared. The man had worked hard to get what he had and was determined not to lose it, and so he insisted that everything be perfect in the four sectors before making a move. Nothing ever was perfect, and the business did not grow. When he retired and turned the business over to his restless son, the bull took over the market. The son, who had just married, worked 22 hours a day, and three new stores were opened within a year. However, expansion had been so abrupt that the hardware market could not absorb it, and the owner could not manage the operation no matter how hard he worked. In a short time, all three stores had failed and he was back where he started. Well, not quite. He had more debts, his blood pressure was perilously high, and his wife had left him.

Those in the middle of the predictive continuum can make sound decisions if they apply the secure sector theory and do not play the blame game, i.e., blame the wife for trouble at home, blame the employees for management problems, and so on. The important point to remember is that when a sector is not secure, it does not matter who is to blame; it is a problem to be solved before the business can move ahead.

The transition to management has been discussed in the context of male drives and how to handle them. The same principles apply to women, of course. As more and more women seek nontraditional employment—that is, work that was once done mostly by men— they will face the same dilemmas. Perhaps they will not make as many mistakes as men have. Perhaps.

The Coach Stage

Having made the passage the right way, the owner of the business is now the manager as well, but it is a family-owned business and the manager needs to get himself into the proper frame of mind. This stage of life could be called the coach stage.

The business world today is inundated with printed material intended to guide the manager. The books enunciate management philosophies and instruct on a variety of subjects such as developing self-awareness in management, and management by objectives. Whatever the titles, the premises on which the books are based are practically always the same: The manager will be a professional manager. The management philosophies and principles are directed at publicly held corporations in which management is responsible to a board of directors which is responsible to large numbers of stockholders. They therefore have little to do with the management practices of privately owned companies. Managers in large publicly owned corporations have the clear, overriding, and universal objective of making a profit. In a family-owned business, management must consider the particular needs of the family as well. In effect, public managers have only one sector in the business world. They are not owners or workers. They are human, of course, and usually have families, but they are definitely expected to either subordinate any needs they have in that area to the needs of the manager sector or give up their jobs. (We tend to cheer for the guys who will not pay this price, as Gregory Peck refused to do in *The Man in the Grey Flannel Suit.*) The manager of the family-owned business must consider the human sector more.

The football coach (who, with rare exceptions, is male) provides a handy analogy. The coach of a team in the National Football League (NFL) is expected to win football games and ignore all other considerations. (Houston Oiler coach Bum Phillips was once quoted as telling his team that he wanted them to concentrate all year on "one word and one word only—Super Bowl.") Those other considerations, of course, include family, friends, personal life, and the long-term welfare of the players. Not surprisingly, if we are to believe any of the stuff from *North Dallas Forty,* both the physical and financial conditions of the players are of little concern to the owners or the coach, if the latter is to retain his job. Like the corporate officer, the coach is judged in terms of how well he performs as an instrument for profit making, not as a human being.

Far too often, the coach of a Little League football team thinks and acts like an NFL coach. When he acts as he is supposed to act, however, he is much like the manager of a family-owned business. He teaches sportsmanship and team spirit and gives everyone a chance to play, not just the ones with the most athletic talent. The players, in turn, look up to the coach and appreciate the chances they are given. Accordingly, he can mold them to a considerable extent in his own image. It is very much a caring situation, as is the family-owned business.

The Little League coach, in addition, sticks with the neighborhood team year after year, while NFL coaches move around from team to team. Likewise, the family business manager is tied to the company he owns. By contrast, the corporation owned by a large number of people, most of whom do not know each other, must have self-perpetuating organizational structure that does not depend upon specific individuals for continuity. These structures, in turn, cause the development of mobile, professional managers whose loyalty is to the management profession and not to specific companies. These executive nomads can fit into any publicly held company, especially with the growth in number of educational programs designed to give them professional training. None of these programs are really tailored for the family business owner; he must learn on the job.

Another difference between the professional and the family manager is that the former cannot control the growth or direction of the company while the latter can. When he is also the owner, a manager can select growth policies that are most suited to the needs of the family. The owner-manager may decide against substantial growth, for example, because of the strains that growth tends to place on family-owned businesses. Although the strains can be dealt with, as we shall see, some may want to avoid them altogether. Many businesspeople who are now managing large companies have their fondest memories of how things were when the company was small. The restaurant owner remembers vividly the first customer to place an order; the water well drilling contractor now tied to a desk yearns for the days when he went into the field as a worker.

It is probably more fun to manage a family-owned business in which values are particularistic than a public corporation with universal values, just as life is more pleasant for coaches in the Little League than for coaches in the NFL. But the fun may not last long. To keep a business secure, the owner-manager may have to work harder and harder. As the business grows, more and more demands must be met. In other words, the owner of a successful family business may soon find himself in the unenviable position of a big-time college football coach torn between his concern for the student athletes and his strong desire for a winning team to appease the alumni. In particular, the owner-manager begins to struggle with the human being.

Does Climb Pay?

After making a successful climb to the top of a successful family-owned business, (FOB), the manager may well ask from time to time whether the job was worth it. The drive of the entrepreneur becomes the drive of the manager, a drive exercised with a view to keeping the business prosperous.

The need to succeed becomes a competitor to human needs—food, air, clothing, shelter, sleep, love[3]—and the human needs do not always win. Perseverance is widely regarded as a prerequisite for success, and it is easily overdone. The hero of the FOB may become an SOB with the tenacity of Sisyphus and the scruples of Machiavelli.[4]

Fearful that hard-won gains will be lost, such a person pushes himself to the limits and beyond.

Work for the manager may become a kind of addiction, and we have coined a word to describe such a person—"workaholic." The word usually has a negative connotation, even when used by psychologists, or perhaps especially then. Workaholics, it is thought, will come to a bad end, physically and socially. Broken bodies and spirits and families await people who singlemindedly devote themselves to business.

Certainly there are many stories of marriages that went on the rocks because one of the mates, usually the husband, could not put in an 8-hour day and let it go at that. He either stayed at the office or brought the office home with him. The business became, in effect, a mistress competing with the wife for the affection of her husband, stripping him of his sexual appetites and driving him to drink. In some cases, of course, workaholics have *real* mistresses stashed away at the office. The end result of all this in the typical scenario is that either the husband drops dead in the arms of his mistress, real or figurative, or the wife (1) leaves, (2) becomes a drunk herself, (3) acquires lovers on the side, or (4) any combination of the above.

There is also evidence that workaholics are not very healthy people, psychologically or physically. Two heart specialists recently advanced the view that the primary cause of coronary heart disease among men in their thirties and forties was not cigarettes, fatty foods, or lack of exercise but a "Type A" behavior pattern. And what are the characteristics of men with this behavior pattern? Among other things, they are workaholics. The doctors asked 150 businessmen in the San Francisco area to select from a list of ten items the complex of habits they believed had preceded a heart attack in a friend of theirs. More than 70 percent of these men believed that the outstanding characteristic exhibited by their stricken friends was "excessive competitive drive and meeting deadlines." (One hundred internists surveyed said much the same thing.) The workaholic's first line of defense is usually that he must work as hard as he does to meet deadlines and beat the competition.

The Type A personality also has emotional traits that many would consider undesirable. He is inclined toward hostility and aggression in his relations with others, particularly those who are not too concerned with meeting deadlines and the like. All in all, the Type A personality, which often surfaces in the workaholic, is not particularly nice to deal with.[5]

Workaholics are beginning to fight back, however, against the traditionalists who portray their habits as emotional weaknesses instead of commendable traits, and they have their spokespersons. Eugene Jennings, who teaches management courses at Michigan State and serves as an executive counselor, argues that hard-driving, successful executives do not have an unusually high divorce rate, do not die prematurely, and do not take to the bottle very often. Then why do so many people think they do? According to Jennings, those who are bucking the establishment in American society have popularized the myth that it is somehow immoral to dedicate oneself wholeheartedly to a corporation. He notes that workaholics are admired in science and the arts.[6] Makes sense. Nobody thought Michelangelo was nuts all those years he spent lying on his back painting the ceiling of the Sistine Chapel.

A Yale researcher notes that workaholics are indeed impatient and energetic but believes they are not money-mad or power-mad; they just want to be number 1. (There it is again.) They do not dread work but enjoy it. Jennings echoes this, contending that executives who work over 60 hours a week are most likely to say they are happy with their lives.[7]

A Georgia manufacturer puts an interesting twist on the matter, considering that workaholics are prone to be apologetic. He is working on his third marriage because he always put the business first and both former wives wanted him home at a normal hour. They felt that fulfilling his family role should be more important to him than any business. He disagreed. Most workaholics would admit sadly that the business caused two divorces. Our Georgia friend feels that the business was the *product* of the two divorces.

Whether workaholism is good for you we shall leave as a matter of dispute about which each can make a personal choice. There is no question that it tears apart many a home. The problem comes about because of the mate's failure to realize that people who climb to the top are not likely to stop climbing just because they are successful and can afford to take it easy. They are workaholics, and they are not likely to change. But many mates are determined to try. Said a nineteenth-century female writer: "Few women understand that in marrying, they have simply captured a wild animal, the taming of which is to be the life's work of the woman, who has taken him in charge." And many mates resist. ("She'll redecorate your home from the cellar to the dome, then go on the appalling job of overhauling you." Rex Harrison in *My Fair Lady*.).

A man or woman contemplating marriage with an entrepreneur turned owner-manager who is likely to be a workaholic must simply make a choice. Although concessions can be, and usually are, made on both sides, either the prospective mate adjusts and finds a proper role in the situation or grief is likely to result. Basic change is not likely; most successful people seem to think that the climb *does* pay. The workaholic, in turn, should take work habits and the way they are likely to be viewed by the mate into account when concluding a marriage agreement.

In the great majority of cases in American business, the workaholic is male and the mate is female, and so we will look at patterns of adjustment in those terms. The number of reverse situations is growing, of course.

There are two basic husband-wife relationship patterns that dominate the family-owned business world. In the first pattern, the man is definitely the lead figure and the woman is an "enabler" who helps her husband by being the proverbial good wife and mother. The second pattern finds the wife as a full partner to her husband in the business. The second pattern is probably more common in small family businesses, but it is found in large family businesses as well. Ford Models, Inc., a large, sought-after New York modeling agency is managed by a husband-and-wife team, Eileen and Jerry Ford. They share a marriage of 37 years and a successful business partnership for 35 of those years.

Blessed Are the Meek

That most famous of all family-owned businesses, the Mafia, furnishes the prototype, nay, the extreme, for the wife who sees her role as serving her husband. She never asks about his business, and he does not discuss it. He is devoted to his wife and children and spends time with them, but the wife is expected to make his life comfortable and shut up about it. In *The Godfather,* when Don Corleone's now-married daughter cries to him that her husband has beaten her, he turns a deaf ear. "But you never beat Mama." Says the great Don Corleone: "She never gave me cause. Go home and learn to be a good wife so he will not beat you." O-o-o-o-kay.

A somewhat less extreme example, Maggie Simmons married John Wesley Webb in 1908 and quickly learned that the wife of a well-drilling contractor had heavy responsibilities. The two men who

worked for her husband also lived with them, and she did their cook-
ing and washing as if they were part of the family. In an interview at
age 85, she stretches out her large hands and says, "These hands have
been faithful."[8]

The typical family structure that still exists in American society—a
dominant male father figure and a supportive mother figure—is
prevalent throughout family business. The wife assumes a role in the
company because her husband needs her help as a worker, but she
must fulfill the wife and mother role at the same time, and she does
so willingly. She is helping her husband create a dream that will ultimately benefit the entire family.

The Mom-and-Pop business may take root in the basement, the
garage, the trunk of the car, or a storefront. Mom's books are found
on the kitchen table, and although she has never heard of a balance
sheet or a profit-and-loss statement, she learns to manage the bills
and keep the family fed. Survival is possible if all profits are kept
within the family. Family members swap sweat and muscle for a
needed job; and since wages are low, the motivation is family loyalty.

The wife's role may change as the business grows and new employees are hired. She may opt for decreasing company responsibilities in order to channel her energies into mothering the children and
enjoying the fruits of the family's labor. The husband may be able to
relax a bit, shorten his hours, and enjoy a personal life with his wife
and children. Or the "mistress" situation may develop and the wife
must adjust to a situation in which she and her husband no longer
work together. She has done her job as the "working enabler," the
business is successful, and she must find comfort in that. Lend an ear
to a few stories from the working enabler. Susan leads off.

"Mark and I started the construction business in the seventies,
there was a housing boom on. Boy, did we work! I did the books,
handled orders and supplies, all the office stuff. For about 2 years, I
guess. But you know, I really wanted to stay home and leave the
business to Mark. I began cutting back my work time, first 4 days a
week, then 3. After about 3 years, I didn't go to the office much at
all. Just enough to see that everything was being done right!

"I enjoyed the free time, got into clubs and community work and
that type of thing. But Mark just worked harder and harder. Lord, I
rarely saw him, even for dinner. I even thought about going back to
work, but I don't even know if I could have gotten a job! The company has over seventy employees now.

"Every year I hope again we can take that European vacation we have talked about for so long. It's not the money, but Mark always says he can't get away. Like they say, I guess he's married to the business now."

Susan decided to accept her life as it was, leaving the man and his "mistress" to themselves and enjoying the limited time she did have with her husband. Joan made a different choice.

"Sam and I set up a little grocery store 10 years ago, and it was quite a struggle. We had competition from the big chains, of course, and really had to work to get people to shop with us. I had to leave the children with sitters while I worked, and I admit I felt guilty about it. So guilty I actually began to hate the business. I thought, if only we could get some money in the bank and hire some people! I could walk out of the store for life. The day finally came.

"They say the grass looks greener from a distance, and it sure did. The kids were older and didn't seem to need me much. Sam was still working long hours because the business was still not out of the woods.

"I decided to go to college and get a degree in accounting so I could go back to the store and set up a real cost-accounting system. It was hard but exciting and I finally got through. I'm back at work now and much happier. Sam and I have a happier marriage. We enjoy working side by side. Like in the song, we 'ain't got a barrel o' money,' but. . . ."

It is, of course, the side-by-side feeling that leads husbands and wives to become partners in business. The wife wants to work with her husband but not in a subordinate position. She does not want to remain meek and inherit the business. She wants a full piece of the action while her husband is still alive.

The Synergy Crisis

The meaning of a "real piece of the action" varies with the situation. Husband-wife "partnerships" may not involve equal influence in business decisions at all. Instead, side by side may mean that the wife is at the husband's side and not vice versa; he is really the manager, and the wife performs specified work tasks, usually office work. (Where the reverse situation exists, as it sometimes does, a sexist society has decreed that the husband is henpecked.) As we have seen, these partnerships are frequently temporary and, for better or worse, the wife tends to move back home once the business can afford to hire a replacement.

Sometimes "partnership" simply means that the wife is kept informed about the business so that she can serve better as an enabler, particularly in emergencies such as the severe illness of the husband. Thus the husband will keep her up to date on the financial position of the business, where to go for legal advice, what major programs the company is involved in, and any changes in basic company policy that are anticipated. Again, the wife is not really a partner but a kind of backup quarterback who never gets to call the plays unless the starter is injured.

If there is to be a true partnership, the wife must be in the manager as well as the worker sector. The two team members may—and probably should—have complementary work skills, but decision making should be joint. The ideal husband-wife team could be characterized by "synergism." This two dollar word is used to describe a situation in which the simultaneous actions of separate agencies have a greater total effect than the sum of their individual effects. The term is used mostly with regard to drugs, but there is a chemistry in the family-owned business too.

Alberto-Culver, a cosmetic company, is run by a husband-wife team. Leonard Lavin, the president, is the idea man and his wife, Bernice, serves as secretary-treasurer and handles the administrative side. However, the couple has shared ideas and experiences for many years, building a successful company while raising three children in the process. They enjoy each other's company and still eat lunch together every day.[9] There are many other happy examples, and it is heartwarming to look at a few.

Joe and Linda Williams did other people's work for years, he as an advertising manager and she as a teacher. They finally decided to quit talking about it and *do* what they really wanted to do—work together in their own business. Excursions Unlimited, a travel agency, was christened. Joe is president and Linda is vice-president; but if the laws governing corporations would allow two presidents, that is the way the company would be organized. No company decisions are made that are not joint decisions. However, they each have some autonomy, traveling separately to set up new accounts and service those accounts. They frequently tell their friends with pride that each is the other's principal competitor. At home, they share domestic tasks such as taking care of two small children. Family life takes up most of their nonbusiness time. Theirs is a total relationship that few couples can match.

Sarah and Richard Vickers have been working together in business for over 20 years. Richard started Vickers Well Drilling in 1942 and hired Sarah as a secretary in 1951. But Sarah Vickers was not content to remain a secretary in the business. She quickly became involved in all aspects of well drilling contracting and has the credentials to prove she can do the job. Sarah holds a master's card from two counties in Florida and a Florida State well drilling license. She is a member of the Contractor's Division of the National Water Well Association. The Vickers have two children and two grandchildren, enjoy deep-sea fishing, and root for the Miami Dolphins.[10]

Despite success stories, it must be recognized that achieving this kind of synergy in a husband-wife relationship is a delicate task that may precipitate a family crisis. It takes work to share bed sheets successfully; it takes work to share balance sheets successfully. When the same two people are sharing both, the strains that accompany most partnerships are increased greatly. A dispute over the laundry or the children may effect a dispute over the inventory or the employees. Each knows the other's personal shortcomings so that when they go to work, neither is likely to be impressed with the other's infallibility. The male professional manager can go home at night and cry on his wife's shoulder about the transgressions that have been committed against him, and she has little choice but to accept his version of events and be supportive. If she was *there,* she may know that the transgressions were partly his, and in discussing the problem, she will possibly be more evenhandedly analytical than blindly supportive.

In a typical case, the husband feels threatened by his wife's assertiveness as manifested by her business interests, and the wife feels she has to put up with too much abuse when she demands to be treated as an equal partner. What happens then is anybody's guess. The wife may revert to meekness to keep the peace; the husband may learn to live with an enterprising wife without constantly sulking or yelling about it. Unfortunately, divorce court is often where the matter ends up, as in the following case.

Some friends of ours on the West Coast recently liquidated both a business and a marriage. They had met in college, though not under the usual circumstances; he was a professor and she was a student. When she completed her master's degree and declared her formal schooling to be over, he decided to leave academe as well. They got married and started a small market research business. It was a truly equal partnership, but there was never really any synergy, at least not in their total relationship. The business prospered but the marriage floundered. The key problem was that the wife no longer saw herself as a student, but the husband could not stop being a teacher. When he insisted that she bow to his decisions on the grounds that he was older (more experience) and smarter (more training), she refused. Eventually, the business suffered too as life became a cycle of feuds. They would have a disagreement at the office, take it home with them for another round of mutual verbal assaults, and bring it back to work with them the next day.

Eventually, they decided to go their separate ways. She decided to keep the business and, after they finally managed to agree on an equitable financial settlement, is running it successfully. She has remained a divorcee, and so it is no longer a family-owned business. He has since returned to college teaching and has married a person of a less assertive nature than his former wife.

Before people get married, they usually discuss their respective attitudes on important questions such as having children. They should have the same kind of serious discussion before they start a business. Is one of them a workaholic, and can the other adjust to this? Will one of them be an enabler, and if so, which one? Will it be a partnership, and if so, can each adjust to a business partnership without letting it disrupt their personal lives? As women more and more exert themselves in the business world, it can no longer be assumed that in a family-owned business the husband will be the boss, the wife will do the dirty jobs when told to, and that is that. If tomorrow's husbands and wives expect to make it in business, they will have to work at it. Synergy takes energy.

Is Everything Relative?

Let us assume that the head of the family-owned business has successfully made the transition from entrepreneur to manager and has come to mutually agreeable terms with the marital partner as to their respective roles in the company. Some dangerous shoals have indeed been negotiated, but there is still choppy water ahead. It is not the waterfall that represents the rise of the children and the problem of succession; that is still well downstream. The immediate rapids are the relatives.

A successful family operation *may* be the envy of the community; it is *sure* to be the envy of uncles and aunts, nieces and nephews, and eventually sons- and daughters-in-law. When a business is called "family-owned," there is the definite inference that it is eager to employ family members. In its gestation period, the business may be in no position to do anything else. Just as Mom must be pressed into service as a bookkeeper, so may other family members be asked to pitch in and help out, often for less money than others would demand.

If they have helped the business in its early stages—and often even if they have not—aunts and uncles assume that the owner will be willing to employ their sons and daughters upon request, first as summer employees perhaps, but later as full-time workers. Family members, in other words, are expected to have an in with the boss that relieves them of the obligation to compete on an equal footing with other job applicants. Otherwise, what is a family for?

Nepotism in hiring practices is certainly not limited to the family-owned business. The professional corporate manager may be pressured by relatives to see that their offspring get a little help from above when they approach the company's personnel department. Indeed, the problem is bad enough that some companies as a matter of policy do not hire any two members of the same family, even if no nepotism is suspected. But the family-owned business is supposed to look with favor on relatives. If a person owns a business and adopts a policy of not allowing relatives, even sons, in the door, the business is not really family-owned as we have used the term. After all, every person who owns a business probably has some kind of family.

The problem for the manager is how to accommodate the family with regard to putting relatives on the payroll and still run an efficient and growing business. The word "growing" should be stressed because some company practices that may not appear to be a problem when the business is small and doing things out of paper bags anyway may begin to eat into profits when hundreds of people are in the company. Accommodating growth is probably the biggest hurdle for a family-owned business to clear.

Relatives create a conflict between the manager and human sectors of the universe of family business owners. They want to run a profitable and productive business, but they want to keep the family happy. People being what they are—often petty and self-serving—it is not always possible to do this. There are several characters that must be recognized and dealt with.

Character Number 1: The Relative Who Is Incompetent

In *The Solid Gold Cadillac,* stockholder representative Judy Holliday discovers that someone in the parent company, for which she works, is trying to put a subsidiary of the company out of business. The culprit turns out to be someone's incompetent relative who did not know the other company was a subsidiary. It happens. Another typical vignette:

Richard Partridge, the owner of a very successful auto parts company, had a moment of weakness when he was asked to put his nephew, Aubrey, on the payroll. It was explained by Richard's brother, who made the request, that Aubrey had experienced some difficulty in finding himself for the past 5 years. He had flunked out of several colleges and had lasted no longer than 6 months at any one job. But he was alleged to have a mechanical aptitude that would certainly make him a model employee in the auto parts business.

Richard rationalized that he could use an expediter in parts and inventory records, and hired an enthusiastic Aubrey. The boundless energy he displayed early on proved to have the bounds of 2 weeks. Despite a salary equal to that of other entry-level workers, Aubrey spent most of his days trying to avoid work. Let Richard pick up the story:

"I knew deep down I should fire the boy, but I hated to have a family war. My brother would be angry and my mother—she's 80—would be upset if her two sons quarreled. So I kept kidding myself that he would mature in his job. Some joke. Two years went by and he still hadn't matured. Took someone else to make me see the light. We had a tough year and, for the first time, the company couldn't give bonuses to the salesmen. One of my long-time employees told me frankly that we could afford bonuses if we got rid of some deadwood, and Aubrey was deadwood. I let Aubrey go, and, sure enough, my brother doesn't speak to me."

If a manager is determined to provide a means of livelihood to an incompetent relative, it may be better business to simply *send* a check than to ask the relative to work for it. A firm in North Carolina recently faced the problem of terminating as bookkeeper a sister-in-law who had been in the business for 18 years. With the growth of the company, it was necessary to computerize all the accounting functions, and the bookkeeper refused to have anything to do with it; she actually attempted to sabotage the system!

Providing a hiding place for unqualified and unemployed relatives can be an expensive drain on a business. Not only do the workers not produce, the owner-manager is likely to be less productive as well because of sleepless nights spent grappling with the question of whether to fire them. The best course of action is to keep the loiterers off the company playgrounds in the first place. As soon as a business is out of its infancy stage, in which it may *have* to put up with a little incompetence, the manager should institute a formal set of hiring policies and procedures that make professional merit the overriding factor in hiring. As the company grows and employment opportunities open up, relatives will be faced with long-standing company policies that they will find it hard to argue against. Even a brother cannot really argue, "Hire my boy even though the written criteria for the job make it clear he is unqualified." Let's face it, the family tie will always be in the back of the manager's mind, and that alone gives the family member an edge. The written policies keep it out of the *front* of the manager's mind—and the company is better off.

Character Number 2: The Relative Who Wants an Important Title

Even when employed relatives are competent, problems may develop as a company grows and it becomes necessary to develop a formal company structure. With five people in the company, the organization chart can consist of you (the owner-manager) and them (the others). With 400 employees, this gets a little messy. Thus there comes a time in the life of every growing company when the job description, the title, and the line of authority rear their troublesome heads. As we shall see, this is especially a problem where heirs are involved, but it is no picnic for the manager in any case. Relatives are apt to want more exalted titles than they deserve, a box on the chart near the top, and overly impressive job descriptions. They are also likely to be jealous with regard to where they stand on these things in relation to other relatives.

Hard choices again. It is tough to tell your brother-in-law that his relationship to your wife does not qualify him to be a vice-president, and even harder to tell your son that his mother is not permitted to promote him over the sales vice-president, who was hired from outside the company.

Often we can tell from titles whether relatives are workers or just family pets. If their titles are superintendent, chief engineer, or sales manager, they are probably workers; but if a lot of brothers, nephews, and sons-in-law are assistants to the president, they are family pets.

This problem is solved roughly the same way as that of the incompetent relative. Get a company structure on paper as soon as possible and attach titles and real job descriptions, with qualifications to them, even if most of the boxes are not filled at first. When it does become necessary to fill them, the manager has ammunition to use in fending off relatives whose ambitions too quickly outrun their skills. By the way, make it a firm policy that the company has no positions entitled assistant to the president and does not intend to have any.

Character Number 3: The Dissatisfied Nonrelative

These persons are dissatisfied because the jobs and titles they should have on the basis of merit are filled by less deserving persons who have some family tie to the boss. This is an easy problem to solve. Just eliminate characters 1 and 2.

As noted, growth usually forces the family-owned business to reevaluate its management structure and employee practices. Relatives working in the company may be unable to adapt to the growth of the organization about them. When their employment began, there were no job descriptions, lines of authority, or titles given to anyone. They were told what to do and when to do it and were left as mindless creations of the company, operating at the command of the chief operating officer. With growth, nonfamily members are employed and the business begins to form a hierarchial structure with a division of responsibilities under the key employees.

Relatives who have had no management direction for possibly a decade are not willing to cooperate in subordinate roles with nonfamily executives. The owner's option is to clean house or teach a new management philosophy to all the people involved. This educational process is made much more difficult by the family personalities involved in the training. Previously, all positions were equal because they reported directly to Dad, and the newly formed authority lines may be resented and resisted by the old-timers. All the relatives want the business to be successful, of course; without a strong organization they may find themselves standing in the unemployment line. But each relative feels that another person in the company should be willing to make the necessary sacrifices.

Frequently, the distribution and responsibilities of personnel are more than the owner can face emotionally. If this situation exists in the business, it will be necessary to seek the outside advice of industrial psychologists or management consultants who can evaluate the company structure and personnel without a biased approach to any family members. Owners may resist calling in outside consultants because they feel that it weakens their authority, but family biases are not easy to overcome. The professional managers can make recommendations for changes, develop job descriptions, and design programs for new nonfamily employees. The growth of the company may depend upon a fresh outlook from an outsider.

The family-owned business in North Carolina hired industrial engineers to analyze the productivity of its construction company. The engineers spent 1 year in the organization, and before they completed their task many of the employees resigned because they could not handle the pressure of the new management structure. A decade later, this is functioning successfully with family members in key roles and nonfamily executives handling the areas of financing, marketing, and sales. Had it not faced up to the need for outside consultants, the organization would have been stymied in its growth.

It is good for family members to work together, build together, depend upon each other's strengths, and shore up each other's weaknesses. But if the family-owned business is to succeed, everything must not be relative.

The Right Chemistry

Just as the family-owned business owner must make the transition from entrepreneur to manager if the business is to stabilize, so the business must make the transition from personalized decision making to professional management if it is to grow successfully. Many businesses never quite find the key, either remaining disorganized and stagnant with relative-ridden management or going all the way to professional management and outside control as the family steps out of the picture. If the former is a tragedy, the latter is not necessarily desirable. A recent study suggests that companies with at least a small amount of family or personal control have better performance records than those from which such influence has disappeared or in which it never existed. The Swifts in meat-packing, the Deeres in farm implements, the Reynoldses in cigarettes, the Firestones in rubber, the Dows in chemicals, the Schottens in glass, and the Wisemans in business machines are all families that continued to hold sizable blocks of stock and take part in the management of the enterprise after it had reached great size.[11]

Du Pont offers an outstanding illustration of how management practices can shift to accommodate growth.[12] The history of this giant firm has been turbulent, but a key figure in the move to modernity was Pierre Du Pont just after the turn of the century. Pierre's major contribution to the building of a large modern corporation was his use of statistical and financial techniques, a trick that few industrialists had mastered at that time. He saw that large-scale enterprises would need experienced managers and administrative systems, but he retained many of the commitments and incentives that existed in the small family partnership.

As far as Pierre was concerned, the large firm did not have the obligation to provide the family with jobs; instead, it should ensure them of large dividends. Of course, when the firm expanded, there would be increased employment opportunities for younger relatives. Family traditions were meaningful to Pierre, and he saw the family as playing a different role rather than being forgotten. The family members remained the major stockholders, and all family members were fully informed of company affairs.

Pierre's ability as a modern manager was instrumental in the building of General Motors, a company in which Du Pont made a large investment, the largest ever made by an American company and family in an outside firm. By 1920, Pierre had become president and chairman of General Motors, and he promptly applied all his experience and knowledge in developing financial policies and administrative methods. By 1928, General Motors Corporation had replaced Ford as the leading American automobile company, a position it still holds.

Pierre's efforts with Du Pont and General Motors were outstanding achievements in a business career. He created two of the most successful American business corporations and did so without losing legal and financial control. The most critical period in the history of any modern corporation occurs when the founder or family must come to terms with the needs of the large-scale enterprise. Few American businesspeople have handled this almost inevitable crisis more efficiently than Pierre Du Pont.

Another large company that has functioned successfully with the attributes of both family business and professional management is the publishing giant Doubleday.[13] Nelson Doubleday is the second-generation president of a privately held company employing 5700 people with reported sales exceeding $350 million annually. The company is not required to file any information with the Securities and Exchange Commission, and up until a few years ago the president would merely chalk the financial results on a blackboard at the annual meeting. Now they have advanced to an annual report that goes to only 300 stockholders.

The corporate officers dodge questions posed by the stockholders, and there are frequent rumors in publishing circles that at last they will go public and all the secrets will come spilling out. But in a day when most book publishers have given up their privacy, the giant Doubleday & Company goes on as a family-owned business which publishes more hardback books than anyone else—700 a year.

Frequently, the downfall of the family operation occurs at the point at which it becomes multifaceted and difficult to control, but Doubleday has sprouted into a publishing octopus with fifteen book clubs (such as the Literary Guild), the Laidlaw Brothers textbook subsidiary, Dale Publishing, the Paperback House, a flock of bookstores, an export operation, a packaging firm, and a radio station. Someone once said that Doubleday is run like a friendly private country club, and indeed Doubleday management has retained the benefits of both a family-owned company and a multifunctional corporation.

For Fun and Profit

We have given you a rather extensive tour of the FOB landscape, following the entrepreneur moving to owner-manager status, sorting out relationships between husbands and wives and mistresses, and getting a fix on the role of relatives in the business. We have also taken a peek at two family-owned businesses that managed to accommodate growth. If you will now all take your seats, we would like to make a few telling points about all of this.

The key point is that the land mines that blow up many family businesses *can* be avoided. The secure sector theory provides a reasonable guide to expansion if it is honestly applied. Workaholics need not destroy the human sector if they begin to understand themselves and get others to do the same. If husbands and wives talk to each other about family and business before they get into either, they can solve the synergy crisis. A family owner can keep relatives on the payroll without ruining the company if the undesirable characters are assassinated. The small business may even act out the Du Pont and Doubleday dreams.

Note that the land mines become activated only when growth becomes a possibility. Very small operations have to worry some, but not a lot, about secure sectors and synergies. The notion is frequently propounded that growth is an imperative, the alternative being death. Hogwash. It depends on what is meant by "growth." Any successful business must change with the times, of course. It must adapt to new markets, products, labor trends, pay scales, and so on. But these are *qualitative* types of growth. *Quantitative* growth—new divisions, new branches, a larger work force, even new types of company work—is a matter of choice.

We would like to stress this because in searching for ways that family businesses can accommodate quantitative growth, we do not wish to intimidate those who have a hankering to remain small. The family can indeed remain involved when a small company becomes a giant corporation, but its role will inevitably change. The owner can no longer be involved personally or even acquainted with the workers. Indeed, the owner will have to cease being a worker and devote full time to managing. It becomes difficult for the company to accommodate relatives as employees. The small family business that becomes large pays a price. For many, the price is worth paying because they can leave a far more extensive set of holdings to their heirs and make it more likely that the family business will extend over many generations rather than one or two. Others may choose to enjoy the pleasures of the family business as it is and let the sons and grandsons—or daughters and granddaughters—make their own choices about growth.

In the popular television comedy *The Jeffersons,* Mr. Jefferson is a black businessman who is determined to make it to the top in a honky world. ("We're movin' on up to the East Side.") His vehicle is the dry-cleaning business, and at this stage of the series he has several dozen stores. This may or may not be a family-owned business—wife Louise is not involved in the business and son Lionel is mostly interested in females—but if it is, it will be a large one.

Perhaps he will make it. There is a dry-cleaning chain in our city that has at least fifty outlets in the city and suburbs. We, however, take our business to Payne Cleaners, a one-location, family-owned business. Mr. Payne started the business and has been at this location about 20 years. His wife sews on buttons in the back of the store; the son and daughter take in and hand out cleaning orders in the front.

Payne, Jr., like his father, has obtained a lot of formal training in laundry and dry-cleaning processes, and the business uses only the most modern techniques.

"Heck, yeah," says Mr. Payne. "I thought many a time about opening stores at other locations; we've been very fortunate here. But I like working with clothing, like meeting the customers, like being with my family a lot. I don't think I could run around from place to place managing a lot of people I don't know very well. Now, my son, Lawrence, I think, will be different. He'll take over the business when I retire, and he thinks maybe we should expand. I kid him about competing with the Nospot people. He says he's up for it. Already has a slogan: 'Dry cleaning is a Payne.' That's okay with me. But I'll stick to being plain old Payne Cleaners."

Notes.

[1]Bernard Livingston, *Their Turf: America's Horsey Set and Its Princely Dynasties,* Arbor House, New York, 1973, pp. 45–54.

[2]John Faulkner, *Dollar Cotton,* Yoknapatawpha Press, Oxford, Miss., 1975.

[3]Abraham Maslow, *Motivation in Personality,* Harper & Row, New York, 1970.

[4]*Why SOB's Succeed and Nice Guys Fail in Small Business,* Financial Management Associates, San Diego, Calif., 1976.

[5]Meyer Friedman and Ray H. Rosenman, *Type A Behavior and Your Heart,* Alfred A. Knopf, New York, 1974, pp. 69–96.

[6]"Workaholic", Columbus *Dispatch,* October 28, 1979, p. 17.

[7]Ibid.

[8]Peggy Webb, "Tribute to a Driller's Wife," *Water Well Journal,* September 1972, p. 54.

[9]William Copulsky and Herbert W. McNulty, *Entrepreneurship and the Corporation,* ANACOM, a division of American Management Association, New York, 1974, p. 50.

[10]"Women In Business: Sarah Vickers," *Water Well Journal,* August 1974, pp. 56–57.

[11]Alfred D. Chandler, Jr., and Steven Salsbury, *Pierre S. Du Pont and the Making of a Modern Corporation,* Harper & Row, New York, 1971, p. 594.

[12]Ibid. p. 591.

[13]"The Sphinx of Publishing," *New York Times,* July 15, 1979, pp. 1ff.

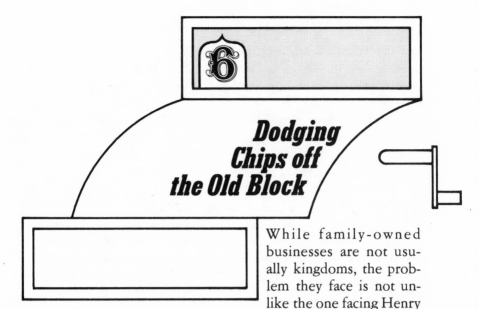

Dodging Chips off the Old Block

While family-owned businesses are not usually kingdoms, the problem they face is not unlike the one facing Henry IV: how to survive as an up-and-coming son moves into his father's domain and ultimately replaces him as the boss. Grumbles Henry to his son, Hal:

> I stay too long by thee. I wear thee.
> Dost thou so hunger for my empty chair
> That thou wilt need and vest thee with my honours
> Before thy hour be ripe? Oh, foolish youth,
> Thou seekest the greatness that will overwhelm thee.[1]

It is a three-stage problem. First, the son looms as a chip off the old block, hurtling squarely for his father's head. If the son lacks his sire's entrepreneurial drive—is not, in other words, a chip off that block—there is not likely to be a problem. If he is, however, Dad will have a troublesome matter to deal with, and there are no easy answers. The son may not be ready to assume an important role in the company. There *are* sons whose ambitions outdistance their abilities. On the other hand, founding fathers are commonly stubborn and reluctant to admit that Junior can now do the job as well as Senior.

The second stage of the transition is essentially a solution to the problem created in the first stage. A way must be found to make use of the son's energies, to let him shine in the business without prematurely tossing Pops into the discard pile. It can be done.

The third stage comes when the father does have to give up an active role in the business. Since death and retirement are two realities that most founders truly hate to accept, the business faces its most severe challenge at this point. Son moves in, Father moves over, Father moves out. A family business must adjust to these moves.

The father-son game that is the major theme of family-owned business in transition is played out against a backdrop of sibling rivalries and son-in-law scheming—confrontations that create no small number of flying chips themselves. Amid all this stands Mom, usually trying to function as a partner to her husband and a peace officer for the family at the same time—no easy chore.

Here and in Chapters 7 through 9, we will look at the way a variety of businesses have dealt with the transition, where they went right, and where they went wrong—and try to glean from this melange a few pointers. First the chip dodging, then the son shining, then the succession.

Some Generation Flaps: Genesco and Johnson

Genesco, Inc., a giant apparel conglomerate based in Nashville, Tennessee, has been an outstanding battleground in the father-son wars.[2] From the day the company began as General Shoe in 1932, W. Maxey Jarman (Maxey to both friends and enemies) sat at the top and called the corporate shots. In 1956, the former shoe company began to branch out into the retail-apparel area, and the Bonwit Teller and Henri Bendel firms were acquired. A few years later, in 1959, Maxey's strong entrepreneurial nature really took hold. He wanted the then $276 million shoe company to become a $1 billion integrated apparel company, and so he changed the name to Genesco and acquired some fifty apparel retailing and manufacturing firms.

Maxey's son, Franklin, a true old-block chip, began to rise about the time Genesco did. He joined the company as an administrative assistant in retailing and moved up through the ranks to the presidency in 1969. At first, Maxey appeared to be moving over if not quite out. Later in 1969 he named Franklin chairman and J. Owen Howell, Jr., president, and he himself became head of the company's finance committee. But who was really in charge? The finance committee held the company purse strings, and according to those in the know, Maxey was still in a position to exercise control, which he in fact did. A 4-year power struggle ensued between fellow entrepreneurs Maxey and Franklin.

When the company's profits began to fall, Maxey decided that his son was not running things properly, and so he came out of "retirement" with a new title—general manager—with the top executives still reporting to him. But Franklin was not finished. As profits continued to go down, the younger Jarman rallied his support on the board of directors. In 1973, Franklin was given complete authority over the company as president and chief operating officer; Maxey was relegated to a board membership position. Franklin was clearly relieved. While grumbling about the tendency of the press to play up the "seamy side" of the situation, he was also quoted as saying that his father would henceforth, as a board member, draw "his salary from the retirement fund."[3]

Clearly, the elder Jarman did not manage the rise of his son very well. Instead, he instituted a game of musical chairs at the top that turned the company's energies to politics rather than business, brought profits down, and lowered the morale of company employees to a dangerous level. Indeed, after Franklin finally took control, about 250 managers either quit or were fired. But the management structure was rebuilt and Genesco's decline was halted.

Although the 4-year Jarman war was undoubtedly a contributor to Genesco's misfortunes, there is no assurance that the absence of such wars guarantees prosperity. The father may move over and out gracefully as his son assumes control, but the star performer of the second generation may follow so closely in his father's footsteps that he fails to make necessary changes.

The Simple Simon atop the orange roof dots the highways of America. As anyone who travels knows, Howard Johnson's has twenty-eight flavors of ice cream and unspectacular but dependable food. Howard Deering Johnson started with a $500 investment and parlayed it into over 900 restaurants and 500 motor lodges and motels.

HDJ was a promoter, and there was never any doubt that his son, Howard Brennan Johnson, would be trained to take over what his father had promoted. Young Howard was appearing in ads at 6, going to annual meetings at 12 and cutting steaks and making sodas as a teenager. His father made him president of the company when HBJ was only 27, and the latter was running the company long before his father died in 1972.

The smooth transition from father to son did not allow the famous chain to escape downturns. HBJ followed his father's fundamental principles—a solid financial base, tight management controls, and a preference for being reactive, i.e., conducting business as usual and trying to exploit trends rather than predict them. As the food-chain competition became more intense—a lot of it from other individually built giants like Holiday Inns and Marriot Inns—and gasoline shortages began to put a damper on family travel, Howard Johnson's earnings dropped.

The younger Johnson has reacted cautiously to these changes. New (for Simple Simon) items such as salad bars, entertainment, and liquor have been added to the basic food service, and two entirely new chains, Ground Round and Red Coach Grill, have been added. But changing the orange roof to something more appropriate for dinner than snacks? HBJ worries that this change, although necessary, may result in a blurred image for the company that could result in its demise. Only in his forties, young Johnson is conservative. But *Forbes* called it complacency in mid-1978. Is the chip too *much* like the old block?[4]

Of the two models for sons moving in described here, the Genesco type is dominant in family-owned business. Dad rarely moves over as easily as did Howard Deering Johnson, and so father-son rivalry is inevitable. The literature is replete with the theme.

The Roots of Rivalry: Society and the Psyche

In Lisa Alther's *Kinflicks,* a young man explains that he does not want to have children because he has always feared they would be his replacement. "I always saw the world as a stage. . . . and any child of mine would be a ballsy young actor wanting to run me off stage altogether, watching and wanting to bury me so he could assume center stage."[5]

Our learned friends of psychiatric bent argue that this kind of fear is by no means an aberration of actors. Says Howard M. Halpern: "In every parent there is a wish that his or her children grow up to be strong independent, effective people. And in every parent there is a wish that his *or her child remain weak, dependent, ineffectual people.*"[6] If this is true, the father in a family-owned business is likely, as with Marx's bourgeoisie, to create the means of his own destruction. He will reward the son who is aggressive and domineering because those are precisely the traits which the father feels that *he* has and which have made him what he is. He will find it hard to relate to a son who is submissive and may well dismiss him entirely as a factor in the company. If an aggressive son goes too far, however, "that's-my-boy" pride is likely to dissolve into defiance. Laudable independence of spirit by the son suddenly becomes unlaudable "uppity" behavior that must be stopped.

The pity in such situations is likely to be heaped on the son. Here the poor lad works as hard as he can to emulate his father, sneers at his submissive brother, and prepares to reap his harvest in the business. Wham! The father who thought he was so cute winning at "Monopoly" when he was young now turns ugly when the money is real. Meanwhile, the submissive son, who has always done what his father told him to do, finds himself the object of scorn. Seems as if nothing pleases the old man.

It is little wonder that many sons are torn apart psychologically about the decision to go into the family business. If they do, they run the risk of parental rejection as the father protects his turf. If they do not, they may be ridden with guilt for life, if we are to believe the psychologists.

The dilemma may be even greater for the children of today than for those of yesteryear. The business the son is entering must survive in a different social milieu than the one in which it was established. In Christopher Lasch's phrase, the Happy Hooker has replaced Horatio as the symbol of success.[7] Lasch's analysis of this new society concludes with the depressing thought that the son going into a family-owned business is in a no-win situation.

The generations before who were involved in the family-owned business stood firmly on the Protestant work ethic as the most important underpinning of the American economy. The self-made man, the founder of most family businesses, lived for the future, shunning self-indulgence in favor of patience and painstaking accumulation. He deferred gratification in expectation of an abundant future source of profits. With an expanding economy, the value of investments could be expected to multiply with time, and the rewards were reaped by those individuals who practiced patience.

In today's age of diminishing expectations, however, the Protestant virtues no longer generate enthusiasm among the young for taking over the business. Inflation erodes investments and savings, and advertising undermines the horror of indebtedness, exhorting the consumer to buy now and pay later. The future becomes menacing and uncertain, and only fools put off until tomorrow the fun they can have today.

This economic surrounding has a profound effect on the heir apparent considering working in his father's business. Time has transformed work habits, values, and the definition of success; self-preservation has replaced self-improvement as the goal of earthly existence. The hope is not so much to prosper as to survive, and survival becomes increasingly more difficult with needs for larger income and expansion.

Today, according to Lasch, children are reared in a self-indulgent society in which they want for little and fail to wait for long-range goals. The son finds himself in a precarious societal position. As he views how others look upon him, he may prefer to be envied rather than respected. Pride and acquisitiveness, the noted sins of historical capitalism and the Protestant work ethic, are no longer in disgrace. This societal change can be a contributing factor in the father's inclination to stymie the growth of the company and the son's overwhelming desire for expansion.

The father has never lost the idea that he worked hard to acquire the level of success at which his son begins. The son, wishing to validate his choice of occupation, would like the business to grow and expand so that he, as an individual, may be envied and esteemed by the community. The son is damned if he does and damned if he doesn't. The community looks upon him as the boy born with a silver spoon. If he takes the company and expands it to magnitudes beyond imagination, the community says: "Why shouldn't he? He got it through the hard work of his father." Should the son lack the aggressive, single-minded direction of his father and the business flounder under his management, the community looks at him with disgust: "His father worked so hard to give him everything and now he's thrown it all away."

Despite the plight of the son, perhaps we should reserve some pity for the father. After all, the business is his "mistress," and people tend to be even more jealous of their mistresses than of their wives. If the son wins her hand, one may be sure that he had to be twice as good as the father, not just as good. In other words, if the son does enter the business, good old Dad will demand perfection from him, even when he does not demand it from others. The situation is akin to that found around every Little League ballpark in the country, if we may return to our coach analogy for a moment. Here is the scenario.

Dad, himself a good football player at one time, has given up his time and energy to coach his son's football team. Dad recognizes that, at the age of 10, the team members are hardly representative of the country's greatest, but he reminds himself daily that the goal of team sports is good sportsmanship and the development of skills in team efforts. The game is close and the plays are sent in by the coach; but under the pressure, many of the boys fail to execute. They drop passes and miss blocks. The team loses and everyone is very depressed, especially the coach, who has put in hours hoping they will be able to experience the joys of victory. As the boys huddle at the conclusion of the game, the coach says: "Guys, don't be upset; it's only a game and it's not whether you win or lose, it's how you play the game." He then proceeds to compliment all the players on their individual efforts and tell them it will be better the next game.

While driving home, the coach becomes a father and begins to show his disappointment and disgust with the lack of ability and skill of his son. He expresses embarrassment and humiliation as a father and can hardly believe that his son has made so many stupid mistakes throughout the game.

Given the complex social and psychological pressures that are exerted on the family-owned business, it is not surprising that father-son rivalry is a frequent occurrence. It is firmly rooted in the logic of the situation.

The Cain and Abel Game

The father who has one son aiming for the top has trouble enough; when there are *two* offspring with similar ambitions, a whole new dimension is added to the universe of rivalry. Different problems take shape, however, depending upon whether the siblings are close or considerably apart in age.

We are told by the authorities in such matters that the best sibling relationships develop between children who are no more than 2 years apart in age. In their youth, they acquire many of the same friends and play the same games, including organized sports. They remain close together in physical size and level of knowledge and thus frequently compete with each other, perhaps for a spot on the baseball team, for top rank in the class, or for the hand of a girl, if they are males. By the time they mature into adulthood, they develop a very close relationship.

The friendly competition that cemented bonds in their youth, however, often becomes less than friendly as they eye their coming roles in the family-owned business. Even when they have chosen different areas of skill in which to excel—one in accounting, the other in marketing, for example—the competition does not cease. Although they are in different areas of the business, they are in the same position as far as advancing to the top management spot is concerned, whatever the job route they have chosen; and a good deal of initiative is called for if victory is to be claimed. For each son, the goal is to establish himself in a dominant position in the family business hierarchy and relegate the other to a subordinate role so that when Dad, willingly or unwillingly, reaches down for a successor, the right name will be drawn from the hat. Such struggles can reach the Cain and Abel stage, depending upon the idiosyncrasies and emotions of the people involved.

The father-founder finds his woes deepening as the conflict goes on below. He must not simply fend off a would-be successor; he must, in the interest of efficient business, try to maintain harmony and balance between two aggressive challengers who seek greater authority and responsibility not only at his expense but at each other's. It will take more than long-range planning and management by objectives to harness two personalities with an intense desire to reach the top. One option is to create more "tops" by expanding the business into new fields that can provide the each surging combatant with opportunities and challenges that do not involve the other's demise. Export divisions and branches in new cities are often business manifestations of internecine sibling rivalry. But many small businesses do not have expansion opportunities that make sense from a financial or business-growth standpoint.

With no land of Nod, Cain and Abel must remain in the Garden of Eden, although it is usually no garden by this time. Sibling business rivalries are, almost as a matter of course, brought home to the wives and children. Family members become sounding boards for warring brothers, sides are taken in the feud, and family gatherings, if they occur at all, are likely to be tense affairs. The familiar "Guess who's coming to dinner?" question is commonly answered: "Like hell, he is!"

Let us visit a water well drilling business in New Mexico that dissolved because of sibling competition. José, only 18 months older than his brother, Sergio, was conservative and rigid in matters of business management. Sergio had a conflicting personality, and the resulting competition led to years of family feuding and eventually to the end of the business.

The two brothers joined the firm in different areas of operation,

José in the pump division and Sergio in drilling, but the two divisions had to cooperate on the drilling site. Once the well was drilled, the pump department was required to complete the job. José and Sergio spent a good deal of time discrediting the work performed by the other. José's conservative approach to purchases and expansion met heated opposition from Sergio, who purchased expensive equipment, hired new employees, and hoped that enough work could be found to pay for both.

The father and founder of the business, Arsenio, was like a frontier marshall, trying to sooth feelings and stop wars that threatened the business. The sibling shouting was sometimes overheard by customers and employees; at drilling sites, the brothers looked more like two people arguing over water rights than drilling for water. Predictably, family relationships deteriorated.

In desperation, Arsenio, despite the expense to his small firm, hired a personnel consultant with experience in a family-owned department store chain to mediate the conflict between the sons. The consultant was ultimately to be the deciding factor in the future of the business. No amount of mediation could bring José and Sergio together. Dispirited, Arsenio, although only 55, decided to retire and let the sons grapple with the matter, with the consultant as referee.

In the end, the referee stopped the bout. He advised that the business was being destroyed by irreconcilable conflict and suggested that the firm be sold, with the two sons splitting the assets and going their separate ways. The business that Arsenio, the first of his family to own anything of value, had hoped to see pass from generation to generation came to an end.

The two brothers, now both working for other people, have never reconciled their differences. At Christmas, Arsenio and his wife visit their sons on different days.

The Elder versus the Younger

When there are two sons and one is a number of years older than the other, different patterns of conflict emerge.

Many family-owned businesses are like monarchies; the oldest son becomes the ruler, and the succeeding brothers, sisters, or in-laws assume roles based on their sex, status, and order of birth. The elder son customarily succeeds the father, and this succession reaffirms the belief of the younger brother that older is indeed better. Big brother often has a condescending attitude toward the younger brother because in their earlier years the older was larger, physically stronger, more competent, and more knowledgeable owing to the difference in age. When they enter a family-owned business in which the toys are to be shared equally, they may end up working out their childhood aggressions within the company structure.

Rarely does the younger brother have an opportunity to match the skills, competence, and experience of the older until they reach adulthood and employment in the business. By that time, their relationship is so well established that the older brother has difficulty regarding the younger as adequate and equally competent. The older child has the added advantage of earlier and longer contact with the parent; consequently, the father's drive tends to be reflected more quickly in him—he pushes himself harder and expects more of himself than the younger brother. Once in control, the older brother tends to judge the younger children harshly.

The younger brother tends to compensate for the childhood relationship by trying to carve out a place in the business that is his very own. He guards his territory with zeal, hoping to keep the older brother out and demonstrate to himself and others that he is indeed competent and can function independently.

The siblings may own equal shares in the organization and sit side by side on the board, but the problems inherent in the older-younger relationship are compounded by their equal role in management. As they sit in planning meetings or board sessions, they can argue policy and procedure from equally strong positions of power; but when they return to the daily operations in which one is subordinate to the other, the younger one is usually subordinate and finds it extremely difficult to think of himself in a subservient role. A self-fulfilling prophecy is achieved in the two roles because the older sibling, distrusting the younger, is likely to give him less opportunity for freedom and responsibility. This in turn hampers maturity and growth in the younger son. The father must be able to compare the business abilities of the two children, but this is difficult because of his long experience in the parenting role.

If for some reason the younger sibling replaces the older in the designated power structure, the younger is often faced with feelings of guilt for having distorted the family structure of power. Unfortunately, far too many enterpreneurs contribute to the existing sibling rivalries with what could be called "seductive secrecy." They fail in the management structure to designate the position and responsibilities of the sibling employees. Subconsciously, they are probably pitting employee against employee and dangling a carrot (the presidency and the company) before each of the sons. Dad encourages competition with the idea that it will make better men of both of them. The story of Acme Supply Company illustrates the problems that result when the father fails to clarify roles in a younger-older sibling situation. (In this case, there was a sexual difference as well.)

Sarah joined the office-supply business 5 years after her older brother, Moe, and her college education in business was a great contribution to the firm's poorly managed finances. Moe, with a glib tongue and a personality to match, fell right into sales and personnel management. The brother and sister worked very well together, and each assumed that Moe would be made president prior to Dad's retirement. There was no professional competition between the two because each had an area of expertise and enjoyed equally the benefits of the family-owned business.

Sarah always jokingly accused her father, Jacob, of chauvinism and felt he never gave enough credit to the job she performed; but her childhood experiences and background never allowed her to consider taking the helm from her brother. Then Jacob had a serious heart attack, and although Sarah and Moe had never discussed succession and the hierarchial structure of the business, they were called in to hear his plan for the future organization of the company. Jacob dropped a bomb. Sarah, with her business acumen, would become president and Moe would be vice-president.

Sarah was elated that she had been chosen for the presidency of the company, but increasingly she had to confess to some guilt, and her husband reinforced that guilt by proclaiming that she should not have a job of such responsibility and that the position should be given to her brother. Moe, in turn, faced an irate wife who would not come to grips with the fact that Sarah would be president although Moe owned equal stock in the company.

For 5 years after Jacob's death, the hostility between Sarah and Moe mushroomed into a situation which began affecting sales and the future of the organization. It was not until they hired an outside business consultant to assist in inventory and management that Sarah and Moe realized that a hostile situation existed. The business consultant explained frankly that the continued operation of the company depended entirely upon their ability to reconcile the personal differences. It took a year of swallowing pride on both their parts to agree that title and structure were relatively unimportant compared with the continuation of their father's dream.

The owner of Acme Supply was a wise businessperson in that he did not allow his business decision to be based on age or male supremacy. Unfortunately, he delayed too long in making that decision, and the business was almost destroyed.

Enter the Son-in-Law

Should the enterpreneur have daughters, he must someday face the fact that sons-in-law may eventually enter the picture. While his dream in life is an heir to carry on the family business, can he rely on the son-in-law to fulfill his dream and carry the family forward with the firm? A father tends to be protective of his daughter and typically wants to believe that the man who marries her is not quite good enough for his princess. Can he trust the daughter to select a husband who is suitable for eventual family business leadership? Few women marry with the thought of choosing a husband to carry on the family business.

The high divorce rate is another factor in selecting the son-in-law as the ultimate successor. If the father and son-in-law have formed close bonds of personal friendship, can the father be assured that there will be no divorce in the future? There are no guarantees, and the entrepreneur must accept the son-in-law as the surrogate son, recognizing that his choice means that the business may not be continued under the family name.

If the father is satisfied with his choice of successor, other problems may develop as the son-in-law begins to manage the firm. The other daughters (if such there are) expect to share equally in the estate and hesitate to accept any financial favoritism toward the surrogate son. Frequently, these situations require that the firm be sold at the owner's death to accomplish a fair distribution of ownership. Alternatively, if the stock can be split, the fragmented ownership will dilute the president's authority and ability to make the company grow. If there is more than one son-in-law in the firm, the selection of a successor may set off violent scrabbles between the two daughters, who feel that they should share equally and that both their husbands should be made president.

The issue of succession is even more complex when sons *and* sons-in-law are in the firm. For example, a franchise restaurant owner in his late thirties was joined by a competent son-in-law, who began at the bottom of the business and worked his way to vice-president, with responsibility for purchasing accounts and personnel management. The restaurant business grew, and the relationship between the surrogate son and the father was steady and harmonious.

The founder's only son had worked for the father prior to leaving for college, but the two had disagreed badly, and the son completed college to begin a career on his own as an accountant. Success in the accounting profession was harder than the son had anticipated and he found that he could not live on the number of clients he serviced. The son, being very familiar with his father's restaurant business, envied the steady income and security of both his father and his brother-in-law. He had indeed shunned a golden opportunity for what he thought was a more lucrative and rewarding profession. The son returned, hat in hand, to patch up differences with his father and rejoin the family business.

Although the father, at this writing, has not named a successor, the family will suffer with almost any decision that is made. At this point, the son is the favorite. If he does gain control, the son-in-law, who has worked long and hard to achieve his position, will be bitter. The son will not develop the support of the employees because their votes are being cast against him. Too frequently the founder in similar situations will die before naming a successor because escaping the conflict seems the easiest route.

Blessed Are the Peacemakers

In the midst of the family rivalries stands the mother, usually trying to make peace between fathers, sons, wives, sons-in-law, and assorted factions but often being drawn into the conflict on one side or another.

The son is deeply dependent on the mother in early childhood because she is the one who holds, rocks, comforts, cleans, and clothes him. She teaches him right from wrong, reinforces him with praise, and controls him with punishment. As the son enters the family business, she may maintain this role of mother and confidant, defending her son's position in the organization while attempting to hear both sides of any argument and determine what is right or wrong. Many of her days are spent extinguishing brushfires to maintain a congenial atmosphere at family gatherings. She, better than anyone else, understands the father's sensitivities and needs and like-wise recognizes his shortcomings in dealing with the son. She considers the son competent and capable and expects him to receive just compensation and responsibility. The father-son relationship is not so easy to arbitrate in business because the entire family faces great difficulties in dissolving the adult-child relationships. Listen to one mother tell the story.

"My son is probably the hardest-working, most competent young man you've ever seen, yet his father refuses to start him in a good position in the company. Now I can understand, because we had many very hard, lean years getting this business going, and Mario feels that handing Tony a major position in the company would be detrimental to both him and the organization. I can't help but feel that if Tony went to work in another company, he would be immediately recognized and advanced accordingly, but Mario continues to hold him down.

"I find myself constantly explaining what Mario or Tony *really* intended to say. It's terribly nerve-racking, and I spend many a sleepless night wondering if they will ever really get along. I didn't do such a bad job handling them until Tony married. His wife is a whole new set of problems for me. She doesn't understand the business or the amount of hours that it takes to make it successful. She is always complaining to me that she doesn't have a husband because he is never around. I want to say to her; 'So what? I've lived this way forever.'

"I hold my tongue and try to explain to her that some day the long hours and hard work will pay off for Tony because he will run the company, but she hates Mario and thinks that he treats Tony poorly and does not recognize his ability. The problems are small now, but our grandchild, who will be born in 3 months, will probably create more problems.

"I remember when we started this business, and I thought it would be the greatest thing in the world to have a company which we all could work in and share the joys and sorrows. Although we are doing okay financially, the sorrows tend to outweigh joys at this point. I'm sure that neither of the two, Mario or Tony, is as emotionally distraught as I am handling the situation because, as they've always told me, I tend to overreact and want everyone to be happy. Everyone cannot be happy in a family-owned business because they must deal with business problems and solve them in a professional manner while handling family personalities and emotions at the same time."

Once again we see the nether side of nepotism in business. The theme here has been rivalry and conflict, and the outcomes have been mostly tragic. But surely there must be ways to traverse the succession minefield safely. Indeed there are, and one way is to know where the mines are. That is what we have shown you so far. The next step is to disarm the mines. Pay close attention now.

Notes

[1]Shakespeare, *Henry IV,* Part II, Act IV, Scene 5, lines 93–97.

[2]"Where Genesco Goes from Here," *Business Week,* March 10, 1973, p. 104; "Genesco: All in the Family," *Financial World,* November 20, 1974, p. 19; "Frank Jarman's Railroad Surgery on Genesco," *Business Week,* May 18, 1974, p. 88.

[3]"Where Genesco Goes from Here," p. 109.

[4]"To Be and What to Be—That Is the Question," *Forbes,* May 1, 1978, p. 25.

[5]Lisa Alther, *Kinflicks,* Alfred A. Knopf, Inc., New York, 1976.

[6]Howard M. Halpern, *Cutting Loose,* Simon & Schuster, Inc., New York, 1976, p. 13.

[7]Christopher Lasch, *The Culture of Narcissism,* W. W. Norton & Company, New York, 1978, p. 52.

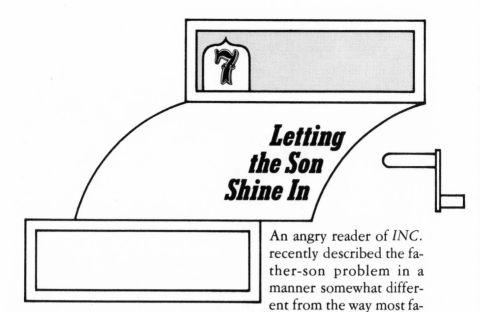

Letting the Son Shine In

An angry reader of *INC.* recently described the father-son problem in a manner somewhat different from the way most fathers do. As this reader viewed things, sons are not aggressive enough: "Family-owned businesses would continue to flourish if 'daddy,' instead of silver spoonfeeding his brats could place a swift kick on the heirs' posterior to motivate their way up the corporate ladder."[1]

This may be overstating the case, but it is true that the rise of the son in business is likely to be smoother if Dad takes a hand in the matter rather than simply letting the chips fall where they may. Danco makes this one of his twelve commandments for the family-owned business owner: "Thou shalt be responsible that thy successor(s) be well taught."[2]

But how best to teach him? We submit seven rules—perhaps "admonitions" is a better word—for the father in letting the son shine in:

- Recognize that times change.
- Avoid talking down the business.
- Resist sentencing the son to hard labor.
- Consider that experience may be the worst teacher.
- Find new worlds for the son to conquer.
- Get—and take—good advice.
- Don't forget to pay the man.

If these rules are followed, the result is likely to be collaborative management and a successful business.

The Times They Are A-Changing

Today's small business owner is likely to have christened the business just after World War II. The moments spent in the sands of Iwo Jima or on the shores of Tripoli remind him constantly that survival is a struggle. If he participated in the war, he probably grew up during the Great Depression of the 1930s as well. The children of that period have tended to learn the value of hard work, the virtue of playing cards close to the vest, and the vital importance of keeping something in reserve. No matter how much the business prospers, its owner, schooled in economic and personal hardship, will probably still be nagged by fears that it could all be swept away in days, that the thrill of victory lurks perilously close to the agony of defeat.

When the father is faced with the need to find a place in the company for his son, these perspectives color his decision. Putting the son in charge amounts to risking hard-earned money on an untested manager. Thus he delays the decision to advance the son, shunting him off to unimportant areas of the business where mistakes are not likely to be costly. Much-needed managerial training is neglected, commonly on the theory that the school of hard knocks is better anyway.

The perspective of the son is quite different. He does not remember the Depression; he knows only inflation. If he remembers a war at all, it is likely to be Korea or Vietnam, hardly the same types of conflicts that his father experienced. And his recollection of the hard work that Dad repeatedly tells him went into building the business in the first place is not likely to be very vivid. He remembers that Dad was away a lot and that there was always food on the table, even though it was not steak. He remembers working at the store on weekends, but his biggest problem was not making weighty financial decisions but concentrating on stacking the boxes on the shelves so that the whole lot would not collapse.

Whatever the circumstances attending the founding of the business, they are vastly different today. Dad won out in a jungle fight, buying cheap and selling dear to beat the competition. Today's business world is still a kind of jungle, but it is far more complicated. Government regulation, civil rights, women's liberation, consumerism, and environmental protection are all forces that have loomed large since Dad succeeded in business. These very forces are where it's at for the son. He grew up in a period of sweeping change; turmoil and uncertainty have been his norm. He neither fears change nor understands his father's fear of it.

If irreconcilable conflict between father and son is to be avoided, the *father must realize that the times they are a-changing,* in Bob Dylan's words, and that he must change with them. Small business is no longer a matter of one truck, one machine and one location. It involves law, finance, public relations—all disciplines that demand understanding and competence. Technology is developing rapidly, so rapidly that today's college graduate will have to be reeducated, in effect, in 5 to 10 years. For the small business, that means a search for new markets, new capital, and new products. Hard work is certainly not passé as a business requirement, but it must take place in a context of change and growth.

The son is likely to understand all this, and the father must be brought to understand it too. It is natural for the father to resist this—to try to stabilize things and to enjoy the things for which he has worked so hard. But he must not indulge himself in this luxury if the business is to be perpetuated. Instead he must train a successor to manage the business in today's world, not yesterday's. The father must cease to see himself as the company's hardest worker; he must become a teacher with a star student—his successor. Danco says it very well: "The term 'president' for a 50 year old owner of a privately held business has to be equated with 'teacher.' And unless he opens up his school, he will not have time to play the graduation march before the requiem sounds."[3]

Don't Knock the Rock

Much of this discussion has proceeded on the assumption that the son *wants* to shine in the business and that our job is to convince the father that a place must be made for him. But sons have something to say in this matter too, and they may not be all that anxious to enter the business. Why? Because Dad, by what he does and says, may turn his son against the business. After building the business into a rock to anchor the family, the owner then knocks it to such an extent that the son wonders whether it is all worth it.

Sometimes the act of entrepreneurship itself can be a turn-off to the son. To recap the scenario, the young entrepreneur works hard, takes risks, and puts together a business. This now becomes his whole life. He spends most of his time minding the store, and when he does manage to get home, he talks only about the business. The wife sees little of her husband and the children see even less. Father is the shadowy figure who does not come to dinner, does not show up to root for your Little League team, and never attends a play at school in which you have the lead role. When he is at home, there are long tirades about the perfidies of employees, of government, of tax collectors, and so on. After years of watching these performances, small wonder that the son doubts that the business is the stage upon which he wishes to perform.

Now a person who rises in business can hardly hide all the unpleasant aspects of this rise from his children. If the business is to be established, long, hard hours must be put in. There is no way the father can operate as the nine-to-five bank clerk who lives next door does. Given this fact, the father must recognize that getting the son into the business will require a deliberate selling act. If there is no deliberate selling, if nature is allowed to take its course, the odds favor the son's never entering the business because nature will tend to take him away.

Here is nature's way: The son starts in the business as a youngster, but usually he only does summer work, and the chores are menial at that. School offers a welcome relief from the tedium and drudgery of the business. Not surprisingly, college is tremendously popular among the sons of owner-managers. The son likes it because he can get away from his parents and postpone a decision about entering the business. Dad likes it because it gets the son out from underfoot while at the same time, Dad daydreams, giving the son the opportunity to grow up and be a man.

But college does not change the son that much. The attitude toward the family business that he brought with him is likely to be around at his graduation. If he was disposed against it to begin with, he is likely to remain so. Of course, he may enter the business for all the wrong reasons, from Dad's point of view. He may be too lazy to try to hold other jobs, or joining the company may simply be the path of least resistance. The father naturally hopes that the son will join the company because he likes the father, likes the business, and genuinely wants to work with the father in it. That is where the selling job comes in.

The selling must come early. In most cases, sons who do not go into a profession decide between going into the family business and becoming an employee of another company almost entirely in response to their perceptions of the father and the business that were formed in high school.[4] If the father waits until after college, when the son is grown up, he may have lost the battle already unless, as noted, the son is simply taking the easy way out.

If the father wants the son to admire the family business and become a part of it, *he must stop knocking that rock* and stress the positive side of things. The son needs to be told and shown at an early age that decision making can be fun, that real pleasure results when a job is well done and one has satisfied customers, and that business planning and management present exciting challenges.

The father works long hours. The son must be convinced that such work can offer as much satisfaction as playing golf, hunting, or other pursuits. Instead of trying this approach, far too many fathers get caught up in the notion of "my kid will have it easier than I did." Why should he want the son to have it easier if having it hard was, in fact, a lot of the fun?

The father has business problems, and it is only human that he should discuss them at home. It is always good for the son to understand that businesses have problems. But they do not have *only* problems. Shoptalk at home should therefore stress the positive as well as the negative side of business decisions. Making decisions is hard work, but being in a position to make decisions is itself a joy. Whatever the problems, the business owner can be proud of the fact that he is, to some extent at least, the master of his fate. It is this aspect of business ownership that the son should learn.

And the father must teach rather than hope that the son learns something from what goes on around him. When plans for the business are made, the son should be invited to comment on them and make suggestions; if there is a sticky employee problem, the son can be asked how he would handle the situation. If the son has a liking for the business at all, he will respond positively when he gets a chance to be on the inside, to participate in management, and to have his ideas listened to and even acted on. These are the things that motivated the father; they will also motivate the son.

Unfortunately, too many fathers teach their sons the wrong things, drilling them in the performance of menial tasks rather than management methods. This happens so often that it is often better if the son does his learning away from the father's supervision. Let us examine these two phenomena.

Take a Hard Look at Hard Labor

One of the most cherished beliefs of today's generation of self-made people is that the only place to start is at the bottom. According to this line of reasoning, before one is qualified to manage any business, one must have experienced the work done in the business at all levels from the loading shed to the executive suite. This is more than a matter of learning techniques. Instead, it is held that hard labor is good for the soul, that those who command must have endured the hardships of those who must follow. Thus, it is said, the best newspaper editors are those who started delivering papers, the best racehorse trainers are those who began mucking stalls, the best restaurateurs are those who first mopped the kitchen floor, and so on.

Going against this tradition are the proponents of book learning, who feel that education provides many shortcuts to positions of responsibility. Great doctors, we are told, need not actually have *had* all the diseases they will be treating. Doing manual labor trains one to do manual labor, not to function as an executive.

What advice should we give the father who is trying to decide where to start his son in the family-owned company? The best rule is to *take a hard look at hard labor.* If the son appears to need the discipline that seems to come with being forced to do menial jobs, start him at the bottom. If he seems to be a self-starter who can work hard and competently without having first calloused his hands, start him much nearer the top. Another factor to consider is personality. If the son tends at an early age to have an exalted sense of self-importance, hard work on the loading dock may be necessary to teach him humility. On the other hand, if he seems to grasp quickly the fact of human frailty, the loading dock may simply be unnecessary punishment. Let us look at a few examples of the hard-labor theory in practice.

When you enter the office of Doersam Marketing, a large chair whirls around and brings you face to face with a very young executive who owns perhaps more than his share of businesses in the town of Chillicothe, Ohio (population 25,000). The third generation of the family-owned business, Jim Doersam, now owns six separate corporations, and under his direction, one corporation—the electric supply company—has doubled its revenue. An automotive parts center experienced revenue increases of 25 percent in a 2-year period, and his petroleum company grew from $1 million to $6 million in revenue. This third-generation son is no sleeper; he sits on a mountain of responsibility.

Upon graduation from college, Jim returned to the family-owned business, which at the time employed his grandfather and father. Wisely, he was placed in a company that was removed from direct supervision by either of them; he became an employee of the Chillicothe Electric Company. Three days after Jim's arrival, the manager became disturbed with his new charge's apparent aggressive desires to learn and work his way up from the bottom. Jim started working on delivery trucks and behind the counter, making low wages and receiving no family perks for his involvement in the family business.

Jim was a star on a local lacrosse team, and every Saturday the teammates sat and waited for him to join them at practice or games. They could hardly believe that his father and grandfather owned one of the largest corporations in the city. How could they if he was not allowed to take off early on a Saturday to meet his teammates and assist them to victory? His lacrosse buddies could not understand his willingness to sacrifice a personal life for what appeared to be low wages in their professional eyes. His college cronies graduated to earn very good professional salaries, setting their own hours and watching Jim driven by a nonfamily manager who demanded the unreasonable.

Jim says: "As I look back now, I'm not sure I recognized the golden opportunity. Upon graduation from college, my decisions and career options were limited since I wanted to remain in Chillicothe. Neither my father nor my grandfather insisted on my involvement in the family-owned business, but I felt it was a job and a way to remain in the area in which I grew up. I swallowed my pride, worked long hard hours, won the acceptance and approval of all the other employees, and placated the manager, who was hostile to me because of my position in the Doersam family. At the time of my grandfather's death, we were running three companies, and each time one of the managers retired, I asked to assume the management role of that business. Dad was a quiet, nonaggressive partner, which, I am sure, was due to the dominant role my grandfather always played with him. There were few power struggles between the two of us because Dad sat back and quietly acknowledged my decisions as the right decisions and reaped the benefits of our growth. Dad officially retired at 67, when I was managing six different corporations. Although he is retired, he comes to the office 6 days a week, but he comes to me for all major decisions. I was allowed every opportunity to grow and expand in the business, but I am sure that had I been the second generation, under my grandfather, we would have had problems."

When asked if there are plans for the fourth generation to follow, Jim explains that his son or daughter and spouses would be welcome to join the family firm, but they would be required to spend 1 year in each company at wages commensurate with their responsibility and no executive family perks.[5]

Starting at the bottom worked well for Jim Doersam, and he plans to continue the tradition. But Marvin Fagel is not so sure that is the way to go.[6]

Marvin's father, Harold, grew up in Chicago during the Great Depression. In 1939, with $5000 borrowed from his father, Harold moved to Aurora, Illinois, and founded the Aurora Packing Company. It was a tough beginning. Harold climbed out of bed at 3:00 A.M. every day, drove to Chicago to pick up meat, then drove back to Aurora to cut and deliver it. With Harold as the hard-driving force, the business grew; in late 1979, 600 to 800 head of cattle a day were being slaughtered. This is not a corporate giant when compared with the likes of Iowa Beef Processors (14,000 to 18,000 head a day), but it is Harold Fagel's life; he still works sun to sun and on weekends. And he is very much the boss. Says Harold: "When you own a business, you live or die by the decisions you make. You cannot run a business by committee. This is mine. I run it."

The ethic that would control the lives of Harold's sons, Marvin and the younger Michael, was predictable: "You may hate me right now, but you'll thank me years from now." What the boys would thank Harold for, in his view, was his having sentenced them to hard labor. From childhood, Marvin and Michael scraped out cattle pens and carried sides of beef to loading decks. Michael was later to become director of safety and security at Aurora, a position that did not bring him into frequent conflict with his father. But Marvin, the boss apparent, had more problems.

Marvin went to the University of Wisconsin. He began his studies in business but found them too theoretical and switched to agriculture. Upon graduation, he was back at Aurora Packing and enrolled in Harold Fagel's "executive training" program, a program that was more like punishment than training. From the Chicago Union stockyards to the western Illinois feedlots, Marvin donned hip boots and thermal underwear and braved the cattle pens during harsh Midwestern winters. Back in Aurora, he worked the "kill floor" (wielding an air hammer), bled and shackled carcasses, cut off hides, and trimmed heads.

Father Harold was harder on Marvin than on any other employee. Marvin always got the worst truck, the biggest load, and the worst delivery jobs. He also got the most riding by his father and was frequently humiliated in front of other people. Although Marvin tried to be one of the boys—driving and drinking with the other employees—he was always regarded as the son of the boss, not really one of them.

It was not a happy time for Marvin. He felt that his father, rather than taking advantage of his education, was actually punishing him for it. Occasionally, Marvin was able to assume an executive role when his father took a vacation (which was not often), but when Harold returned to work, Marvin was always banished to hard-labor-dom again. Marvin finally found a way to escape (as we shall see below), but it is not apparent to this day that he thanks his father for having sent him to the executive suite by way of the chain gang.

Commenting on this situation, the Cleveland-based Center for Family Business said: "You don't insure competence in your son by sentencing him to hard labor. Pretending nepotism doesn't exist by crushing your son only ends up crushing your son. People can't stand up under that kind of treatment, not even sons. They need a healthy environment, good working conditions, encouragement, and positive feedback. Employees aren't going to accept a son as boss just because he can shovel sand. They'll accept him only if he can run the business."[7]

Remember, however, that we have only asked the businessman-father to query the hard-labor route, not necessarily to reject it. As we mentioned, the personality factor must be considered. A case in point:

David Donovan worked hard to build his small cotton and soybean farm into a 1000-acre plantation. A Catholic in a largely Protestant Southern environment, David had more than his share of personal motivation, and he tried to transfer this to his sons, Perry and Art. Despite his own lack of education, he was convinced that modern agriculture, to be a successful pursuit, would require the application of the new science and technology being espoused by the land-grant universities and carried into the field by extension agents.

His sons appeared to be complete opposites as far as appreciation of education was concerned. The older son Perry, played hooky, lost his books, and consistently made low grades. His father allowed him to quit school as soon as it became legally possible—at age 16—and put him to work in the fields—driving tractors, hoisting sacks of soybeans, and exercising some supervisory responsibilities over other (all black) workers. Meanwhile, Art, who seemed to take to the books, was encouraged in every way to continue. He finished high school, took a degree in agriculture at the state university, and returned to the plantation to be groomed as the successor to his father. When David Donovan turned 60, he gave the business over to Art. Perry continued to work as a day laborer.

There was one problem, however. Art had learned a lot about agricultural machinery and hybrid corn but very little about people. He proved to be a poor manager, was capricious and unreasonable with his workers, and refused to do anything other than be the boss. He had never been asked to work with his hands and showed only impatience and even contempt for those who did so. Predictably, worker turnover increased and there was a decline in farm productivity and profits. Friction between Art and Perry increased because the workers looked to Perry, who had always worked with them rather than above them, for advice.

David Donovan finally realized that he had made a mistake. Perry was given operational responsibility for the farm, and Art was put in charge of the company office in town, where his principal jobs were to keep abreast of new agricultural techniques and track the futures market.

Both of David's sons are now considered successful; one did it through education, the other primarily through hard labor. The key in this situation is the fact that Perry was not sentenced to hard labor against his will; he chose it as a way to maturity.

Experience Is the Worst Teacher?

The Fagel family also provides a good illustration of another good bit of advice for father: *Recognize that experience is often the worst teacher.*[8] In other words, the best way for a son to learn the business is not necessarily at the side of his father. In fact, this is often the worst way. Better that the son should seize upon any opportunity to go out on his own, even in the same line of work, and then return to the family business if he chooses. Not only will this spare him the pain of doing it Dad's way, it may also give him a greater appreciation of Dad's problems.

When we left Marvin Fagel, he was frustrated and angry, still hauling beef when he thought he should be helping to run the company. One day Marvin made a delivery to Chicago's North Side and met George Pasek, part owner of the meat-packing firm. At 63, Pasek was getting ready for retirement, and the idea of a partnership with a younger man seemed attractive. He and Marvin talked it over, and within a short time the two of them had launched Midway Meat Co., a meat-packing plant on Chicago's South Side. Marvin financed his part of the deal out of his savings, and his father gave his blessing to the venture and a promise of credit backing.

Midway's fortunes bobbed up and down. At first, Pasek rarely came to the office, Marvin ran the business, and Midway began to show a profit. Then Pasek started coming in every day; dissension soon resulted between the partners, and profits began to drop.

Although his own company was not doing well, Marvin's relations with his father were better than they had ever been. He was in constant contact with his father, and since they now headed separate companies, they could talk as colleagues. And Marvin's respect for his father grew. He had learned before that when his father could not answer all his questions, it was not because he was putting his son off; it was because there were no quick and easy answers.

When the situation at Midway did not improve, Marvin finally bought Pasek out. His father, in turn, offered to buy Midway—the supreme compliment for a businessperson. Marvin's specialty (processing beef navels into skirt steaks and trimmings), said Harold, would fit nicely into Aurora's line.

The merger improved Midway's financial position; and although Marvin and his father still have some problems, their relations have improved tremendously since Marvin left Aurora for Midway. Harold feels that his son has finally learned the meat business, something of which he was never convinced before. And Marvin feels he has done some learning. "Having been in the hot seat at Midway, I find that I can appreciate the position. I guess it's like the old saying: "When I was 25, I couldn't believe how stupid my father was. Now I'm 32, and I'm amazed at how much he's learned in only 7 years.'"

The Center for Family Business again: "The best way to learn how to be a manager is to learn on your own. The second-best way is to learn from someone else. The worst way is to learn from your father. It's better to make your mistakes outside the family."[9]

Would that we could simply let it go at that. However, things do not always have a happy ending when the son learns the business elsewhere. Bill Margate, for example, a business school graduate, always intended to go into his father's business, an electronic components company. But he decided to get his first business experience elsewhere, and so he worked for 4 years with a large manufacturing firm. Both his education and his experience convinced Bill that his father's business was very unsophisticated; when he joined the company, he set about shaping things up.

This has led to a nasty business and family situation. In his son's eyes, the elder Margate can do nothing right. Mrs. Margate encourages her son in these attacks on the father, and whenever Bill's ventures have failed, as they have on several occasions, she blames the failure on the father's interference. However, when the father-son battle becomes serious, Mrs. Margate shifts to her husband's side.[10]

The problems of this family-owned business are obviously not all caused by the fact that Bill worked somewhere else first, but that is a factor because it was not properly planned. Working in the manufacturing firm was a unilateral decision made by Bill without he and his father ever having agreed upon what Bill needed to learn and how this could be useful to the family business. Outside experience can bring insights and fresh ideas into the family firm, but if no attempt is made to make the new ideas mesh with the old, a Margate-type situation is likely to result. Experience outside the family business can be most useful when it is done deliberately and is part of a plan developed by the father and son together.[11]

New Worlds to Conquer

One way to accommodate onrushing sons in a family business without first farming them out to other employment is to create new divisions so that *the son has new worlds to conquer* and is not tempted to interfere with the old man's world. Our advice to the father-owner is thus simple: When the son is young and eager, establish a branch store, set up a new operation, buy out a defunct competitor, or make the business grow so that it is big enough for father and son or even father and sons.

An interesting and illustrative, though by no means typical, example of letting sons shine through expansion is provided by the

Rooney empire.[12] Art Rooney, Sr., the legendary founder of the four-time Super Bowl-champion Pittsburgh Steelers, purchased the National Football League (NFL) franchise in 1933 for $2500 and kept it afloat by betting on horses. He has lived for 30 years in a neighborhood that could be considered a slum, walking from his house to Three Rivers Stadium, wearing baggy pants, smoking a cigar, and usually trekking in the company of a group of black youngsters with whom he jokes.

Art, Sr., boasts that he never borrowed a dime in his life, but his sons—Dan, Artie, Tim, John, and Pat—have borrowed over $60 million and, with their father, control not only the Steelers but Shamrock Farms in Maryland and a variety of racetracks—thoroughbred, harness, and greyhound.

The elder Rooney is still very much the boss. It was only in the last few years that the boys dared to drink in front of their father or appear in public without a white shirt and tie. Although their mother, Kathleen, allows that none of the boys is really the man the father is, they all have shown talent in the managerial area. However, they have never, so far as is known, dreamed of overthrowing their father and have also managed to suppress any dissension among themselves. When they were young, the boys did engage in some furniture-smashing fights; but as adults, they talk to each other on the phone nearly every day, slip away from sessions to drink milkshakes, and follow the fortunes of the Steelers.

Since all the boys were ambitious but were faced with a father who was unlikely to give up his position, they have expanded around him, and each appears to have accepted his place in the empire. Naturally, all the sons would have liked to head the Steelers—the franchise is a sort of family heirloom—but the mantle was passed to Dan, the oldest. Art, Sr., had wanted his oldest son to be an electrician, but Dan only wanted to be at Steeler training camps, and so his father did not push. Dan is now the team's general manager, and he has brought the football championships to the Steel City that Art, Sr., was never able to do when he was active head of the organization. Dan has been voted NFL Executive of the Year.

Artie (Art, Jr.) wanted to be an actor after he finished college and did go off to New York to try his luck, carrying both his father's blessings and misgivings. The theatrical career flopped, and after a stint working at William Penn Raceway in Pennsylvania, Artie returned to the Steelers. He headed the four-man scouting team used by the Steelers to supplement their scouting service and was thus responsible for the acquisition of such household sports names as Franco Harris, Terry Bradshaw, and Mean Joe Greene.

Of all the boys, Tim, it is commonly said, is the most like his father, but he could not stay in Pittsburgh because there was no more room for Rooneys in the Steeler organization. After working for a few years as a stockbroker, he went to West Palm Beach to help run the dog track and then moved up to head Yonkers Raceway, a New York harness-racing track that the family bought.

The twins, John and Pat, found no jobs in sports when they finished college. John taught high school for a few years and Pat worked as a copper salesman. But when Liberty Bell racetrack opened up in Philadelphia, both boys worked their way up from ticket punchers to managers, John becoming president of William Penn, the nighttime harness operation, and Pat becoming president of Continental, which handled the daytime flat racing.

The Rooney story can be summed up this way: The father-founder of the business made it clear as his five sons began to emerge from childhood that he did not intend to move over anytime soon and that the sons, rather than fighting each other for control of his holdings, should begin to carve out places for themselves somewhere in the organization. They did.

Such expansions are obviously more difficult if the Rooney fortune is not available, but the case history does provide a helpful perspective for even the smallest of family businesspeople when considering expansion. Dollars-and-cents market analyses might indicate that a move to multiple locations or to a new line of products would be risky. In deciding whether to make such moves, however, the father-owner should consider more than the dollars and cents. Are there up-and-coming sons who could be stashed peacefully in a new location or a new division until Dad is ready to retire? If so, expansion may be a way of saving money in the long run because the father-son conflicts that usually lower productivity and profits can often be avoided in this way. Where more than one son, or even son-in-law, is involved, expansion is an especially effective way of muting conflict.

Help with the Hard Ones

All the rules laid down here for letting the son into the business with a minimum of bloodletting are, we modestly suggest, good ones, but even those who apply them most diligently may still be faced with situations in which the correct course of action is not crystal-clear. In such cases, it is a good idea to get—and take—advice. This book, in other words, should help you with the easy ones, but you may need *additional help with the hard ones.*

An entire organization was created to help sons whose fathers are bosses in a family business. After hearing so many sad tales about life with father, Gerald Slavin, who headed a subsidiary of his father's business in Boston, decided to form an organization to stimulate and formalize tale telling. He called it the Sons of Bosses and described it as a "very casual social group" to discuss father-son business problems. The organizational meeting in 1969 drew thirteen hardy members, drawn together by the common woes described in their anthem, "S.O.B. Blues." A sample:

> He calls it my allowance
> but I'd like a salary.
> I'm ready to take over
> 'cause Dad is 93.

Slavin collected so many sad experiences through the S.O.B.'s that he began to write a book with the working title of *The S.O.B. Syndrome.* The S.O.B.'s became a national organization, and the name was changed to the National Family Business Council. By this time, the group was inviting fathers as well as sons to the meetings, serious affairs usually concluding with case-study discussions in which members seek advice about father-son relationships in business. Members listen sympathetically as cases are described, sometimes admitting that they have had the same experiences as the speakers.[13]

Marvin Fagel, the meat-packer discussed earlier in this chapter, sought out the S.O.B.'s for assistance when he was struggling to make Midway Meat Company a prosperous concern. A chapter was being formed in Chicago. Says Marvin: "At the S.O.B. meetings, I found people I could identify with, people with the same problem. In discussing our troubles, we had to define our father's problems, and we learned they weren't so simple. Also, the S.O.B.'s were a tremendous source of solace—misery loves company. There, it was clear that my father wasn't the only dirty bastard around." Marvin eventually became president of the Chicago S.O.B. chapter and discovered strength in himself that he never knew existed before.[14]

The basic tenet of the S.O.B. movement is that every family business can benefit if there is better mutual understanding between father and son. Those readers who are having problems in this area that they cannot seem to solve might wish to look in on the local chapter or start one if none exists.

There are also other groups with perhaps more sophisticated methods than the case-study approach that comment on the father-son situation. The Center for Family Business, whose observations on the Fagel situation were quoted earlier, is dedicated to the perpetuation of successful family businesses by the provision of educational services to its family business owner members. The Levinson Institute and the Independent Business Institute are also groups that can offer advice. In addition, there are many consultants in private business who specialize in father-son problems. Nor should educational institutions such as the Harvard Graduate School of Business Administration be overlooked.

In the end, of course, father-son problems, like other personal problems, can be solved only by the persons in the situation, drawing upon such outside help as they can. Rather than stewing in guilt and anger, the family member must take steps to solve his problems. If reasonable attempts do not work and he continues to feel bound to the family organization, the problem is largely psychological. To free himself to make choices about what he wants to do, he must talk his feelings out with whoever is his rival in the business, a conversation that is often most usefully pursued in the presence of a neutral third party. Sometimes professional counseling will be necessary. Talking the matter out will reduce the emotional intensity of the situation and make it possible for alternatives to be more sharply perceived and choices more freely made. Of course, if a contending family member has a need to expiate guilt by punishing himself, that is his personal problem and not necessarily the problem of the family business.

Dollars and Sons

We have saved for last a subject that is sticky in all family businesses: How much should the crown prince be paid while he is being groomed to assume the throne? It will be hard for nonfamily employees to accept the fact, but the most common finding is that father-owners are underpaying their son-successors and the latter harbor some resentment because of it. Fathers usually deny this and cite a number of reasons why the cash being shelled out to the son is adequate:

"I do not want the other employees to feel that I am showing favoritism to my son."

"I never had much money when I was coming up and I don't think he should either."

"Because his father is the boss, he gets some benefits that others do not, so he should be willing to work for less money."

These arguments are rarely compelling to the son. He feels that being paid a day's wage for a day's work is not favoritism, that he already knows the value of money, that inflation has made his father's salary experience irrelevant to the needs of the son, and that there are not nearly enough benefits connected with being the son of the boss to justify the lost income.

Our advice is: *Don't forget to pay the man.* Make sure, however, that the salary the son receives is commensurate with the responsibilities assumed by him and is on a par with the salaries of others with similar responsibilities, neither above nor below them. Furthermore, limit the son's compensation to salary (except for stock ownership, of course); compensating the son through family favors is likely to rankle the employees even more than overpaying him would. The son should have the same fringe benefits, working hours, and company bonuses as others.

If the father pays the son the money to which he is entitled but no more, can the father justly ask the son to give more loyalty and dedication to the firm than other employees? Indeed he can. After all, the son will someday inherit the business and thus has more at stake in its fortunes than other employees. The extra work should be thought of as work for future financial rewards, not current ones.

If there is more than one son in the business, should all be paid the same wages? The best rule is to make sure they all have equal opportunity to assume positions of responsibility and then pay them in accordance with responsibility. If one son wants to remain on the loading dock, he should not receive as high a salary as the son who is willing to move up to the boardroom. Of course, it will not always be easy to decide exactly when responsibilities are equal and thus deserving of equal pay, and all wives concerned are likely to hold that their husbands are being discriminated against, but these are simply hardships that the father must endure.

Toward Collaborative Management

What we are striving for in this welter of rules and admonitions is a path through the minefields of father-son conflict. The objective is a presuccession phase for the family-owned business that could be called one of collaborative management. In this situation, the father is still in charge of the business, but he is collaborating with his son in its management and training the son to take over completely when he retires. Achieving this blissful state is no easy matter. It may help both father and son get there if they are willing to pause and reflect on the stages their relationship is likely to go through. Since the concept of collaborative management involves one or more people working to formulate a strategy, perfection may never be attained. Factors such as personality, age, and degree of maturity all affect the stages of the father-son relationship. (Figure 1 presents the stages schematically.)

Stage 1: All Is Well

In years 1 to 4 in which the father and son work together, Dad is the leader and the son follows loyally, questioning neither business practices nor methodology. The heir apparent is working in the family business to earn wages and help make his career decisions. The age of the father is irrelevant to the relationship if the heir apparent is handling part-time jobs, developing a college curriculum, and setting his goals to graduation. Should the son choose not to go to college and enroll immediately in the school of work, he considers the years 1 to 4 or 1 to 6 a training ground for the technical experience and a rudimentary introduction to grass-roots experience.

Stage 2: Trouble on the Horizon

The collaborative management in stage 2, years 4 through 10, is characterized by decreased cooperation between father and son. This period in the father's life reflects an unstable environment in which he attempts to teach the son how to manage the business while still not releasing any responsibility and authority. The technical training aspects which occurred in the early years have now progressed to management training techniques. The decline in collaborative management is a result of aggressive action with the son as a doer, wishing now to expand the company or change things as he thinks they

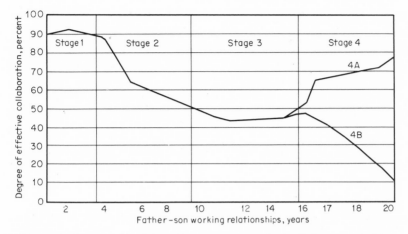

Figure 1   Pattern of collaborative management in the father-son working relationship.

should be done. He moves slowly so as not to confront his father openly with the problems he may see in the company.

Stage 3: Something's Gotta Give

When the son or heir apparent has dedicated 10 years of his life to the family business, he is ready to validate his decision with expansion into new, uncharted territories. While many businesses may move through the stages more rapidly, they find themselves caught in a struggle against the nurturer of the business (the founder) and the budding executive who wishes to make it grow and expand.

Stage 3 presents the most open hostility and conflict in the father-son relationship. The father may be referred to as tyrannical—protecting his love, his mistress. While he wants the son to succeed, he does not want to part with his creation. The impatient son cannot understand his father's resistance to growth, change, expansion, and his ability to manage. Stage 3 is a critical one for the development of collaborative management.

Stage 4: At the Crossroads

A. As the father and son solve their personality conflicts and ameliorate their power struggles, they move to a situation needed for collaborative management and the ultimate growth of the organization.

Some family businesses may never make it to 4A but instead fall into 4B.

B. This represents the route to total conflict if the combatants do not reconcile their differences and join efforts collectively for the growth and stability of the company.

Thus the father has dodged the chips off the old block; he has let the son shine in (increasingly, the daughter also). There is another reality that awaits every business owner; its presence has been a brooding part of the father-son drama all along. This is the grim specter of succession.

Notes

[1]Letters, *INC.*, August 1979, p. 11.

[2]Leon A. Danco, *Beyond Survival*, University Press, Inc., Cleveland, Ohio, 1977, p. 188.

[3]Ibid., p. 14.

[4]Frank M. Butrick, "Don't Turn Your Son against Your Business." Reprinted with permission of *Trailer/Body Builders* by Independent Business Institute, Akron, Ohio, p. 63.

[5]Based on a personal interview.

[6]See John R. Halbrooks, "Handling the Boss When He's Your Dad," *INC.*, October 1979, p. 76–80.

[7]Ibid., p. 80.

[8]Ibid., p. 76–80.

[9]Ibid., p. 80.

[10]Harry Levinson, "Conflicts That Plague Family Businesses," *Harvard Business Review,* March/April 1971, p. 93.

[11]Frank Butrick, *Survivorship for the Family Business,* Independent Business Institute, Akron, Ohio, p. 6.

[12]Roy Blount, Jr., "An Unsentimental Education," *Sports Illustrated,* vol. 39, July 16, 1973, pp. 34–35.

[13]Robert Levy, "Chips off the Executive Block," *Dun's Review,* August 1977, pp. 30–31.

[14]Halbrooks, op. cit., p. 78.

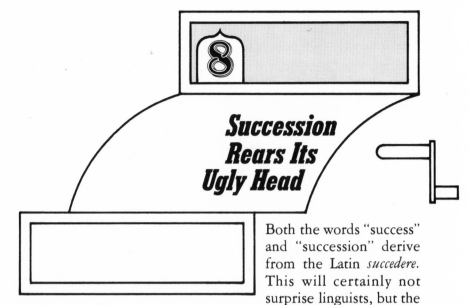

Succession Rears Its Ugly Head

Both the words "success" and "succession" derive from the Latin *succedere*. This will certainly not surprise linguists, but the juxtaposition of the two words sounds strange in the world of family-owned business. For if it is true that nothing succeeds like success, it is equally true in family business that nothing fails like succession. Succession is a creature that inevitably rears its head in such business concerns, and the head is often an ugly one because the business is likely to undergo some traumatic experiences before things quiet down and there is a new boss in place, even if the latter position is achieved at all. In Chapters 8 and 9, we shall examine various facets of the succession phenomenon and see whether there are ways to achieve it without tears. Succession presents both organizational and financial problems. We will first explore the organizational problems—e.g., how to get Dad to retire—and then look at the financial matters—e.g., estate planning—that must be dealt with.

The Concept of Succession

It should first be clarified that when we use the term "succession," we are referring to a change in the top leadership of an organization. In other words, when succession occurs, an old boss is out and a new boss is in. There are, of course, changes taking place at lower levels in organizations all the time. New department heads are selected, lower-level employees are promoted, and new divisions with new people in charge are established. All such changes may exhibit some of the same symptoms as succession at the top, such as resentment, hostility, loss of continuity, and so on. Those are all matters for the boss to deal with. But the real problem comes when the boss position itself is the place where change is in process. Who will boss the boss? It is only at this level that the concept of succession becomes relevant.

Succession is a problem for all organizations, not the least of which are governments. Different forms of government handle the problem in different ways. In the monarchies of old, dynasties were established and clear procedures for succession were laid out. The usual rule was that the eldest son would always succeed his father as king. If there were no sons, the eldest daughter would become queen, although there commonly were squabbles about that in the chauvinist days of yore, and so fathers went to great lengths to make sure they had a son waiting in the wings. (Not all were as heavy-handed in the matter as Henry VIII of England, of course.) If the eldest son was not of age at his father's death, a regent would serve until the son grew up.

It was always the *death* of the monarch that was the occasion for succession. Almost no monarch ever went out alive, with Edward VIII, who renounced the English throne to marry a commoner (and a divorcée at that), being a notable exception. Occasionally, a kingdom would be left without an heir to the throne, and then a crisis would ensue. A new dynasty had to be established, and there were usually disputes, sometimes quite bloody, over which dynasty that would be. Also, revolutions sometimes interrupted the established succession patterns. On the whole, however, monarchical rules of succession worked fairly well and brought stability to the kingdoms.

When monarchy fell into disfavor as a form of government and divine will was replaced by popular choice as the source of the right to rule, the new governments still had to grapple with the problem of succession. Democratic governments constructed elaborate electoral processes to choose their top leaders, be they presidents or prime ministers. Such processes have had mixed success in attempting to provide the final word in the filling of leadership vacancies. In the United States, fortunately, the established procedures for determining a new President have never been rejected. No Vice-President has ever attempted to overthrow a President in office. In other countries with democratic forms—Latin America, for example—the experience has been quite different. Elections were (and are) sometimes simply the first stage in deciding who would rule the country, and the overthrow of established leaders has been the rule rather than the exception.

Despotisms (whatever their legal form of government) have had perhaps a more difficult time with succession than democracies. By definition, modern despots rule because they have the informal power—army, secret police, and so on—behind them. Any electoral processes are simply manipulated to bring about the results desired by the person with the power. Since ruling power is gained, held, and lost informally, succession at the top becomes an unpredictable series of events. The ruling despot who designates a successor is in all probability creating a competitor who will not necessarily wait for his patron to step down before moving to take over. If a successor is designated, other claimants may not accept the choice of the deceased despot, and a power struggle will ensue. Succession in the early years of the Soviet Union provides many examples of this process. Lenin, Stalin, and Khrushchev all gained control by besting their rivals in bitter and sometimes bloody contests; elections were after the fact.

The family-owned business has some of the features of all these governing forms as far as succession is concerned, but it is probably closest to despotism. The boss rules, and there are no established procedures for replacing him. Except for constraints imposed by the government or unions, he makes the decisions as he sees fit and designates successors when and if he chooses. There are some hints of the old monarchical style because the eldest son is likely to be the designated successor, and there may even be some elements of democracy since if no successor is designated, possible claimants may have to make a collegial decision; even the board of directors may become an independent factor. On the whole, however, succession in the family business is an informal matter.

There are four ways by which the top spot in the company may be vacated so that a succession must occur: The boss may die, retire, resign before retirement, or be dismissed. Resignation and firing are not common ways for bosses in family-owned business to leave office. They usually want to stay at the helm as long as they can, and there is usually no one to oust them against their will, although there are exceptions to the latter, as the Genesco story recited in Chapter 6 indicates. Mostly, however, a succession occurs because the old man dies or decides to retire.

Before drawing morals and maxims from the literature of succession, let us look at succession as it has occurred over the years in one family-owned business. The case history suggests where the pressure points are in the succession process. The business is the Neiman-Marcus Company.

Minding the Store: Neiman-Marcus

Neiman-Marcus is a Dallas-based retail firm, and we are privy to the story through a book, *Minding the Store,*[1] written by a key participant, Stanley Marcus. By and large, the power transitions in this company, perhaps best known for its bizarre Christmas gifts (his and hers elephants, for example), have been successful; but there have been enough anxious moments that illustrate the problems that other businesses may encounter.

The Neiman-Marcus Company was formed in 1907 by Herbert Marcus, his sister, Carrie, and her husband, Al Neiman. Like all entrepreneurs, Herbert Marcus was charismatic and unmindful of the risks he was taking. He was also a good merchant but a bad delegator of authority, a condition that could have meant trouble had Herbert not been right so much of the time. In addition, both Carrie and Al Neiman were capable so that a considerable pool of talent was available to carry the business through the early years.

But it was Herbert who was the life force of the business, and his son admired this quintessential entrepreneur a great deal:

> He was a remarkable man in that he represented the combination of so many antithetical forces: he had the tenderness of a woman and the sternness of a commanding general; the courage of a lion and the wariness of a panther; he was religious but a nonbeliever; he was a visionary but at the same time a pragmatist; he was uneducated but had an appreciation of all that was fine and beautiful; he was understanding of the personal problems of a stockboy, but not of his wife's inability to balance a checkbook.[2]

As the store grew from a shop into a business, the delegation problem was solved by having the principals assume responsibility for different areas of the business. Al concentrated on buying suits, coats, and apparel for the new misses' department. Carrie devoted her time to the better women's clothes salon; Herbert merchandised the whole store but particularly the new men's and boys' departments and the new accessory division.

Nepotism and paternalism were firmly ensconced at Neiman-Marcus. Nieces, nephews, and brothers-in-law who could not find jobs elsewhere could always come to the store to work, but they repaid this generosity with loyalty and honesty. Herbert's elderly father, a retired cotton merchant, was even given a seat of honor near the front door, and Herbert presided benignly over the entire scene.

Stanley Marcus, Herbert's first son, literally started in the business on the ground floor. His mother could not afford a maid, and so when she went downtown to the store, she deposited young Stanley in the dress-altering department. In a way, then, he started in the business at age 2. As Stanley grew up, it was a foregone conclusion that he would go into the business; certainly Herbert never considered any other options for him.

"While I was debating the various aspects of the book business, my father had no doubts at all that I was going to enter Neiman-Marcus. This was a foregone conclusion with him, and he told me very frankly he expected me and my brothers to follow in his footsteps."[3]

Like so many sons, Stanley felt that his college training was not utilized sufficiently when he entered the company. He wanted to apply some of his ideas concerning the use of statistics and advertising in business but got little opportunity to do so. As the first college-trained Neiman-Marcus executive, he was suspect.

Meanwhile, Al Neiman left the business. He and Herbert had disagreed for some time, and Marcus finally bought out his partner's interest, although the Neiman-Marcus name was retained. (One of the Neimans also stayed; Carrie divorced Al, who had admitted to having an affair with a buyer.) Al's departure created an opportunity for Stanley Marcus. The number-two administrative man in the company left with Al Neiman, and Herbert decided to give his eldest son a crack at the job. His other brothers, Eddie and Herbert, Jr., also came into the business eventually, and Stanley was used as the model for them to follow.

"Consciously or unconsciously, I was the model by which they were constantly being measured. There were no problems between the brothers in the early years, but later, unhappy tensions did develop, as egos expanded, marriages occurred, and pillow talk exerted itself."[4]

Although Stanley's relations with his father were generally good, waiting in the line of succession proved a great frustration for the younger Marcus. Stanley confessed that the greatest single disappointment in his life was his father's failure to name him president of the company before his fortieth birthday. He had completed high school at 16 and college at 20 so that assuming a business presidency while still in his thirties would have completed his track record. Even when his health began to fail, Herbert Marcus remained in control; to promote his son at that time would have been recognition of his declining physical capacity, something to which no founder-father wants to admit.

Stanley Marcus's wait did not end until his father died. But the new president faced a different situation than his father had. Herbert could rule by dictate while Stanley had to use persuasion—all four brothers had equal shares of stock. However, his role as first among equals was accepted by his brothers, and they were able to operate the business successfully.

> After the board meeting at which I was made president, I gathered my brothers together to reiterate the need for continuing family solidarity and to caution us all that the test of this concept was about to begin. Heretofore, we had been held together by the colossal strength of a great man, our father, who was both the head of the family and the controlling stockholder of the company. "Now," I said, "we stand as four brothers with equal shares in the company, with theoretically equal rights as stockholders. I have been named president and chief executive officer and I shall be forced at some time in the future to make decisions which may be contrary to the judgments of one or the other of you. I shall attempt at all times to be fair and objective, but as long as I am the chief executive officer I shall expect you to accept my decisions, even when you may disagree." All three of them recognized my seniority in both age and experience, and pledged their sincere cooperation without reservation.[5]

Remembering well the hard road he had traveled in the business, Stanley did not repeat the process with his son, Dick. The latter was not pressured into going into the business, was given room and time to experiment in other areas, and came into Neiman-Marcus by his own choice. He did well in the company, and his father eventually named him president. Stanley moved up to become chairman of the board, where he could continue giving Dick on-the-job training so that he could take over completely at his father's retirement and carry on the business in the manner of his father and grandfather. Ultimately, the company merged with Broadway-Hale and became a multicompany corporation. The merger was an unusually successful one.

If I were doing it over again, the only thing I would do differently would be to have merged five years earlier. It was a good deal for both our stockholders and for Broadway's. It gave us the financial ability to enter into a large and significant expansion program. And it relieved me of having to name my successor by myself. I would imagine that in the whole history of American corporate mergers, this is one of the few in which neither of the parties has suffered any disillusionment after five years of association.[6]

In sum, the first generation at Neiman-Marcus resisted succession until overtaken by death; the second generation was amenable to succession and assisted in the transition; and the third generation is yet to be heard from. What does this tell us about succession problems and patterns?

The Pain of Departure: Naming a Successor

One lesson seems to be that the founder of a business is not likely to go quietly. Only death could move Herbert Marcus from his store, no matter how much it appeared that his son was ready to take over.

The pain that accompanies departure, or even the suggestion of departure, by the founder is usually caused by the fact that the father and son perceive the situation quite differently. To the father, the business is "his thing," something that he has built and that requires a strong dynamic leader such as himself to survive. His son is able, to be sure, but young and inexperienced and not ready for such a demanding job. At a less conscious level, the father feels that giving up his position means premature aging and a loss of self-esteem. The loss of his primary purpose in life, he fears, will lead to despair and death.

The son takes a quite different view of the matter. He thinks that his father is too unyielding, that he should retire, and that he (the son) is perfectly capable of guiding the business. He views his father's aging as a natural process that is accompanied by growth in the father's prestige. His father has earned respect, has paid his dues, and should be eager to take life easy for a while.

Because the father is in the commanding position, his views are likely to prevail. Since the thought of leaving is very painful to him, he will wait and wait before naming a successor because that would mean acceptance of something that he is not willing to accept.

Examples of this are legion. "I have no plans to retire," said the chairman of Continental Telephone at age 68. "I'll fight 'em, I'll set up a bazooka patrol, but I'm only leaving feet first." The chief executive of Tampax, Inc., refuses even to discuss succession, though he is 70. "People don't ask me about things like that," he says. Said one employee of Edwin Land, then 70, "To talk of a successor is to acknowledge that Land himself will die. That is not spoken of at Polaroid."[7] Preparing for a successor is like putting one foot in the grave, and many, many bosses will not do that.

When a successor is named before the death of the owner, the latter may even frustrate his efforts to succeed. Take the case of Maurice Vickerman.

Maurice started with a small ski repair shop in the Rockies, which grew to a chain of ski apparel and repair shops in several resorts in Colorado. Both his daughters (he had no sons) expressed no desire to be involved in the family-owned business, but upon their marriage, each of the sons-in-law was asked to join the family firm and train to assume the top management position of Maurice's company. As Maurice approached his sixties, he decided to give each son-in-law a 1-year opportunity in the role of company president. During this testing period he removed himself from the day-to-day operation of managing the shops to allow the son-in-law an opportunity to blossom in the situation. At the end of the first year the oldest son-in-law had completed his term, and Maurice asked the board of directors to evaluate his performance. The profit-and-loss statements and growth in management problems throughout the year were analyzed by the board, and the result was a unanimous disapproval of the son-in-law as manager.

Maurice fired the first son-in-law and moved the second son-in-law into the experimental position for 1 year. At the end of his year, the reports were taken to the board of directors, and again the board voted the son-in-law incapable of managing the corporation. Maurice fired the second son-in-law, creating a hostile situation between him and his second daughter. The event shocked the whole family.

Maurice seemed intent and sincere on the surface, but the results certainly raise questions as to whether Maurice really intended for the two sons-in-law to fail. They felt that they had done a very good job, but the results reaffirmed Maurice's position as head of the family and the firm, and no one will ever probably know if he provided a true testing ground for the sons-in-law.

Of course, it is easy to make the father in a succession situation look like the villain of the piece because he so frequently is. However, sons and other family members dealing with Dad in these troublesome times probably do not take sufficiently into account the severe psychological wrench that retirement is likely to represent for a hard-driving businessperson. In addition, they are often guilty of "ageism," equating advancing age with incompetence without reflecting on individual cases. They should recognize that retirement for Dad should be well planned and that it does not have to occur at some specific age.

Preparing for the Pasture: Retirement Planning

In *The Three Boxes of Life,* Richard Boles says that life is really in three boxes—education, work, and retirement—and that these periods become more and more isolated from each other. Life in each period seems to be conducted by those in charge without much consciousness of preparation for the next period. The family-owned business founder is a person predominantly accustomed or addicted to work all his life, deriving from that work some sense of importance. Retirement to him means being deprived of both the work and a sense of self-worth. "The cultural expectation that your life should consist of first an orgy of learning, then an orgy of work and finally an orgy of leisure or play is very strong."[8] To break from this requires a preplanned life which involves all three phases: education, working, and leisure. For those now approaching retirement, it is already too late for all three, but at least retirement can be planned.

The business owner faces the same problem all members of society face as they begin to age and think of getting old. According to Dr. Howard P. Rome, former president of the World Psychiatric Association, Americans spent $5 billion in 1970 for beauty aids, and much of this expenditure was for cosmetics, a fact that attests to the enormous effort people in a youth-oriented society make to improve their appearance and hide the signs of age. This does not include the additional millions of dollars that are invested annually in cosmetic surgery.[9]

As the business owner ages, he sees that many of his old customers and friends are in retirement communities or have died. There is a terror connected with the concept of the great unknown of death, and attempts are made to avoid the approaching end. Society softens the terms of old age with gentle euphemisms such as "elderly," "advanced in age," "senior citizens," and "golden age," and the word "death" is circumvented with an array of synonyms: "passing away," "departure," "demise," "loss." Loved ones insist that the aging entrepreneur accept a new life of leisure and travel, thus contributing to his well-being, but they may be hastening his earthly departure. The family members feel he should be willing to give up the business and allow his son the opportunity to manage it without interference, but they must be sympathetic to the emotional problems this causes. Should the family force him into retirement and idleness without proper planning, they may be ridden with guilt when he dies shortly after retiring. A frequently quoted statistic is that those who make no plans for their retirement years receive, on an average, just 13 Social Security benefit checks, and seven out of ten die within 2 years.[10]

The rules of mandatory retirement at 70 are no longer followed strictly. Government and industry have looked at older workers and recognized that sending them out to pasture may not be advantageous for the company or the workers. In some industries, a worker is discharged at 65 and rehired on a free-lance basis. Other companies have raised the retirement age to 68, and in several fields retirement is much later. Professionals and academics may work until they are 70 years old. Some government employees are prepared for retirement over a 5-year period. The first year they are given 1 month's vacation; the second year, 2; the third year, 3; and so on until the day they must retire. During these extended periods of leisure time, they have the opportunity to acquire new interests and skills.

These extended vacations work very well in the family-owned business because by the time the father is fully away from the business, his successor has had the opportunity to function successfully in the management position. As the period of time is extended, both founder and successor become more willing to accept the absence of the founder from the firm. A perfect example of this is Howard White Well Drilling of Waterloo, Iowa. As Howard's annual vacation increased from 1 to 6 months over a decade, his son, Buck, nestled into the top spot with the greatest of ease. The family and business founder must remember one thing in preparation for the retirement years: "A pilot cannot make a smooth landing if he waits until he runs out of gas." Planning is the key to a successful retirement.

Retiring from the business does not mean the end of the owner's life but only the end of one phase of life. There are different challenges and opportunities for recognition and satisfaction in other areas. The continuity of the business is a monument of one kind of success, and it is now time for the owner to channel his efforts elsewhere. This transition is a family effort.

One answer may be another business. A case in point is Maurice Vickerman, the man discussed earlier, who devoted most of his life to his ski shop.

When Maurice made his retirement exit, he found in a very short period of time that travel, golf, and warm climates were a colossal bore. More than anything else, he desired to get back into the business. Maurice had served as chairman of the board of directors but found this labor unsatisfying. A sympathetic and understanding board recognized that Maurice was in need of another career to fill his days. They assisted him—in his sixties now—in establishing Ski Bunnies, a business that would teach young children to ski, rent beginning ski equipment, and function primarily as a baby-sitting agency for parents vacationing with their young children. When the suggestion was first made, Maurice looked 10 years younger, and he spent the next 3 months hiring instructors, purchasing new equipment, and establishing his new business, which would be only three doors from the old ski shop to which he had devoted his life.

Successions Gone Astray

In the Neiman-Marcus case, the succession from the father-founder was not easy—it did not occur until Herbert Marcus died—but the succession to the next generation was accomplished effortlessly and the business continued to do well. Whatever fears Herbert Marcus may have had about seeing control pass to others proved to be ill-founded. If all successions turned out this well, perhaps fewer fathers would be reluctant to retire. But successions sometime go astray. There are two good examples from vastly different areas of business—the drug industry and professional football.

G. D. Searle & Co. was founded in 1888 but was little known until the 1960s, when it pioneered in birth control pills and developed new drugs for motion sickness, diarrhea, and peptic ulcer—all unpleasant aspects of modern American life. John G. Searle was the dominant—and domineering—force behind the rise of the company. His son, Dan, went to work for Searle at age 12, washing bottles in the lab as a summer job. His father withheld $12 from each weekly paycheck and gave Dan a $5 allowance, justifying the low wages on the grounds that Dan broke too many bottles. (Dan got the money back, with interest, as a wedding present.)

In 1966, Dan, now possessing a Harvard M.B.A., finally took over as president of the company, but the elder Searle stayed on as chairman of the board and continued to second-guess and overrule his son. He finally removed himself from the picture in 1971 (and died a few years later), and the "Searle boys" tried to manage with a troika at the top. Dan was chief executive officer; his brother, William, became chairman; and brother-in-law Wesley M. Dixon was president.

With the strong-willed father gone, Dan was in a position to assert himself, and he embarked on a campaign of diversification, acquisitions, and mergers. Friends felt that Dan was actually trying to outdo his father. The competition proved to be unhealthy. Diversification never paid off, and the company got into serious trouble with the Food and Drug Administration.

At this point, the Searle boys knew that something was wrong, and they went outside for help. Don Rumsfeld, a former Secretary of Defense and chief of staff in the Ford administration, was given carte blanche to put the company's affairs in order. Rumsfeld became chief executive officer, with the Searle boys remaining as company directors, although with greatly reduced salaries. And all employees took their marching orders from Rumsfeld, not from Dan Searle or his kin.[11] John G. Searle, now dead, must have been smiling. He had always suspected the boys could not make it without his strong hand, and Rumsfeld appeared to represent his reincarnation.

The Los Angeles Rams, perennial winners of the National Football Conference's Western Division, provide an unusual illustration of the perils of succession. In this case, the owner-father died suddenly, but it was widely assumed he had already anointed his son as his successor as team boss. Steve's stepmother, Georgia, had other ideas.

Carroll Rosenbloom was worth several million dollars at age 71 and had everything except peace of mind. Winning the Super Bowl was an obsession with Rosenbloom, an obsession practically warping his life. Despite all his material possessions, pro football was his identity. "When I was just rich no one knew me," Rosenbloom once told a Rams executive. "Now that I own the Rams everyone knows me."[12]

Rosenbloom was born rich, the son of a successful textile manufacturer in Baltimore. In 1953 Rosenbloom bought the Baltimore Colts, and in 1971 he traded the Colts for the Los Angeles Rams. Rosenbloom actually made little money from the football team because it consumed his every moment. He monitored everything from equipment purchasing to game planning. Rosenbloom did not disguise his dependence on winning. "There's nothing sweeter than a win," he once said. "Losing tastes like cardboard."[13]

Rosenbloom was grooming his son, Steve, 33, to take over the Rams, but he was not about to make an early gift to him. "I've given my children a great many things" he said, "but I've kept the football team for myself."[14]

In April 1979, Carroll Rosenbloom drowned in Florida. A press release which appeared in the New York Times, April 8, 1979, said that Steve would take full charge of the Los Angeles Rams in place of his late father. He already had been running the club for several years in a quiet, self-effacing way. Steve Rosenbloom had been introduced to pro football at the age of 12, when he started working in the equipment room of the Colts.

When the will of Carroll Rosenbloom was disclosed, the bulk of the estate, guessed to be worth as much as $100 million, went to his wife, Georgia, along with 70 percent ownership of the Rams. The remaining 30 percent of the Rams was divided equally among the five children—Steve, Danny, and Suzanne by his first wife, and Lucia and Chip from his marriage to Georgia. It was assumed that Georgia would inherit the money while Steve inherited the team. Then came the bomb. Georgia was to oversee the entire operation of the Rams.

This was a blow for Steve, who had learned the football business from the ground up and had spent more than 20 years working with his father. But more was to come. At the start of the 1979 season, Steve was fired by his stepmother. The firing occurred because Steve attempted to relieve the Rams' general manager, Don Klosterman, of some of his duties. Klosterman was Georgia's man, and she was the boss.[15]

Did Carroll Rosenbloom intend for this to happen? Most sports observers think not. It is believed that Carroll observed proper form in leaving the bulk of the estate, including control of the Rams, to his wife, assuming that Steve would be the de facto boss, what he had always wanted to be. But there was no such stipulation in the will, and Georgia Rosenbloom had ambitions of running a football team herself. We will never know if Carroll Rosenbloom would be pleased with the way his succession has gone.

The saga of the Rams almost has a storybook ending. Despite the front office upheavals and multiple injuries on the team, the Rams of 1979 managed once again to win the Western Division title. Always before, they had lost the first game of the playoffs, but not this time. This time they went all the way to the Super Bowl; their first time ever. Close, but no cigar. Art Rooney's Pittsburgh Steelers won the game.

Summing Up

Let us conclude this trip through the father-son succession minefield with the reiteration of some key points:

- *To all hands:* Perhaps the most important thing for all those present at the succession scene to remember is that open conflict should be avoided at virtually all costs. Differences of opinion are inherent in the situation, but rarely do hostile confrontations lead to solutions. More often they lead to schisms in business and family. So keep talking to each other.

- *To the successors:* It is natural to be impatient, but demands, threats, and ultimatums will not expedite the transition. They will only encourage the father to dig in his heels and hold on longer. As heir apparent, you must understand the father's psychological dependence on the firm and work with him in breaking these bonds. The bonds cannot be broken by life in a retirement community; they will not be broken simply because you have become a shining example of management. Father's separation anxieties are natural and perhaps inevitable, and you must work with him to create a meaningful life in retirement.

- *To the reluctant fathers:* Your reluctance to let go is nothing to be ashamed of. However, if you are reluctant to the point of outright refusal, you are likely to be accused of premeditated murder of the family business. And you will probably be found guilty—by yourself if by no one else.

- *To third parties:* You may assist in the transition. You may be a family member or a friend, but you can also be an outside professional—a lawyer, an accountant, or a business consultant. Whatever your role, you will know that the firm cannot survive unless succession occurs in a timely and orderly manner. A good way to start the process is to pressure the founder early to think about succession and a plan for the estate. Father will certainly understand the folly of wasting money, and so he probably will be able to accept succession better when things are put in financial terms than when it is simply an organizational matter. In other words, if succession rears its head and the eyes are dollar signs, it may not be so ugly.

Notes

[1] Stanley Marcus, *Minding the Store,* Little, Brown, & Company, Boston, 1974.

[2] Ibid., p. 40.

[3] Ibid., p. 39.

[4] Ibid., p. 66.

[5] Ibid., pp. 147–148.

[6] Ibid., p. 357.

[7] Paul W. Sturm, "Choosing the Next Boss: Why So Many Bosses Do It Badly," *Forbes,* October 2, 1978, p. 44.

[8] Richard N. Boles, *The Three Boxes of Life,* Tenspeed Press, Berkeley, Calif., 1978, p. 373.

[9] Howard P. Rome, Psychiatric Annals: *Geriatrics,* Part I, vol. 2, no. 10, October 1972, pp. 7–11.

[10] *Leaven,* Newsletter of National Network of Episcopal Clergy Associations, vol. 6, no. 14, June 1977, p. 2.

[11] *Managing to Succeed: Success Stories from the Wall Street Journal,* Lawrence Armour, ed., Dow Jones Books, Princeton, N.J., 1978, pp. 3–10.

[12] Philip Taubman, "Carroll Rosenbloom's Obsession," *Esquire,* November 21, 1978, p. 112.

[13] Ibid.

[14] Ibid.

[15] See Paul Zimmerman, "L.A. Goes Marching behind Georgia," *Sports Illustrated,* August 13, 1979, pp. 44–47.

When the Business Outlives the Owner

The British actor Robert Morley used to do a two-sided monologue involving God and the angels having a discussion about how the death of mortals would be handled. All agree that every mortal should know that death is certain; the specific point at issue is whether the exact *time* of death should be made known to each person beforehand. A majority of the angels argue that a specific time should be made known to each individual. Left with uncertainty, they feel, people will never devote themselves to serious work but will spend most of their time getting their affairs in order in preparation for death. God overrules the majority and decrees that no one will know the time of death beforehand. His prediction is that most mortals would worry very little about the subject and certainly would do little planning for it. The angels shake their heads in disbelief, but, as usual, God has called it correctly. People who worry about their coming departure from life before it becomes an imminent fact are regarded as odd. And as for being prepared . . .

Thousands and thousands of people die each year with their worldly affairs in total disarray. Their financial affairs are particularly likely to be in a mess. They leave no wills behind, have inadequate insurance, leave their property exposed to the ravages of the tax collector, and sometimes even fail to indicate how they should be buried or where the money for the funeral is to come from.

The heartache for the heirs in such situations is more than apparent. Each may feel compelled to grab whatever possible before the other heirs, or the government, make off with it. The ensuing struggle hardly presents humankind at its best. In a family-owned business, one would hope, the property owner would rarely fail to look ahead because he or she would have particular motivation for wishing the property to be passed on in an orderly manner. If not, the family business that has taken a lifetime to build is unlikely to remain intact. Alas, even in family-owned businesses in which the owner bears no malice toward spouse, sons, daughters, or others, financial arrangements are often not what they should be.

The Widows: A Lot in the Dark

Given our understanding of the sorrows of succession, this fact should not come as a surprise. Succession only ends in the *retirement* of the big boss, yet the boss frequently refuses to plan for retirement by naming and preparing a successor, carving out a new role in the business, and otherwise adjusting to a coming new situation.

On the contrary, the studies show, or certainly imply, that the boss holds on as long as possible. Older workers constitute a disproportionate share of the self-employed. One investigator who looked at the figures reports that over 28 percent of covered (by Social Security) workers over 65 were self-employed; only 6 percent of those under 30 fell into this category.[1]

A business owner's chances of hanging on longer are much better. Self-employed workers are in an institutional environment quite different from that of workers who toil for wages and salaries paid by someone else. Compulsory retirement rules do not loom as a threat, and the self-employed can more easily juggle work weeks and vacation times in order to vary the amount and kind of labor supplied, a move that increases longevity. Also, the self-employed can withdraw from labor more gradually than their wage-earning friends; given the trauma that usually accompanies retirement, there is great temptation to do so.

Do we really expect that death will be handled any other way in the absence of some special urging? To strong-willed entrepreneurs, retirement and death are virtually the same thing; both are intruders whose sole purpose is to take away the business. The Grim Reaper is no more than a compulsory retirement rule to be evaded, certainly not an inevitable event for which the way should be cleared.

All too often, the burden of this wishful thinking falls on the unhappy widow(er)s because they may be a lot in the dark. They are left with the spouse's business affairs to clear up and may not know how to go about it. A business crisis is thus heaped atop their personal bereavement as another cross to bear. They do not know any of the firm's advisers, board of directors, bankers, accountants, or key employees. They may well not know what the husband's goals and wishes for the business were since these may have been a major target for secrecy.

But surely this happens only occasionally and then only in the case of unlettered individuals who have no reason to appreciate the importance of looking ahead? Hah! A Utah lawyer did an informal survey of the wives of a large group of attorneys of diverse ages. Get this: Over 30 percent of the wives did not know whether their husbands had made out wills; over 60 percent had not themselves made out wills; over 35 percent did not know where to find their husbands' wills or other important documents; and about 85 percent reported that they had never had meaningful conversations with their husbands about such matters.[2]

The last-cited figure is particularly astounding. "Oh, well, lawyers," you say. "The ethics of the profession would predispose them toward secrecy in all matters." Perhaps. But the same Utah attorney interviewed forty successful businessmen with a broad range of professional backgrounds, incomes, and estate sizes. Over 95 percent of these people—who spent about 2000 hours per week accumulating things for their estate—had not had an in-depth, serious, meaningful discussion with their wives regarding what to do with the estate if the owner should drop dead.[3]

"Que Sera, Sera": The Doris Day Story

For a real-life illustration of a spouse in distress under precisely these circumstances, we need look no further than the movie (or TV) screen or our record collection, where actress-singer Doris Day is still prominent. She has previously shared her experiences with the readers of *Ladies' Home Journal*[4] in the hope that others might learn from her mistakes and thus should not mind if we spread the word again. The characters she sometimes portrayed, like Babe *(The Pajama Game)* and Jane *(It Happened to Jane)*, fought for the union and ran a lobster business, but Doris herself was not so business-minded; she was more like her hit song "Que Sera, Sera."

Her agent, Marty Melcher, helped make Doris Day a star, moving her from a traiier to a hotel to a house in the San Fernando Valley. When stardom proved not to be enough without someone to love and lean on, Marty was there, and they were married in 1951. Doris assumed the role of wife and star, and Marty became husband and manager. He made the decisions and she found out later. For example, a friend once called to ask Doris whether she was excited about working with *him*. "Who is 'him'?" she asked. Nobody had told her that she was making a movie with Cary Grant.

In 1968, Marty Melcher came home from work and said he thought he might be catching a cold. He went to bed and was there for 2½ months. When he finally agreed to see a doctor, it was too late; he was in the hospital less than a week before he died of an acute virus infection.

It was as if the earth had simply opened up and swallowed Marty, and Doris was in panic. She had never concerned herself about business details because Marty took care of them and she felt that asking questions was not a woman's place; it would only make Marty regard her as a nuisance and a "buttinski."

Now she paid the price. Although she had a grown son, Terry Melcher, to help her, she did not know where to begin. She could not find Marty's will or any of his business correspondence; Marty's office was bare, and a search of Doris's house turned up nothing— except that she apparently owed the Internal Revenue Service $500,000 in back taxes. Luckily, she was able to do a television special to help pay her debts, but it was years before the financial mess could be straightened out.

Doris Day learned her lesson, and presumably other ladies did too—her article concludes with a ten-point checklist for wives to use in finding out about the financial affairs of their husbands. But there is a lesson here for the husbands of the world as well and, in our case, for the owners of family businesses who want to pass them on to their heirs. The message is that they should do some estate planning, painful though it may be psychologically.

Passing It On: Postmortem Business Strategy

The term "estate planning," although commonly accepted as the proper phrase by lawyers and accountants, should perhaps be avoided when the subject is being discussed with the owner of the estate. It conjures up visions of strangers pawing through desks, scattering sacred papers, and treating as a set of figures a business that has been a life's work. One might just as well expect the owner to discuss the technical details of the cremation of his or her spouse matter of factly. Besides, there is a ring of finality to the term "estate"; that is what is always being disposed of. The owner does not want to dispose of the estate but rather pass it on to loved ones.

We prefer the term "postmortem business strategy." The term "strategy" is more appealing to entrepreneurs than "plan" or "planning." It is an active, not a passive, term, and they are active persons. See clever businesspeople plotting ways to guarantee that the business will go smoothly even after they are gone. That is what it is really all about—arranging affairs in such a way that life will be easier for the spouse and other loved ones. The owner may well be able to be content with the fact that if this is done well, he or she will be around in spirit if not in body. That is one way of beating the Grim you know what.

If the psychological hurdle can be cleared, there are some other threshold matters that are pertinent to postmortem business strategy. The first is the status of the business. If it is not a corporation, it should be incorporated forthwith. This act has no estate tax consequences (if properly carried out), involves minor expenses, and puts the owner in a position to consider moves that would not be available if the business remained unincorporated. When a sole proprietor dies, no one else has the right or power to continue the business operation unless there is a will or instrument that confers such power. This may mean problems. For example, in order for the owner to give someone (children or grandchildren) an interest in an unincorporated business, a partnership must be created. Partners are probably the last thing the owner wants. Besides, minor children, the most likely donees, are usually not eligible to receive an interest in an unincorporated business.[5] With the assistance of a lawyer and accountant, incorporation ensures perpetuation of the family business.

Second, the owner should clearly identify all those who will have an interest in the future of the business. Unless he or she is the soul of selfishness, a look at this list should illustrate the importance of strategizing wisely. If the owner does not do this, the spouse will have to shoulder a tremendous burden, the children may lose their inheritance, the employees may be out of work, and the customers, suppliers, and potential investors may find their plans upset.

There is one party with an interest in the business who must be added to anyone's list, even though not many people are specifically concerned about this person's well-being—the tax collector. The Internal Revenue Service will have been a partner in the business all along, keeping a close eye on the earnings generated and the yearly "dividend" received. This partner will be the first on the scene as soon as the funeral is over, insisting that its interest in the business be satisfied before anyone else's. Suppose, owing to lack of foresight by the owner, this somewhat unwelcome partner absconds with most of the loot and leaves only pennies for the loved ones? It would be the ultimate in business defeats. What self-respecting entrepreneur could treat this possibility with a lack of concern?

This brings us to a third threshold item—a list of objectives to guide the formulation of postmortem business strategy. The general objective, of course, is to pass the business on to the heirs intact. However, no business is likely to be 100 percent "intact" when it gets to the heirs because of the need to satisfy the interests of the tax collector. Thus, when it comes down to the financial nitty-gritty, postmortem business strategy objectives are usually stated in terms of taxes. Objective number 1 is to reduce to the extent possible the amount of taxes that must be paid. Objective number 2 is to make sure that there is enough cash available to take care of the taxes (and other financial obligations) that fall due when a business changes hands. Objective number 3 is to develop a cash-benefits system in the business that can help support the family during the transition period. Objective number 4 is at least to ensure that the financial posture of the business is such that control does not pass to the hands of nonfamily members who need it to satisfy their financial demands.

It would be better for all concerned if business owners during their lifetime took the responsibility for choosing and installing their successors and for making the arrangements for the use of their assets after their death. If owners fail to do the former—and we have already watched them agonize over this successor matter—they can at least do the latter.

Fouling It Up: Two Sad Stories

Between the warnings of threshold problems in passing the business on and some handy suggestions for doing it right, it is probably well to lay in a heavy slice of sad stories to indicate what happens when the whole thing is fouled up.

Ken Korchinsky devoted his adult life to establishing a successful auto dealership ("Used or new, Korchinsky's who"). Along the way, he acquired a wife, Helen, who knew nothing of cars except how to drive them and nothing of business except how to spend the profits. Ken also sired two sons, John and Arthur, who *did* know about the car business and who were anxious to know more, particularly how the dealership looked from the owner's perspective. Each saw room for only one at the top, however. The two sons, in turn, acquired wives, Lois and Mona, both of whom never ceased to remind John and Arthur, respectively, of the great things they expected from them. Accordingly, both John and Arthur avidly sought the blessing of father Ken, especially his blessing as successor to the business.

Poor Ken could never decide between his two sons but covered himself with the oft-repeated statement that decisions as to his successor were premature. He was still saying that when he died in 1966. His estate, consisting of the family home, the business, $50,000 in insurance, and $5000 in cash, passed to his widow after the estate taxes and probate expenses had siphoned off $70,000.

Whereas Ken had acted like Hamlet, Helen decided to be Solomon. With attorneys, accountants, bankers, sons, and daughters-in-law creating a chorus of dissonant voices, she threw up her hands and came down with the sword, cutting the firm into two halves and making each son a general manager of one half. She even gave both sons raises because of their new responsibilities.

The business survived, but only temporarily. To settle the estate taxes, Helen had borrowed money and then increased her own draw by enough to cover the payments. The new profit was zero. When Helen died in 1973, she left insurance of $25,000, taxes and probate costs of over $100,000, and the firm—such as it was by then—equally to the two sons.

John and Arthur were hardly left with a gold mine. They were forced to sell the family home and other possessions to settle the estate, but even these sacrifices left them $30,000 short. John wanted to borrow the money and keep the business; Arthur wanted to sell the business, pay off the taxes, and start over. John finally prevailed, but in the process the two brothers made Cain and Abel look like Donny and Marie. Arthur finally sold his half interest to his brother, but by then John's inheritance was so heavily mortgaged that the business was hardly worth owning.

This unhappy conclusion—two brothers who were mortal enemies and a business up in smoke—was brought about by a chain of circumstances originally set in motion by the father. Not only did he not name a successor, he failed to develop a viable financial plan for the business. He should have chosen between John and Arthur, left

the common (voting) stock to his chosen successor, provided a right-
ful share to the other heirs through the creation of a new class of
stock, and let control of the business pass to the person who would
actually run it.

Since the reader is possibly in tears by now, we will make the
second case somewhat shorter. Michael Pignatano was the owner of a
prosperous trucking firm ("You call, we haul"). He had a young second wife, Donna, and his only children were two married daughters,
Katherine and Mary. Since none of the three women were interested
in pursuing the trucking business, Michael made arrangements
whereby, at his death, the firm would be bought by one of the company vice-presidents. The latter acquired an insurance policy on Michael's life to provide the purchase price, which was agreed upon at
$350,000.

In his will, Michael left half the value of the firm to his wife and
the balance equally to his two daughters. Seems simple enough—but
not so. Enter the Internal Revenue Service. Estate taxes were fixed
by the buy-sell agreement at $350,000, but IRS was not bound by
this valuation. This worthy agency decided that the firm was worth
$660,000. (It happens.) The probate court, dutifully following the
terms of the will and the IRS valuation, awarded Donna $330,000 of
the income from the sale of the business, which was, remember,
$350,000. Poor Katherine and Mary were left with the balance—an
inheritance of $10,000 each. This result had obviously not been the
father's intention, and the two daughters fought the probate decision. The winners and still champions—the lawyers.

Again, it was the loving father who made the mistake. When arranging to sell the firm at his death, he should have made the price
contingent upon the actual value of the firm at that time. He did not;
and when the IRS valued the firm, it could not be proved wrong. Can
you bear another sad ending? A short time after Katherine and Mary
walked away with their meager inheritance, minus lawyers' fees, the
vice-president who had bought their father's trucking business decided to sell it. It went for $400,000. (No, that didn't really happen
in this case, but it could have, and there would have been nothing
Katherine and Mary could have done about it.)

Since even the most undiscerning among you should easily be able
to guess the punch line from these two case studies, let us repeat in
unison: *A good postmortem business strategy is essential to the survival of
the family-owned business.* (You can substitute "estate plan" for "postmortem business strategy" if you prefer.) The owner must face up to

the reality that although death is only historically certain, it is about as certain as anything we know about, and preparations should be made accordingly.

As a final point in terms of fouling things up, probably the worst mistake that can be made is to assume that reasonable people will work things out without formal arrangements. Many people labor under this misconception and pat themselves on the back at the lawyers' fees they are saving. They would kick themselves later—except that they are dead.

When there is an estate to be settled, it is truly amazing how rapidly siblings can turn against each other, how doting parents can devour their offspring, and how—conversely, children can disavow their mothers. Families in which a quarrelsome word has seldom been spoken can become the scene of bitter shouting matches. (In the example just cited, Katherine and Mary went quite a few rounds with Donna, who refused to share her windfall inheritance with them.)

Most of us would like to think otherwise. In the family-owned business, the owner would like to think that when he or she is gone, everyone involved will be able to sit down like reasonable people and do the right thing by everybody—including Gertrude, who is not a relative but has been with the company 20 years. The chances of that happening are about 1 in 20. Sometimes the reason is that people are simply avaricious. More often, however, everyone concerned *means* to do the right thing but cannot agree on what that is. Is it possible that a solution that is clearly fair cannot be found in a situation in which all are reasonable and well intentioned? You bet it is.

Given the human condition, the wise owner will give justice a helping hand by making the future plans for the estate clear and by making formal arrangements to see that those intentions are carried out. Love, not having to conquer all, can thus continue to prevail in the family.

If the business owner has taken care of the threshold problems—including psychological ones—involved in postmortem business strategizing and is sufficiently impressed with horror stories to wish to avoid the same mistakes, what happens now? The number of items to be taken into account in such a strategy is obviously considerable, and there is no intention here to write a textbook on the subject. However, a good basic way to develop a postmortem business strategy is to get together a team of experts, work out a plan, and then engage periodically in "death drills." (This term makes owners squeamish; you can call it "postmortem practice.")

Estate Planning: A Team and a Drill

The team concept is based on the notion that two heads are better than one and four are likely to be better still. No businessperson is likely to be able to do a postmortem business strategy (estate plan) alone because it is a complicated area in which the typical business owner is unlikely to have expertise. Thus, wise owners will decide what they want to accomplish through the estate and then bring in experts to tell them how to do it. The firm's lawyer, accountant, and trust advisor from the bank should obviously be consulted. If insurance is to be a part of the estate plan, a life insurance expert may be sought.

While it is possible to find all the required expertise in one able estate planner, better results are likely to come from a team of people with different specialties. No matter how competent the single estate planner, one person is likely to have some blind spots—who among us does not? Besides, if there is a group of experts involved, the business owner will have to become involved more closely in the process whereby a plan is developed, and the entire exercise will become more real. With one estate planner, the owner either accepts or rejects a plan or chooses among "options"—pretty passive stuff that enables him or her to lapse back into the immortality syndrome.

Since estate planning, from a legal and accounting perspective, is a specialty, your company lawyer and accountant may not have the experience to represent you adequately. If not, they can, of course, recommend a specialist; this is no small matter because lawyers and accountants do not list themselves by specialty the way doctors do. By one means or another, the owner should put together the team.

As always, cost is a factor when it comes to seeking the services of experts, and this helps explain some of the reluctance owners have to engaging in estate planning. Of the four people who may be on the team—lawyer, accountant, trust advisor, and insurance advisor—two sell their time and two have products to sell. The attorney and the accountant have only their time and advice. The trust advisor has a trust service, a trusteeship, an executiveship, or a corporate-agency relationship to sell. The insurance advisor is selling life insurance.

However, banks usually do not get paid until they are actively a trustee, and very few life insurance people charge for consultation. This does not guarantee that you will get something from trust and insurance advisors that will be worthwhile, merely that they get paid only when you buy their products. By contrast, as soon as the lawyer sits down to talk, the meter starts running. In any case, when a business owner spends money for an attorney or accountant, or for purchasing life insurance or arranging a trust, the cost is small compared to the savings that can result when the business changes hands.

Although the postmortem business strategy should be worked out in consultation with the family members who will be affected, the experts should not be expected to solve basic problems regarding who gets what. That is for the owner and family to decide, and the experts should not be called in until these matters have been resolved. All the lawyers and accountants can do is point out the legal and financial consequences of the courses of action decided upon. Whether Bill or Jill should become the company president is a business question. Thus, while the owner is advised to use the experts, they should not be made scapegoats for personal indecision.

A useful device, if the owner can get up for it, whereby future business strategies and the response of the family to them can be tested is the "death drill."[6] In this little number, the owner meets with the family and advisors and is declared dead. Then a drill is conducted, working through the procedures that are to be implemented in the event of his or her death.

Imagine the following monologue, owner speaking: "We are going to put ourselves in the future. I am dead, and I want to see how well you are able to handle the situation. The first topic of discussion is the current financial position of this company. Accountant, can you advise my spouse of outstanding debts and assets? Will my spouse have enough income? What is my total estate tax bill? Attorney, please ready my will. Do we all feel these directions are fair and reasonable? What future changes do you feel would date this document? Is the chain of succession well defined? Let's discuss alternatives. To be prepared, the family should know where to find the safety deposit box, life insurance policies, wills and trusts, location and value of real estate, all deeds, titles, stocks, and bonds. Do the family members know where to find these things?"

The death drill can be a rewarding experience for a family; the members may be surprised to find out how little they know about many of the items. (Doris Day certainly did not know the answers!) The practice may be chilling to some, but it is a dispassionate way of looking at a plan whose implementation depends upon the death of a loved one, evaluating it, and seeing that it is kept up to date.

Is it emotionally possible for a family to go through such a death drill? Those who are reluctant should remember that the easiest way to deemotionalize most things is to talk about them in a practical, matter-of-fact way. The family that cannot endure the rigors of practicing a postmortem business strategy probably cannot endure the rigors of making one up in the first place. This is too bad because the personal grief is only being postponed and the business grief will soon pile up.

The Power to Will: Some Interesting Examples

Long, long ago, when the concept of property itself emerged, there came the companion concept of the will. The owner of the property, said the rule, should be able to decree what was to happen to it once he or she shuffled off the mortal coil. In the age of paper, the "will" of the property owner became synonymous with the document in which it was expressed. In the age of lawyers, property owners were advised to prepare such documents well in advance of their probable demise, have them drawn up by experts so that they would stand up in court if challenged, and see them witnessed by someone who could testify that the preparer of the will was of sound mind at the time.

We are not going to tell you how to draw up a will, how to challenge one in court, or how to do anything that would get us into trouble with the minions of the law for practicing without a license. Certified lawyers have long since obtained a monopoly on the provision of this service. Instead, we want to talk about the importance of wills in postmortem business strategy and bring out some pitfalls in willing by reciting some tall tales about what others have done.

Now, any business advisor will tell you immediately that a will by itself is not an estate plan; it is simply a formal mechanism for the distribution of the property that a person owns at the time of death. By itself, it does not save taxes or do any of the things a good estate plan is supposed to do. However, it is an important vehicle for achieving these objectives and is thus a key feature, perhaps the centerpiece, of the estate plan.

Just for the record (and so you can show off to your lawyer), note a few terms. The "testator" is the person who draws up the will. Any action that occurs with regard to the will is "testamentary"; for example, a trust included in a will is a "testamentary trust." Those who die with a will all drawn up are said to have died "testate"; those who fail to perform this crucial act must bear the shame of dying "intestate." Willing, like marrying and divorcing, is a social as well as a personal act, and so the courts of law are involved. A court may have to "probate" the will, i.e., determine that it is genuine. The "executor" is the person named by the testator to manage the distribution of property after the testator's death; if no executor is named, the court will appoint an "administrator." An important part of the power to will is the power to appoint an executor because this presumably will be someone who knew the testator intimately and can carry out instructions correctly.

It all sounds very tidy, does it not? The fact is that the process is often very untidy. People draw up wills in some very weird ways and put some very weird things in them. An executor or administrator is thus often less a person who "carries out someone's instructions" than someone who cleans up the mess left by the testator.

We are eternally indebted to Millie Considine and Ruth Pool for some juicy stories about wills.[7] For starters, there are the "let 'em eat cake" people such as actor Walter Huston (*The Treasure of Sierra Madre*), leaving nothing but a gold watch to his son, actor-director John Huston (*Chinatown*), with the explanation that "John can always earn money." Indeed, John has.

Then there was the great Pablo Picasso, an example of the "let 'em scramble" set. Whether it was because he was ornery or because he was superstitious about death is not certain, but he left no will at all (and thus died how? Correct, intestate). Picasso predicted a scramble, and the prediction came true, what with some $90 million lying about in bank accounts, investments, real estate, and works of art, not to mention the thousands of treasures scattered around in the artist's many houses, which included a forty-room castle. The claimants included two legal heirs—his second wife and his son by his first marriage—and the illegitimate children Picasso fathered with his mistress.

Then there is the "keep 'em guessing" school typified by the famous columnist Drew Pearson. He believed in drawing up wills—did he ever!—but not in lawyers' offices. He wrote his wills on hotel stationery whenever the mood struck him—and apparently it struck him often, at least seven times because seven wills were found after his death. All were handwritten, none had been witnessed, and no two were alike. Since there was obviously some question as to which was the *last* will and testament, it took years to straighten out the estate.

Whimsical or unfair testators may run afoul of "like-hell-you-will" heirs, of course. There was the lady in Boise, Idaho, who put up a late-model Cadillac in first-class condition for sale at the bargain price of $50. A misprint? Not on your life. Seems the lady had recently been widowed and her cheating husband had specified in his will that the car or the proceeds of the sale from the car were to be bestowed upon his girl friend.

In this connection, we cannot resist regaling you with a horse-racing story. There was a bookie at the New York tracks (where pari-mutuel betting was not legalized until 1939) who amassed a sizable fortune through his ability to size up the horses and quote odds that put himself in the winning column and the horseplayers on the losing side. Given his reputation, there was great surprise when he suddenly began to quote bargain odds. He was giving 6 to 1 or 8 to 1 on natural 2 to 1 horses. As would be expected, horseplayers leaped at this bonanza, and the bookie was broke in record time. He died soon after—but with a smile on his face. Why was he smiling? After discovering that he had terminal cancer, the bookie had wanted to divorce his shrewish wife and marry his loyal girl friend of many years. The greedy wife had refused, anticipating her inheritance. Not trusting the courts to be fair in such matters, the bookie made sure before his death that the wife would receive no payoff at his window.

If potential heirs are sometimes surprised, so would some testators be if they lived to see the results of their bequests. A case in point is Eleanor Medill (Cissy) Patterson, a case that also shows some of the pitfalls in drafting wills. Cissy came from a newspaper family (her daughter married Drew Pearson), and after some backing and filling in her youth, she went into the newspaper business herself in a big way. In 1937, she bought both the Washington (D.C.) *Times* and the Washington *Herald,* combined them as the *Times-Herald,* and began to make money.

Cissy's will was a reflection of her love for the newspaper profession. The original document left the *Times-Herald* to eight loyal employees, but one was later dropped through a will amendment (a codicil) so that the "instant millionaires," as they were later called, turned out to be seven in number. (Thereafter, Cissy had some second thoughts, but a proposed new will leaving the paper to a relative was never legalized.)

It had been Cissy's intention that the seven beneficiaries would carry on the newspaper, but the will was drafted in such a way that this proved unlikely. There was a clause in the will specifying that all beneficiaries had to agree before the paper could be sold. But there was also a clause under which the interest of any beneficiary, at his death, would pass to his personal representative. To forestall this possibility, the seven heirs quickly sold out to Bertie McCormick of the Chicago *Tribune;* each heir received $1.5 million—seven instant millionaires. (As a footnote to the story, the seven heirs paid off Cissy's daughter $400,000 when the latter contested the will on the grounds that her mother was demented.)

The Woolworth saga is another story in the best-of-wills anthology. Frank W. Woolworth, a self-proclaimed born-loser farm boy, built the multimillion dollar five-and-dime chain from scratch, but he worked himself into ill health in the process, and so apparently did his wife, Jennie. The year 1918 was tragic for the first dime-store Woolworth generation. Frank's daughter and granddaughter died that year, and he was forced to declare his wife, who had been regressing for some time, mentally incompetent. A short time later, just before turning 67, Frank died of uremic poisoning.

The will situation turned out to be unbelievable. Frank's only will, handwritten, was dated 1889. It named Jennie, who was to receive the entire estate, as executrix without bond of the estate, then valued at $27 million after taxes. Over the years, Frank had changed the wording of his will many times but had never signed his name to any of the changes. Romantics speculate that he could never bring himself to change the will because whenever he started to do so, he remembered the happy time when two poor lovers had exchanged wills—Jennie's was a duplicate of Frank's will except that she left everything to him.

Poor Jennie did not even know that Frank was dead. She died herself 5 years later, and since Frank was already dead, her will was totally invalid. The estate had to be probated by the courts. As Considine and Pool ruefully note, "What took Frank and Jennie a little over a page to write, took several hundred pages and about six years to consummate."[8]

The Woolworth wills continued through the generations—to daughter Jessie (whose husband was a hopeless gambler), to her son Jimmy (a homosexual who committed suicide like his father), and so on. In addition to bequests to friends, relatives, servants, and assorted individuals, there were gifts to the American Cancer Society, the Salvation Army, the New York Association for the Blind, the American Red Cross, Southampton Hospital, United Cerebral Palsy, the New York Foundling Hospital, the Metropolitan Opera Association, the Archbishopric of New York, and the American Museum of Natural History in New York City. The Woolworths were catholic in their charities.

No will discussion would be complete without Eleanor E. Ritchey, oil-refining heiress (Quaker State), who left her entire $4.5 million estate to her 150 stray dogs in 1968. Five years of will contesting by relatives, during which the estate grew to $14 million, ended in a bizarre settlement under which the dogs (only seventy-three were left) got $9 million, relatives got $2 million, and the tax collectors and lawyers got the rest. The dogs were separated by sex to prevent any enlargement or continuation of the beneficiary pool (although accidental offspring were to receive benefits). The bequest, apparently still valid, is to stay in effect until the last dog is dead or for a maximum of 20 years, after which the estate is to pass to the Auburn Research Foundation at Auburn University for research in small-animal diseases.

So what can the business owner (the potential testator) learn from this hodgepodge? Try these on for size.

1. If you really want to cause trouble for your heirs, do not make a will at all or make several wills and leave them all undated.

2. If you make strange bequests such as leaving the business to your parakeet, expect the relatives to contest the will; the parakeet may well be dead before the matter is settled.

3. Whatever you want to accomplish, make sure the will is carefully drafted to accomplish it. Many lawyers specialize in finding loopholes in wills. Make sure yours is drafted by an attorney who specializes in closing loopholes.

4. If you want to do right by your heirs, draft a good will as soon as you have some property to pass on, revise it whenever you feel the need, but do so legally—i.e., in the lawyer's office and not a hotel room—and make sure everything is dated.

5. Ideally, the drafting of the will and later revisions should be a part of the death drill process. That keeps everything on the table where the heirs can see it. Surprises when the testator dies sometimes have disastrous results. A fictional (but not too far-fetched) illustration drawn from the once-popular television se-

ries *Hawaii 5-0:* In one episode, the dying family patriarch so detests all his potential heirs that he devises an ingenious if somewhat gruesome plan for doing them all in. His will specifies that any person named as an heir who is still alive 1 year from the reading of the will is entitled to collect the spoils. Before his own demise, however, the vengeful rascal arranges delayed-action deaths (e.g., a cyanide pill hidden deep in a bottle of allergy pills) for all the heirs save one. The latter presumably will be convicted of the murder of the others and will himself pay the supreme penalty. Some death drill.

Death and Taxes: Principles

The National Family Business Council and its state chapters lobby around the country for governmental relief for family-owned businesses. Says a spokesman from the Minnesota chapter: "We must work together if our businesses are to survive in the face of increasing government regulation, punitive estate tax law systems and a general psychology in legislatures of equalization." He explains equalization as the tendency to "take from the haves and give to the have-nots."

That tendency has certainly been prominent in America since the Progressive Era beginning before the turn of the twentieth century. Estate and gift taxes, income taxes, antitrust laws, and so on, all sprang from the same premise: Those who obtained great wealth were allowed to keep it all and pass it on from generation to generation; the rich would get richer and the poor would be poorer, since those who start out in life with considerable wealth have a much better chance to get even wealthier than those who start with nothing. The idea was not to equalize incomes and wealth but to equalize the opportunities that people have to obtain these things. This could only be done, the reasoning went, by lending a hand to the have-nots through transfer payments of various kinds, and these payments could best be financed by taxing those who already had wealth.

The virtue of this principle is a moral matter about which people obviously feel differently. We shall not debate the point here but only note that the taxation of the haves in society is a firmly established practice that is not likely to be discontinued, although taxes and tax rates can certainly go up or down. The family-owned buiness owner who prospers will not only pay a lifetime's worth of taxes but will also find a special tax collector waiting for the estate when he or she dies. Small business persons will grumble that the tax laws that are strangling them were meant for the Fords and Rockefellers, not the small fry, but they will still have to pay taxes.

There is another firmly established American principle called the "principle of tax avoidance." Tax *evasion,* a failure to pay taxes legally due, is a criminal offense, but tax *avoidance,* paying no more in tax than the law absolutely requires, is not only legal but socially acceptable. In other words, the taxpayer is entitled to devise any means within the law to avoid a tax. In practice, it is the lawyer who finds the means of avoidance.

So it goes with business estates. That an estate will be taxed is as certain as tax itself, but this does not mean that the business owner must invite the tax collector in to take the spoils. Instead, the owner uses a team of experts to develop a postmortem business strategy that includes a plan for reducing taxes on the estate to the lowest point possible and otherwise arranging the taxation so that it has the least possible deleterious effect on the business. A business owner who does not do this is imprudent.

Mind you, these taxes are not insubstantial amounts of money. The following table indicates the amount owed on the taxable estate. The taxable estate of a spouse who inherits a house, personal property, cash, and stock valued at $250,000 would incur no tax because of the marital deduction.

Value of Estate	Tax
$ 250,000	$ 23,800
500,000	108,800
750,000	201,300
1,000,000	298,800
1,500,000	508,800
2,000,000	733,800
5,000,000	2,503,800

Estate taxes, like income taxes, are progressive. Note that the tax rate is about 10 percent on a $250,000 business, jumps to about 30 percent for a $1 million business, and rises to a flat 50 percent when the business is worth $5 million. The prospect of the tax collector taking away fully one-half of what has been accumulated through a lifetime of work sends the sensible business owner scurrying for an estate planner and tax lawyer in a hurry.

A problem for a business, especially a small business, is not just the amount of tax itself but the speed with which the tax must be paid. If the deceased owner in a $1,500,000 business has a share valued at $1,000,000, the estate will owe nearly $300,000, and this will be due 9 months after death. Such a short-term tax bite can put a crimp in small business's operations by depressing its liquidity. Thus the tax expert must not only lower taxes as much as possible but also spread them out over time to the advantage of the business.

In moving now to talk about some ways of saving money, we should emphasize that this book should not be used as an estate-planning manual. By the time this material is read, laws may have changed to invalidate some of the propositions put forth here. Our intent is to spur the reader into seeking expert advice in developing a postmortem business strategy and suggest some possibilities that may be pursued with the experts. We implore the business owner to accept our suggestions in this spirit.

Another anxiety point. If you hope to gain anything at all from the following discussions, you will have to read carefully. There is no way to avoid figure citing and hairsplitting in tax discussions—that's what tax law is. We suggest you read one section at a time, reflecting on and digesting each before going to the next. Otherwise, you are likely to end the chapter with a dazed look on your face and nothing in your head.

Gift Taxes: 'Tis Better to Give

When an estate tax is computed, there is a marital deduction of $250,000 or one-half the estate, whichever is greater. In addition to this off-the-top saving, gifts may reduce the size of the taxable estate. In 1976, estate and gift taxes were integrated; both gifts and assets left in an estate are now taxed at the same rate (gifts had been taxed at a lower rate). Also, with certain adjustments, the value of gifts made prior to death is added to the estate to determine the total amount of tax due.

Here are some key points to remember. First, anyone can give $3000 per year to any number of recipients and none of the gifts will be subject to the federal gift tax, which is paid by the giver, not the recipient. Second, as of 1981, a $175,625 exemption will be in effect; any combination of gifts and property equaling this amount contained in an estate is not subject to the unified estate and gift tax. Third, in addition to the $175,625 exemption, there is a $100,000 lifetime exemption for gifts between spouses. Fifty percent of the value of gifts above $200,000 are subject to the unified tax; gifts between $100,000 and $200,000 are subject to an adjustment.

Two particularly effective estate-planning tools should be mentioned in connection with gifts when a large estate is involved. If the estate is small (generally under $250,000), there is no estate-planning reason to make gifts. One technique is simply to bestow gifts of $3000 on those of your choice; that is an effective and simple way of reducing the estate and thus reducing the tax to be paid. A second ploy is to give away property that is expected to appreciate in value in cases where the size of the estate for tax purposes is expected to be a prominent concern.

We are willing to bet that the typical business owner will not make full use of gifts as a tax-saving device without being prodded into it by a persuasive accountant or other expert. Entrepreneurs did not get where they are by giving away money, and so there is bound to be some psychological aversion to simply dumping the load they have been adding to all these years. In appreciation of this, the estate plan should spread these gifts over time and make sure they are tossed in deserving directions. Otherwise, the gifts will be made only to the tax collector under duress. And why not? Is government less deserving of largesse than individual wastrels who stand around waiting for the gifts to drop from the sky? We make this point particularly for the expert readers. Accountants must understand that although it is only money to them, it is not their money.

Trusts and Inflation: To Guard We Trust?

One time-honored device for saving on estate taxes is the testamentary trust (the one in the will, remember?). The explanation of this gets a little heavy, so pay attention. Under law, different people have rights to the income (i.e., withdrawals from the principal, and the principal itself). The basic tax-saving idea is to avoid one round of estate taxation by separating the *income* beneficiary of the estate from the *principal* beneficiary because it is the principal who is whacked by the estate tax.

An example: Suppose the husband has an estate of $800,000 and his wife has an estate of $50,000 and they have two children. If the husband dies first, a testamentary trust can save substantial amounts of money. Here is how it works:

The First Tax

The tax on the husband's estate will be $32,000—the tax due on $244,375. Where did the latter figure come from? Well, before we arrived at the taxable amount, we made some deductions, just as the taxpayer does on his or her income tax. There is the marital deduction of $250,000 or one-half the estate, whichever is larger. In this case, one-half is $400,000, a larger amount, and so the wife has $400,000 free and clear. Then, assuming that the husband had made no gifts over $3000 in his lifetime, there is an exemption of $175,625. When the deduction and the exemption are subtracted from the original estate, $224,375 is all that is left to be taxed.

The Trust

The wife, having inherited her husband's estate, now has an estate of $818,000. That is the husband's original estate ($800,000) plus her own estate ($50,000) minus the $32,000 in estate tax she had to pay. Excluding her own estate and subtracting the $400,000 marital deduction, there is $368,000 left. This is put into a trust. The two children have the right to the principal, and the wife has the right to the income for life.

The Benefits

The trust can be structured so that the wife receives full benefit for the money while still keeping it safe from the estate tax. Without losing benefits, she can withdraw $5000 or 5 percent of the trust principal, whichever is greater. In addition, she can withdraw the principal if she needs it for her support, health, or maintenance. In effect, she has the benefit of outright ownership, even though the principal, if any remains, technically belongs to the children. The value of the principal is not included in her estate.

The Savings

When the wife dies, her estate will also be subject to taxation. Assuming that she never needed any of the principal and that the value of the principal in the trust ($368,000) and what she inherited directly stayed constant between the time the trust was set up and the time when she died, there would be $450,000 subject to taxation. The tax on this amount would be $59,800. If the $368,000 safely in the trust were subject to taxation also, the total tax would be

$227,820. The trust has created an estate tax saving of $168,000. A trust is a good way to guard the estate against taxes.

One problem with putting large chunks of the principal into trusts and letting the money sit there is the inflation factor. Trusts often use bonds as the principal. A bond is an instrument with a fixed monetary return, and today's skyrocketing inflation can erode the value of such instruments quickly.

The basic problem with fixed-return devices, assuming an inflationary spiral, is that the user pays out quarters and gets back nickels. For example, suppose we assume a 1980 average salary of $10,000 and an average rate of inflation for the next 10 years of 10 percent— an optimistic assumption. At this rate of inflation, the average salary would increase to $38,906 by 1990. However, a decade of 10 percent inflation would reduce the value of $500,000 to $134,339. Thus if money is allowed to sit, there will be a staggering loss in relative terms, i.e., the relationship of average salary to the arbitrarily chosen amount of $500,000. In 1980, the $500,000 would be 33.3 times as much as the average salary ($15,000); in 1990, the real value of the $500,000 would have shrunk to $139,339, only 4.5 times larger than the average salary ($38,906). If the inflation rate should be 20 percent—definitely a possiblity—the losses would be even more devastating. The average salary in 1990 would be $92,876, and the $500,000 would be reduced in real terms to $53,687.

Even if bondholders receive interest equal to the rate of inflation, they still get killed in real terms. The government taxes "interest," which in all probability is below the rate of inflation; in reality, the government is taxing on a loss. Assume that the interest received is 20 percent compounded and that the interest is taxed at a 40 percent rate. If you start with $500,000, the money theoretically increases to $1,552,924. However, just to keep pace with inflation, the money would have to increase to $3,095,900, and so there will be a 50 percent loss in real purchasing power in 10 years. If the money is not compounded—and many bonds and trusts do not compound—the losses will be even more enormous. In this case, with a 10 percent inflation rate, the principal would lose 65 percent of its value; at 20 percent, it would lose a whopping 89 percent.

In addition to trusts which use bonds as principals, the value of whole life insurance also declines precipitately during inflationary times. The purchaser of $100,000 worth of insurance in 1980 will find that the value of the coverage in real terms decreases with each passing year. Insurance firms, of course, encourage people to update their coverage regularly to take inflation into account, but many experts still do not believe that whole life insurance is a good way to put money aside. (Okay, let's hear the squawks from you insurance folks.)

In sum, the trust may guard against the pillaging of the tax collector but may be overwhelmed by inflation. So why can't someone do something about inflation? It's like cancer; the cure hasn't really been discovered yet.

A Matter of Deferment: Sections 6166 and 6166-A

We have noted that estate taxes are normally due 9 months after the death of the estate holder and that this often creates cash-flow (liquidity) problems for small businesses. Some significant relief in this regard has been provided in the Internal Revenue Code.

Under Section 6166, the estate of a person with a 65 percent interest in a small business can totally defer the payment of any taxes for 5 years after the death of the estate holder and pay only 4 percent interest on the tax due up to $298,800 of tax. When the tax exceeds this amount, the current (mid-1980) interest rate that must be paid is 12 percent. The code calls for periodic adjustment of this interest rate to reflect the prevailing prime interest rate, but there can be gaps between the two. With the current prime rate of 20 percent, the 12 percent government figure is obviously a bargain. At present rates, an estate can make money by paying the government its interest due on an outstanding tax and investing the money in money-market instruments or bonds, the current rate for which is 16 to 19 percent.

To qualify for these windfalls, a business must have fifteen or fewer owners and be a business in which the decedent (the person who died) owned 20 percent or more.

Section 6166-A does not provide benefits as great as those under 6166, but it is easier to qualify under 6166-A. Under 6166-A, owners of small businesses are permitted to pay their tax in up to ten installments, with the first installment rather than the total amount being due 9 months after the death of the former owner. For the business to qualify, 35 percent of the decedent's gross estate, or 50 percent of the taxable estate, must be attributable to small business holdings. (As under 6166, if the decedent owned 20 percent of any business, the holding will be considered a small business for 6166-A purposes, no matter how large the business is.) An alternative way for the business to qualify for the tax deferment under 6166-A is to have ten or fewer employees (6166, remember, permits up to fifteen).

With inflation and high interest rates, these two provisions of the Internal Revenue Code are exceptionally good bargains and tax savers. For instance, assuming that $98,800 in tax is due, a deferment to the full extent permitted by Section 6166 and the receipt of 10 percent interest on payments being deferred would amount to an accumulation of $128,627, a sum that would more than pay for the tax. The savings under 6166-A would be less but still very substantial.

A final point on tax deferment. If 6166 or 6166-A is not applicable, it still may be possible to defer the payment of the estate tax for up to 10 years if there is "reasonable cause" for the IRS to extend the tax deadline. Reasonable cause is determined by the facts of particular cases.

The Basis for Valuation: Sections 2032-A and 303

In addition to tax savings obtained through reducing the size of the estate and deferring tax payments, there are some further possibilities in terms of the basis used for valuation of the estate.

Section 2032-A offers some hope in this regard. It permits an estate to be valued at its *actual* use value rather than at its highest and *best* use value. For example, a farm may be worth only $200,000 as a farm but may have a potential value of $1,000,000 as a housing development. If the extra value attributable to the value of the land is included in the valuation of the estate, taxes will increase and the farm will probably have to be sold to pay them. Section 2032-A prevents this.

There are qualifying rules, of course. Twenty-five percent of the value of the decedent's adjusted gross estate must be attributable to the farm or closely held business property, the real property must pass to a close relative, and the decedent or a family member must have participated materially in the farm or business operation in 5 of the last 8 years before the decedent's death.

In addition, there are restrictions on the sale or transfer of property that receives benefits under Section 2032-A. If the heirs transfer the property to nonfamily members or if the property is not used for farming or closely held business purposes, the government will recapture the amount of the tax that was avoided through the use of 2032-A. Section 2032-A restrictions on the transfer of property are not lifted until 15 years have passed. In the first 10 years there is complete recapture, and between years 10 and 15 there is partial recapture. Since the "special use valuation" provision places more restrictions on the property than Sections 6166 and 6166-A, it is not always as valuable as those sections as a tax-saving clause. However, it can be valuable when family members expect to continue the business for a long period of time.

Another tax saver related to valuation crops up in Section 303 of the code. This provision permits a corporation to redeem shares of the family business to equal the extent of death taxes (e.g., state inheritance taxes) and funeral expenses. The redemption is in terms of the current value of the shares, not their original value.

For example, suppose a deceased owner has 800 shares in the company and they were originally worth $100 each, or a total of $80,000. However, the shares have increased in value and at the time of death are valued at $1000 each—a total of $800,000. If the death and funeral taxes amount to $120,000, the family corporation can cover this amount by redeeming 120 shares, and this is a goodly tax saving. The $100,000 profit on the 120 shares is not taxable. For estate tax purposes, the value of property is determined at the date of death and any appreciation in value prior to the date of death is not taxed.

Restructuring the Enterprise: Buy-Sell Agreements and Preferred Stock Recapitalization

Because each individual is so important to the welfare of a family business, planning for departures—expected or unexpected—is crucial. Failure to plan for the departure of key people may result in higher estate taxes, inadequate compensation for the survivors of one who dies while still active in the business, and entry into the business by outsiders.

The buy-sell agreement is the preeminent means for dealing with the problem of restructuring the enterprise after a key person leaves. In the simplest form of the agreement, two owners of a small business each agree to buy or sell the other's share upon the occurrence of a specified event. For instance, two partners may agree that whoever survives the other will purchase the departing member's share at a specified price and that each will agree to sell under these circumstances.

When more people become involved, the agreements can become quite complex; however, the intent remains the same. When the family business is incorporated, there are two basic types of agreements: (1) an entity-type agreement under which the corporation agrees to buy the shares of the deceased person and (2) cross-purchase agreements, which provide that each individual shareholder, and not the corporation, enter into an agreement to buy out the person who leaves the business.

For the buy-sell agreement to be effective, three provisions must generally be present. First, a solid price or method of valuation must be agreed upon. Second, each party to the deal must agree not to sell to anyone other than those who signed the buy-sell agreement. Finally, the method of funding the agreement must be specified.

Valuing the interest of an owner in a family corporation is a difficult matter. Since the corporation's shares are not traded publicly, there is no handy reference source as to price. However, there are three indicators of value which are often used either separately or in combination—book value (rarely used by itself), appraised value, and capitalization of earnings. The first two are commonly understood indicators. The third involves finding a multiple of earnings which is linked to the expected rate of return in a particular industry. For instance, suppose that in a furniture business the average amount of earnings during the last 5 years was $100,000 and that the rate of return in the business is $12\frac{1}{2}$ percent. to find the multiple, $12\frac{1}{2}$ percent is divided into 100 percent; the result is a multiple of 8. Then 8 is multiplied by $100,000, and a figure of $800,000 results. The $800,000 would be the value of the business as determined by the capitalization of earnings.

Another way of setting the value is to have the prospective parties to the buy-sell agreement simply agree to a specific price. So long as the agreed price is updated at reasonable levels, possibly yearly, it is a practical way of setting the value. However, if it is not kept current, it can lead to serious inequities.

In addition to helping protect the family business from the damaging effects which can ensue with the loss of a key person, the buy-sell agreement, if properly structured, can be a means of setting the value of the business for estate tax purposes. Although what will bind the

IRS is subject to some interpretation, basically two factors are necessary for the buy-sell price to hold up. First, the agreement must in fact be a bona fide business agreement and not a device to pass property at bargain prices to family members. Second, the agreement must absolutely require that the estate sell the property according to the prearranged price or method of valuation.

Suppose an owner does not die but wishes to ease out of the picture gradually. By doing this, the owner can allow the successor or successors to become acclimated to increasing responsibilities, can minimize estate taxes, and can make it easier for the successors to pay for their share of the business. A popular vehicle for achieving those ends is a preferred stock recapitalization. As with all other estate-planning tools, its effect is skewed by inflation. However, in some instances inflation actually makes it a more attractive estate-planning device than it would otherwise be because it is so flexible.

A preferred stock recapitalization permits the immediate transfer of control to the younger generation but at the same time leaves ownership in the hands of the founder of the business. In very simple terms, the owner's 80 percent of common stock is exchanged for preferred stock. To avoid tax consequences, the value of the preferred must equal the value of the common stock which was given up in the exchange. However, this can be done by setting a fair rate of return on the preferred stock. The beauty of this agreement is that the use of the preferred stock will allow the younger people to gain control immediately and will lessen estate taxes. It is perfectly proper as part of the exchange to shift control to the common shareholders. Therefore, any changes in the control of the corporation can be brought about easily.

Furthermore, through the use of a preferred stock recapitalization, one can freeze out any appreciation in the value of the corporation and keep it out of the founder's estate. For instance, suppose that the business is currently worth $1 million. If the business appreciates in value to $1,500,000, the $500,000 increase will escape the estate because the value of the preferred stock is frozen by the fixed rate of return. By moving the $500,000 out of the estate, the family can save hundreds of thousands of dollars. It should also be noted that not only does the money escape taxation, it is available (in the hands of the heirs) to help finance the operations of the corporation.

We hope that this short tour through the estate-planning maze has opened up some of the avenues down which the family business may glide when the founder-owner departs. It is still the owner who must set the vehicle in motion in the proper directions. We close with a plea to that worthy one. Look at it this way: You have applied a good deal of the proverbial blood, sweat, and tears to building the family business. You have wondered and blundered and thundered your way to the top. The real test comes now. Will you create a new wonder by seeing that the business is passed on to other family members in an orderly way? Or will you see it rent asunder as you shun the death drill? You know what the answer must be, so call your lawyer and accountant. As Robert Morley would say: "They'll take good care of you."

Notes

[1]Joseph F. Quinn, "Labor Force Participation Patterns of Older Self-Employed Workers," *Social Security Bulletin,* April 1980.

[2]Max B. Lewis, "Surviving Quarterback of the Estate Planning Team," *Trusts and Estates,* October 1978, pp. 694ff.

[3]Ibid.

[4]From the article "Doris Day: My Most Costly Mistake as a Wife," by Ronnie Cowan. Copyright 1973 LHJ Publishing, Inc. Used with permission of *Ladies' Home Journal.*

[5]Jack Jeffries and Carter Howard, Jr., "Estate Planning for Water Well Drillers," *Water Well Journal,* March 1975, pp. 38–39.

[6]Pat Alcorn, "Death Drill," *Water Well Journal,* July 1978, p. 38.

[7]Excerpts from *Wills, A Dead Giveaway,* by Millie Considine and Ruth Pool. Copyright 1974 by Millie Considine and Ruth Pool. Reprinted by permission of Doubleday & Company, Inc.

[8]Ibid., p. 49.

Some Unsung Heroes

Chapter 10 presents a defense of nepotism. We want to be up front about this because when the dishes are being cleared, we do not want to be accused of having surreptitiously brought an unsavory character home to dinner. Defending nepotism is no easy task because those to whom the case is made are likely to have an emotional bias against it, even to the point of feeling that it should not be discussed in public. It is somewhat like defending adultery; everyone knows that it happens all the time, but rarely do we hear a principled justification. We leave the readers to their own thoughts about adultery, but we do have some principles to assert about nepotism.

The word itself has an ignoble origin. It stems from a Latin word used to describe the practice of medieval prelates, particularly ecclesiastics. The practice was to show favoritism toward "nephews" in appointments. If the truth be known, many of these nephews were in fact the illegitimate issue of the lust of bishops. (The American South has a similar subterfuge—undercover girl friends are often introduced as "cousins.") With such a history to live down, it is small wonder that nepotism is in disfavor. The word has now been generalized to all family members and is used, commonly as a disapproving term, in most large organizations. Educational institutions, for example, typically ban nepotism in hiring. It is in business firms and governmental entities, however, that the term crops up most often.

We will define "nepotism" here to mean taking family connections into account when making business decisions, whether these decisions involve hiring, expansion, the making of wills, organizational arrangements, or a variety of other matters. It is the contention of

191

Chapter 10 that nepotism thus defined can be a good thing for the business and a positive force in American society and that the people who put the family and the firm foremost when they make decisions and make them work out right are—ready for the punch line?—the unsung heroes of American business. With this motion on the floor, let us briefly review the changes over the years in the nepotic nexus.

The Extended Family Compressed

What we know as civilization is about 5000 years old, and for most of that time, human beings had to struggle to tear out a livelihood from the earth and protect life and property from wild beasts, both the two-footed and the four-footed kind. People had to band together if any significant number of them were to make it through life successfully. This need to gather together in order to achieve common goals resulted in the establishment of tribes, city-states, and finally nation-states. (The world state is perhaps the ultimate in social togetherness, but nation-states do not seem to be ready for this despite the ever-present danger of the destruction of the planet.) At the root of all this was the family.

At the irreducible minimum, a family is two people living together and sharing work and play. The traditional conception of the family in America is a man and a woman married and living together and raising 2.3 children, all born in wedlock. This view is being challenged, of course. A recent national conference on the American family was disrupted when the majority in attendance refused to recognize unmarried heterosexual couples and homosexual couples living together as families. We do not propose to enter *this* dispute and will only note that anything said here about nepotism would probably apply to nontraditional families as well as to the unit consisting of Mom and Dad and Dick and Jane. No one really knows because we have had limited opportunity to study nontraditional arrangements in circumstances where they were accepted as legitimate.

In any case, the small family unit is a fairly recent model for human interaction. Earlier, a larger family unit was considered necessary for defense and survival. As humankind passed from the "primitive" to the "civilized" stage and its members fell upon each other less often with intent to do bodily harm, economic factors tended to force the large family grouping. The pursuit of agriculture, which was to a considerable degree the root of civilization, required many hands. Thus people lived in multigenerational households with children, grandparents, aunts, uncles, cousins, and in-laws all sheltering in the same place and working together in an economic production unit. This was called the "joint family" in India, the "Zadruga" in the Balkans, and the "extended family" in Western Europe.

With the coming of the industrial revolution, economic production shifted from the field to the factory. Workers were freed from the soil but were chained to machines. The soil had been a stern master demanding group effort; the machines could be operated by individuals, and the output of many individuals was combined at a level much higher than that of the workers themselves. The new mode of economic production required mobility in the labor force—workers who could follow jobs from place to place. Sons acquired skills different from those of their fathers and left home to apply them. Eventually, the role of women was to change. More and more, they did not simply stay home, tend the household, and bear children; they entered the labor force instead. The family ceased to be the basic unit of economic production.

Social patterns kept pace with the economic changes. The functions that had been performed by the family were parceled out to specialized institutions. The education of children became the responsibility of schools; the aged were turned over to poor houses or "homes" for the elderly or, in time, to retirement plans. The first stirrings of life itself even began to occur outside the family bounds. Children had always been born at home with possibly an outsider with experience in such matters, e.g., a midwife, lending a hand. Often childbirth was handled entirely by family members. With the new society, hospitals were established as the typical places in which people were born and in which they died.

The result of these economic and social forces was the breakdown of the closely knit multigenerational unit—the compression of the extended family. It was replaced by the "traditional" family—mother, father, and children who were not yet old enough to leave home and join the labor force. Grandparents were people who had retired to Florida or Arizona; aunts, uncles, and cousins were people who visited on occasion.

There were those who resisted these trends because they perceived the world of machines and stock markets to be every bit as threatening as the world of capricious weather and wild animals. A good example is the Joads in *The Grapes of Wrath*. Driven from their home in Oklahoma by dust storms, banks, and tractors, they flee to

California, a land of opportunity, but they try to keep the family together. In one scene, after a vehicle has broken down, Ma refuses to let part of the group push ahead to find work while her sons stay to make repairs. It would mean splitting the family.

> What we got lef' in the worl'? Nothin' but us. Nothin' but the folks. . . . The money we'd make wouldn't do no good. All we got is the family unbroke. Like a bunch of cows, when the lobos are ranging, stick all together. I ain't scared while we're all here, all that's alive, but I ain't gonna see us bust up.[1]

Most families did "bust up" because they could not withstand the forces of progress. The extended family came to be regarded as an artifact of backwardness because it survived only in places—e.g., Africa—where modern economic development had not occurred.

In American society, the extended family has survived mostly in the form of the family-owned business. The children are brought up in the business; other family members hold key positions; and all work together as an economic production unit. The entrepreneur in the family firm seeks not only the assistance of the family members but their emotional support, and they are rewarded with preferment in the operation of the business.

The practice of sharing and caring, however, generally extends to nonfamily members as well. The family business does not really hire employees; it adopts them. It also adopts their families and their problems. The firm becomes a social group in which people genuinely care about the well-being of their cohorts. Parental instincts toward the employees become more the rule than the exception. When a child is born to an employee, the business founder opens a savings account for the newborn and makes the first deposit into it. Baby blankets are made for the infants. The personal element lives as the unit becomes an extended family operating as a business organization.

As the business grows, this familial attitude toward the workplace is carried over to all levels of management and down to new employees. The supervisors (the second-level managers) remember the early days and the special care and interest in their families shown by the firm. Accordingly, they commit themselves not only to the founder personally but to the task of making the company grow.

To sum up, the extended family, once the foundation stone of society, has been dispersed by economic and social pressures. It survives primarily in the family business, where nepotism, of course, is alive and doing well, thank you.

The Maybe Boom: Attitudes toward Nepotism

The survival of nepotism has its defenders. Says one college professor matter of factly: "It is great. The people so vehemently opposed to nepotism are actually speaking out against hiring incompetent relatives. Why are any of us in business? To help our families." In a more flowery vein, the executive director of a trade and professional society proclaims: "Nepotism is the ingredient that can turn a cold corporate structure into a warm familial environment where the boundary between work and play dissolves."

Many other observers adopt a "yes-but" or "no-but" attitude. One attorney goes the yes-but route: "Nepotism can be very beneficial because of the high level of trust in familial relationships. I see two significant defects. First, the father and son may not have a healthy relationship. Second, incompetent relatives may be given management positions because of their bloodline." For the no-but school, a certified public accountant: "As a financial advisor to a variety of small businesses, I recognize that problems can develop. The salient advantage, however, is loyalty, and small businesses desperately need loyal employees."

Negative thoughts about nepotism abound, and so we will cite only the most commonly used argument. The general manager of a small business: "Nepotism decreases management's ability to fairly appraise the performance of employees."

In 1965, the *Harvard Business Review,* noting that nepotism was frequently viewed as an unprofessional practice that would, to the betterment of all, ultimately be replaced by an intellectual and analytical approach to management, decided to check with some businesspeople.

The magazine surveyed 2700 executives about their attitudes toward nepotism. The results were a little surprising. The businesspeople were impressed by the advantages of having relatives as a part of management and were aware that many companies, large and small, had prospered with uncles, nieces, in-laws, and the like on the payroll. A good many of the respondents had themselves been involved in nepotic exchanges at one time or another, either on the giving or the receiving end, and over half reported that relatives were at present employed in management positions in their companies.[2]

We should toss in a word of caution about this generally favorable report on attitudes toward nepotism: The study is 15 years old. As colleges continue to turn out business management graduates, a less supportive attitude toward nepotism may appear because academe frowns on showing favoritism to relatives.

Business hiring practices are much more sophisticated today because of attempts to comply with Equal Opportunity guidelines. Today the Department of Labor would not accept hiring practices based strictly on nepotic credentials.

Despite the bad press, the record of companies that hire relatives is not that bad. The roster of American companies that fall into this category is impressive—Oscar Mayer, Pillsbury, American Can, Gulf Oil, and Great Lakes Paper, for example. The problems that nepotism brought these corporations are clearly not insurmountable. Nor has nepotism created major obstacles for corporations in other countries. In Japan, for example, firms tend to adopt employees for life and sons regularly follow in Dad's footsteps. In 1960, James C. Abegglen and Hiroshi Mannari found that over half the sons of major executives of large corporations were in the same organizations as their fathers; the figure for the United States was estimated at under 20 percent.[3] Japan has risen to the top ranks of industrial power. In West Germany, a country whose economic achievement since World War II has often ranked first among European nations, nepotism is also common. The great Krupp steel empire has a long history of relatives in top management.

Clearly, relatives are doing something right because the businesses they dominate are not all failing by any means. The dynamics of family business seem to be productive. These facts are forcing many people to take a second look at family-oriented business. With a second look, they often can be moved from a "hell-no" to a "maybe" position. Beginning with a case study, let us examine the dynamics that are apparently producing this "maybe boom."

No Place like Home:
A Case Study in Business Dynamics

Entrepreneurs should be quick to credit their success to their loyal employees. True, it is their dream and largely their efforts that turn the dream into reality, but they do not do it alone. Employees caught up in the excitement of a new venture are a rich asset that often spells the difference between success and failure. The entrepreneur and the small but loyal group band together in the cold, cruel marketplace. Emotional bonds grow naturally, and the relationship becomes that of an extended family. A complex set of human relationships and commitments is created. Take the case of Feinstein's Fast Print Company.

Steve Feinstein worked as the marketing director for a medium-sized consulting firm. Among other duties, he had the responsibility for coordinating all printing, publicity, and advertising for his firm. The job was fraught with frustrations, missed deadlines, and poor printing quality. One day Steve decided he could do a better job if he had his own print business. Gathering together a few friends with whom he had worked, he described his dream and promised a lucrative venture for those who joined him. Staking his whole life savings and money borrowed from relatives, Steve and six friends opened the door to Feinstein's Fast Print.

There was an atmosphere of pioneering, team spirit, and together-we-can-make-it independence in the new business. The firm was more than just a job to both the owner and the employees. The latter identified with Steve and his dream, and they considered themselves members of a close-knit family that could survive against threats inherent in the environment. In return for sharing the risk of Steve's dream, they asked for security. The team was involved in all the management decisions, and together they made the business a success.

When paper costs rose and profits fell, Steve tried to avoid sharing these problems with his team. His reaction was a decision that the employees who shared in the wealth of the organization would also share in the loss; there was a cut in their wages. An immediate uproar ensued, and there was even talk of a strike. The employees called a special meeting—the first one ever without Steve present—to discuss how they would react as a group to the cut in wages. After 3 hours of debating the unfairness of it all, the group concluded that their anger was aimed not so much at the reduction in pay as at the fact that Steve had decided to make the cuts without consulting anyone. "I felt betrayed," said one of Steve's workers. "We'd always been one big happy family; all of a sudden, he was asserting his authority over us as though we were just any group of fellows." Another employee expressed a feeling of psychological loss with the change: "I feel that the shop is suffering a lot from business success; it's a less homey, comfortable place to work. Steve has become less a fellow worker and more a manager, owner, or controller of the business. The employees here had always enjoyed a work atmosphere of participation and management, and we were shocked at his lack of communication with us in the problem areas."

After a second meeting and a period of cooling off, however, the employees changed their tune. They decided that Steve too had been betrayed; they were not supportive as they had been in the past. Members of the old family would have stuck together and never threatened a strike to close the shop. The temporary decrease in wages, while not exactly applauded, was accepted, and the employees asked for a meeting to discuss the financial position of the firm and what they could do to remedy the situation.

Steve assembled the financial information and reports on his plans for the future and called a planning meeting with his six original employees—his extended family. Six hours later, some concrete plans emerged. Two men volunteered to spend their lunch hours making contacts for new clients in town. Another volunteered to meet all the old clients, discuss with them the increased price of paper, and offer the options of cheaper quality or higher prices. The meeting concluded with a spirit of renewed enthusiasm for strengthening the financial position of the company and for continued participative management by all those involved in the dream.

What are the lessons of this case study? First, the familial organization and its members may be largely responsible for the success of an entrepreneur. Second, as the organization grows and develops a tendency to hierarchical structures, the original employees can be shaken by the transition. They remember an informal place to work with few rules and a shared understanding of management policies rather than a written personnel manual. The growth and sophistication of the organization sometimes comes as a shock.

Third, entrepreneurs should be constantly aware of the dependency their employees have on the success of the business. They "adopted" those on their work force and, as good parents of adoptive children, they are charged with the duty of ensuring their workers' economic livelihood. This is a heavy burden that entrepreneurs feel each payday when they analyze the bank account to see if there is enough money there for the workers.

Mary Elford of Elford Construction Company had this feeling of responsibility when her husband unexpectedly died in 1949 and she was faced with the prospect of dissolving his construction company. One day she was an executive's wife who loved to play bridge, and the next day she assumed the management of a construction company that she had only visited previously. Mary refused to liquidate because to liquidate would have "put too many old men out of work." Her desire to provide security for the people who had worked so closely with her husband sent her into the corporate whirl when feminism was only a word in the dictionary and women executives were practically unheard of.[4]

Do the employees of a family business risk their future security by assuming positions in a business that could run out of cash tomorrow? No doubt, but they also satisfy their need to be involved in the corporation, and they tend to accept the possibility of financial failure as a challenge to be faced.

Beyond Bureaucracy: The Work Force Revolution

What the reader has no doubt surmised by now is that the tenor of this discussion is placing us on the side of the growing number of heretics who call for a reevaluation of some basic assumptions about business performance. We plead guilty, Your Honor. The conventional wisdom has been that efficiency should be the sole test of business performance, that bureaucracy is the most efficient form of business orgnaization, and that human motivations are such that people will adapt, or can be adapted to, such organization. All this leaves the family pretty much out in the cold—hence the aversion to nepotism. A sneaking suspicion is developing in certain quarters that while the principles just enunciated may be valid to a point, they have been pushed too far.

The family business is indeed a work organization with the purpose of producing goods and providing services efficiently. We do not mind the word "efficiently" because efficiency is instrumental in all free enterprise work organizations if they are to make a profit and thus survive. Members of the organization—be they related or non-related—must perform a variety of functions to maintain stability and continued growth. Specialization of these functions has been the key to efficiency in modern business organizations. This fact is reflected in the titles of the top executives—vice-presidents for public relations, marketing, research, and so forth. This specialization often requires that jobs be divided into simple components with tasks that are performed repetitively.

With specialization, there is an inevitable counterpart in the organization—the coordination of different functions so that they can contribute jointly to the end result. In large corporations, the role of the individuals as persons may be quite incidental to the fact that they are cogs in the machinery. Workers are more or less taken for granted; they are expendable, replaceable, and interchangeable, and they are expected to fit into place and not foil the grand design of the organization. The learned sociologist Max Weber coined the term "bureaucracy" as a label for this type of formal organization in which impersonality and rationality are developed to the highest degree. The term "bureaucracy" since that time has come to apply negatively to any kind of organizational inefficiency or waste, particularly in government. (There is a moral here.)

The motivational corollary to the organizational principle of bureaucracy is that humans are basically creatures who respond to rewards and punishments of a pretty tangible sort. The beast was well described by Adam Smith, who gave us the "economic man." Smith assumes that: (1) people are near-perfectly rational and (2) people are guided by a near-exclusive desire to maximize their economic well-being. So motivated, people will buy cheap and sell dear; they will abide by rules that enhance their economic position. They will seek the greatest benefits at the least possible cost because that course of action will maximize their profits.

The work result of the cost-benefit conception of human behavior is that modern institutional life is dominated by "X organizations." As revealed by Douglas McGregor in *The Human Side of Enterprise* (and popularized more by Robert Townsend in *Up the Organization*), X organizations operate on the assumption that people hate to work but love to be paid. It is thus incumbent upon the organization to force them to produce as the price for receiving a paycheck. Rules regarding hours of work, vacations and sick leave, pay and promotions, reports by supervisors, and so forth, are all founded on the belief that people will try to get something for nothing and must be prevented from doing so if the business is to be efficient. The key management feature of the X organization, as described in another context by Frederick Herzberg, is the KIT method. KIT stands for "kick in the ass," and it is this approach that is favored by supervisors of plants in large organizations.

Are folks really this way? The evidence suggests that people are not nearly as simple as the economic man. They appear to be, and thus respond to X's and KITs when they are at the bottom economically. Whenever they get a little ahead of the game, they show themselves to be complex beings with varied needs. They seek approval and status and inner satisfaction—all tangible rewards—as well as wealth. The attempt to satisfy these needs inevitably induces them to struggle against the bars of the cages that were constructed to hold economic man.

The conflict between employee and organization has been the subject of much social philosophy. Rousseau predicted that with industrialization the destruction of the individual's true and better nature would occur. Marx stressed the frustrations imposed on people by the very nature of the industrial organization, the essential frustration being lack of control over their destiny. In Marxist terms, workers are separated from the means of production and thereby suffer alienation, a sense of powerlessness, and a lack of positive identity with their work. The typical organization demands conformity, and corporate pressure toward conformity has been portrayed in the extreme in the fiction of Huxley and Orwell. "Round pegs in square holes," as Huxley put 'it, tend to have dangerous thoughts about the social system and to infect others with their discontent.

The family-owned business is reaping the harvest of this discontent. This type of business does not face many of industry's problems because it is human-oriented. A great tidal wave is sweeping through the workplace, wiping out traditional attitudes toward work, flooding companies with litigation, battering the walls of educational establishments, and altering the nature of our working lives. It is neither violent nor political, but a new kind of revolution—a human resources revolution—based on the changing views people have about their work and their employers and their rank and aspirations. Large corporations are in an age of activists in which everyone is a litigant.

The family-owned business escapes this turmoil because it is the most humanistic of all organizations. While many such businesses have grown to a size where they can be classified as large organizations, their executives and leaders have not forgotten the days of their grandparents and the needs of the employees around them today.

Business faces a social change as labor unions, consumer activist groups, new technology, and other disturbers of the status quo come to the fore. Employees are taking the opportunity to rebel. One form of their rebellion is a deepening antagonism toward business itself. In *The Age of Uncertainty*, John Kenneth Galbraith identifies the corporation as a major source of uncertainty. The faceless corporate giants leave people wondering how and by whom and to what end they are ruled. This uneasiness may have persisted for a long time in America, but it appears to be deepening and hardening so that an antibusiness syndrome is one of the readily identified new maladies of society, at least if we are to believe opinion polls.

A key reason for the general lack of confidence is that business is widely perceived to be grossly insensitive to human needs. Working people are painfully aware that when the economic balloon begins to lose altitude, it is the workers who are expendable. Junglelike hiring and firing are the norm rather than the exception. People are hired for their ability to deal with a given project, and they fall victim to the American tradition of waste when they no longer are needed; they are as expendable as a paper cup. There is growing opposition not only to the practice of forced early retirement but to *any* mandatory retirement in an inflation-plagued economy. The prevailing view is that business treats people like so many statistics to be manipulated in the same way that engineering data are run through a computer. Says Galbraith:

> Media reports suggest that industry is willing to tolerate lethal conditions in the work place unless government forces them to do otherwise. Only a few years ago a small chemical plant producing a dangerous chemical was found to have conditions that led to the crippling and death of a number of workers. The top executives were interviewed on a television program and their smiling defense was that the legal responsibility was not the company's. This tendency to divorce the legal from the moral is a major factor participating in antagonism to business.

The rise of entrepreneurs and interest in small family business may continue to spread as a result of the work force revolution. The popularity of franchising is one indication of this. Franchising has already become a major part of the national marketing system. There are more than 900 franchising companies in the United States with at least 400,000 franchised businesses. They account for nearly 30 percent of retail sales, or nearly $160 billion. Franchising is already providing jobs for 3,300,000 Americans.

The family-owned business can survive the work force revolution because it can satisfy basic human needs. People want to think well of themselves and develop self-respect and self-esteem. In general, they need approval, acceptance, respect, recognition, attention, and appreciation. A bureaucratic organization is not designed to feed the egos of employees; the family-owned business, on the other hand, thrives on making all employees of the firm feel like they are part of the family, including those who *are* part of the family.

Staying on the Job

In the last 10 years, job security has been a touch-and-go matter in the United States. Headlines in newspapers and magazines help tell the story: "59-Year-Old Executive Terminated"; "Automobile Company Lays Off 600 Workers"; "XYZ Company Moves to Japan—300 Workers Looking for Jobs." As business takes a coldly objective look at its location, its marketing future, and its financial bottom line, jobs are put in jeopardy. Many business executives today can no doubt sympathize with the NASA scientists and engineers after the moon launches, who thought they would be staying on the job right up until the minute the ax fell. The number of business acquisitions is increasing each year, and every merger puts some people on the streets, particularly management people.

Is job security greater in the family-owned business? We have no hard data on the point, but the information that is available does allow us to put forth some hypotheses. Hypothesis number 1 is that family members certainly have greater security in family firms. Providing such security is at least one of the *raisons d'être* of such firms. The family has committed itself to moving ahead as a group. If there is a financial downturn, the family retrenches and figures out a way to protect everyone until the picture improves. Uncle John may be able to make it on half salary and still do his job as service manager because his kids are grown now and his cash-flow needs are fewer. Cousin Tommy may be farmed out to another firm with the understanding that he will return to the family business as soon as the money loosens up. Daughter Agatha may go off the payroll as bookkeeper for a while and draw upon savings to get in that additional semester of college work she has been pining for.

When a business has to scramble like this to protect jobs, there are always many possibilities. The problem for most businesses is that opting for short-term job-security solutions is not usually the wisest course of action from a strict balance-sheet point of view. It is simpler, and usually less costly in the long run, to lay off workers when times are hard and hire new ones when the downturn swings up. This may well cause some economic hardships for the workers, of course, but that is *their* problem, not the firm's. In the family-owned business, it *is* the firm's problem. The overriding concern is to preserve the *family* business, not just the business.

The position of people who work for a family-owned business but are not themselves members of the family is somewhat different. Hypothesis number 2 is that their job security may be greater or less, depending on the situation. It follows that such employees are likely to view their security differently. Both points of view are reflected in interviews with two employees of the Booth Fire Equipment Company, a twenty-two-employee firm in Columbus, Ohio, that is owned by brothers Dick and Mike Widdis.

Eddie Basso left Taft Broadcasting to come to work at Booth. He started on a delivery truck 13 years ago and is now manager of service and customer relations. Eddie Basso feels very secure, and nepotism does not worry him: "Should either of Mike's or Dick's children take over, I know they would be qualified. We have relatives working now, and there never has been any favoritism." And job security? "The turnover at Taft Broadcasting was scary. I know that as long as Mike and Dick are in business, I will have a job."

David Thomson has been sales manager for 4 years. He left American District Telegraph because he was unhappy in a large company, and he got the opportunity to come to Booth Fire Equipment because he was a friend of Mike Widdis. Davis is happy with his job, but he is aware of some of the downside of family business. On nepotism: "It has frightening aspects because you always wonder if the business can grow enough to provide income for the six children of Mike and Dick." As for job security, he zeroes in on the Achilles' heel of family ties as a means of staying on the job: "I feel the job security in a family firm is largely based on your personality and ability to fit in. Even if your performance is outstanding, you could be fired because you develop personality conflicts with the owner. Large corporations offer you the opportunity to transfer to other departments in situations like this."

Job security is guaranteed in two ways. There may be formal guarantees embodied in written agreements and officially established arrangements regarding hiring and firing. The alternative is informal guarantees based upon personal relationships with the people who do the hiring and firing. In large segments of the American economy, workers have chosen formal guarantees such as multiyear contracts and tenure rules backed by organizations that speak for the worker—unions or civil service boards. The economic sectors in which these procedures are much in evidence are areas where the family-owned business is not found at all—e.g., government service—or is a minor factor—i.e., the major industrial occupations. Small businesses are increasingly feeling the pinch of unionization, of course, but the bulk of family business is still operating without such institutional devices for worker protection.

That these devices have been beneficial to American labor is hardly a matter of dispute. However, neither union rules nor civil service laws can keep people on the job. When there is no work to be done owing to plant closings or budget cuts, there are layoffs. Such rules may ensure that workers are separated from their jobs in a fair manner, but they cannot ensure the jobs themselves.

This is where informal guarantees have the edge. If the business is committed to keeping people on the job, or at least to seeing that they do not suffer economic hardship, this represents better protection than fair layoff procedures. As we have seen, family businesses are likely to make such commitments because they tend to adopt their workers. Layoffs are a last resort when the business is collapsing. In Chapter 1, we watched a drilling business go down the drain while workers stayed on the job, polishing rigs at $9 an hour. Obviously, all family businesses are not so generous. Obviously, some firms fire nonfamily members first. On the whole, however, family business represents a set of dynamics that may afford workers stronger protection than their unionized counterparts receive.

Whether a person feels secure in a family business with only informal job guarantees is largely a matter of temperament. Detractors of such arrangements say that they are paternalistic and totally subjective—the job is secure as long as you are in good with the boss; if not, you are out. Others argue that a long-time friendship and a close working relationship are stronger reeds on which to lean than paper agreements drawn up among strangers. Both arguments may be on the mark, depending on the business. A person considering working for a family-owned business should try to read the situation correctly. One must not assume willy-nilly that a job will be more secure in a unionized, nonfamily business.

And Justice for All

The most common complaint lodged against nepotism in business affairs is that it creates a situation in which rewards—promotions, raises, perquisites—may be passed out on the basis of family ties rather than merit. The word "may" should be spotlighted because reward without merit does not *necessarily* occur in the family business; the potential for its occurring is simply greater than in other types of business. If such does occur, say the management consultants, it is a very bad business practice and should be condemned for that reason. We could not concur more, and in Chapter 5 we laid down some strictures for handling relatives on the payroll from a business standpoint. The general proposition put forth was that incompetent relatives should not be hired and kept in positions of responsibility lest the business suffer.

There is another aspect to this matter of reward without merit that should be discussed in the context of nepotism as a principle. That is the question of fairness as opposed to business efficiency. People in general believe that reward should equal merit and merit should be defined in terms of performance, not status, such as position in the family. The most oft-heard cry from family businesses—emanating from both family and nonfamily members—is that such and such action was "unfair" or "unjust." "It's not fair that cousin Terry got a raise and we didn't." "I don't think it's right that he can play golf every day while I sit here slaving over his business." "Just because she's the daughter of the boss doesn't mean it is right for her to get free gas from the business when we don't." "It's not fair that he makes more money than I do when we are brothers in the same business." And so on.

The players in the fair-right-just game tend to keep detailed scorecards on the progress of the contest. Two brothers maintain tallies on approvals they have received from Dad; two daughters add up the wealth to make sure they are being paid the same. In the end, the whole thing does become a business matter because all the scorekeeping, jealousy, and backbiting are not conducive to a good work atmosphere or to good relations between superiors and subordinates—and none of this is good for business.

Of course, jealousy is not an emotion whose expression is limited to the family-owned business; it is a universal human phenomenon that is likely to keep occurring, a fact often overlooked by the detractors of nepotism. This is not fair to family business. (See, no one is immune.) But there are certainly times in these businesses when rewards are bestowed in one direction and merit may appear to lie in a different direction. For example, the father-founder gives a top management spot to his eldest son rather than to a nonfamily employee who has more experience and seniority. Faced with a challenge on such decisions, many—perhaps most—businesspeople do not have a ready defense because, like most people, they have grown up with garbled notions about the meaning of justice and fairness.

Let us see if we can ungarble them, taking our text largely from Western political philosophy. First, there seem to be no illustrations in human history of people being opposed to justice. Certainly they have disagreed as to what was just in given circumstances, but whatever was just should be done—that all agree on. Said Marcus Aurelius: "In the whole constitution of man, I cannot see any virtue contrary to justice, whereby it may be resisted and opposed." No one has resisted or opposed it.

In Western constitutional thought, justice appears as the purpose for which governing entities are established. James Madison said it succinctly in *The Federalist Papers:* "Justice is the end of government. It is the end of civil society." Western theorists recognized, however, that no one short of God was in a position to determine in advance— for all people, for all time, and for all circumstances—what was just. How, then, was government to seek justice? The answer was to determine, on the basis of what was known and what people felt and would stand for, that which was just for the short run and for defined sets of circumstances. The principles thus determined were written down as rules to be enforced by government. The body of rules is known collectively as "law." Laws would be changed as times changed to keep the two—law and justice—in balance. Thus constitutional governments do not enforce justice, they enforce law. Persons are said to have received justice in a given case if their affairs are handled in accordance with due process of law.

A latter-day part of this due process of law was the concept of "equal protection of the laws." Now, equal protection never meant that everyone would be treated equally in the sense that they would be treated the same way. Murderers and jaywalkers are both lawbreakers, but their sentences are likely to be very different. Why? The principle is that not all crime should receive the same punishment. Instead, the magnitude of the punishment should equal the magnitude of the crime; and murder is considered worse, and thus deserving of more punishment, than jaywalking.

The question comes up every time someone is asked under the law to assume a heavier burden than others, as in paying income taxes. Says the well-to-do person: "It is unfair (i.e., it violates equal protection of the laws, which is a denial of due process of law, which is unjust) that I should pay more taxes than others; all people are equal under the law." Wrong. The principle of justice that underlies the tax laws is that people should pay in accordance with their ability to pay. The legal deduction from this principle is simple: The rich must pay more than the poor.

The point is that in the Western concept of justice, it is acceptable (right, fair) to make distinctions between people when laying down rules for making specific decisions as long as the principle underlying the distinction is one that people are willing to consider legitimate and as long as there is logic and consistency in the application of the principle.

We have taken a long time to get around to it, but there is the point for the family business person. The principle is that the business is to serve as a vehicle for family enjoyment and betterment. If this is so, then logically, decisions about the management and perpetuation of the business must take family ties into account. For the founder to name a relative as successor over the heads of more experienced but nonfamily workers is not unjust. It is a decision perfectly in keeping with the underlying principle of the business.

Those who complain most of unfairness and injustice when family members are given preference in a business are operating from the principle that merit—in the sense of training or experience or ability otherwise demonstrated—should be the sole basis for decision making. Is this true? The question is wrongly put. Principles are not more or less true, they are more or less acceptable or logical or useful. One can make business decisions purely on the basis of merit as defined—business efficiency often dictates that this be done—but the principle itself is no more worthy than the principle of family preferment. The better principle is the one that better serves the stated objective.

Let us come down off our philosophical high horse and talk some plain language. A family business should, as a matter of justice, give preference to family members. The owner should be straightforward about this and not mislead people with hogwash about how "we play no favorites here." If no favorites are played, it is not a family business. Nonfamily employees are thus forewarned. Certainly, some good potential employees may be lost to the firm because they prefer not to have the family standing in the way of their advancement. There is nothing wrong with their declining such jobs; what is wrong is to take the job and then constantly moan about unfairness.

Within the family, the same principles can apply. Thus if the founder wants the business to be perpetuated in the family, and if offspring A wants this also while offspring B wants to sell it off to the highest bidder, the business should be left to offspring A. Offspring B has no cause to scream foul; given the principle involved, it would be unjust if the business were split between the two.

Those who have not read carefully will probably say about now, "My God, I have just been told that merit should be ignored in family business decisions." We did not say that. We said that there is no shame in using family ties as a principle for bestowing rewards in a business that was founded and is being perpetuated in the interest of the family. Merit cannot be ignored to the point where the business is destroyed by inefficiency; if it is, it cannot be perpetuated. But the rewarding of merit based on performance is not a categorical imperative.

Alas, the concept of meritocracy is so entrenched in American society that it will probably never be rooted out. An accountant of our acquaintance, an otherwise very sensible person, recently resigned as a partner in a firm because one of the firm's senior partners insisted on bringing his son—apparently a well-qualified accountant—into the business at a level higher than that of employees who had been with the firm for some time. "It is simply not fair," we were told. But why should seniority be a universal principle for high office? What is wrong with paving the way for a relative if one is in a position to do so? "It is not fair to the others." We gave up.

The Pros and Cons of Family Hiring

The manager of a family business, who will probably be its founder or the successor of the founder, is going to practice nepotism. Steps will be taken to fit a prospective successor into the business. Other positions will be filled according to merit, but relatives will have the inside track if they are close in terms of merit. If these things are not done, it is not a family business.

This process is likely to go more smoothly if the manager clearly recognizes the fact that there are advantages and disadvantages to hiring family members. This recognition is not likely to deter the manager from hiring them, but it will point out the things that will make the job easier as well as those which will make it harder. Relatives are not going to be "just like any other employee," particularly if they have positions of responsibility, and the sooner the manager faces up to this fact and stops trying to placate critics by saying it isn't so, the sooner steps can be taken to minimize the disadvantages. For handy reference, we offer a summary of the important pros and cons.

First, the pro factors:

1. *Adaptability.* The relative joining the firm is more likely to fit socially into the current management team. In a closely held corporation, it is imperative that personalities mesh because companies are small enough that employees are like members of an extended family, depending upon each other emotionally as well as socially. Relatives hired into the firm are likely to have similar backgrounds and at least a rudimentary understanding of the company's policies, objectives, and focus. The hiring of any new employee—relative or nonrelative—is a chancy situation even if the best recruits are available. Personality quirks and problems may not surface for months after the employee has been hired. Social acceptance and personality meshing are of grave importance to the corporation acting as an extended family.

2. *Interest and participation.* A relative is inclined to take more interest in the job and feel a deeper responsibility than a nonrelative. With relatives working together, the business becomes a way of life, and each family member accepting a position in the firm feels a deeper obligation to perform above the average so as not to discredit the family name as well as the family business. Of course, one can never assume that each relative is eagerly waiting to join the family firm; many sons and daughters of relatives choose not to join the family business and elect professions outside it. Those competent employees analyze the pros and cons of joining the family firm, as does the owner when he considers hiring them. When every related member—owner and employee—accepts the commitment to work together, their dedication and responsibility exceeds the norm.

   Relatives who are executives can actually save time because they do not have to "play up to the boss." They can set their own pace, develop their own potential, and save the countless hours employees tend to spend vying for the attention of the manager. In addition, relatives can afford to be more outspoken about company policies and procedures than any other employees of equal service. In some corporations, the unwritten law is: "Do not express your opinion unless asked." The relative who understands the personality of the family members is in a better position to express an opinion without fear of being fired or ostracized.

3. *Continuity.* Relatives in management help assure continuity and effective implementation of company policy. The long-range programs and objectives of the entrepreneur can best be fostered by those extended family members who understand the course and route of the business. The most outstanding advantage cannot be understood by people unless they are working in a business which becomes an extended family. The psychic rewards of jointly paddling your own canoe through rough waters and calm periods can be expressed only by those members who have experienced them.

Now, the disadvantages:

1. *Jealousies.* The biggest disadvantage is almost certain to be jealousy on the part of other employees. It is normal that an offspring someday assume the presidency and that relatives reach a much higher level of management than nonrelated employees. The very purpose of the family-owned business is to continue the family reign in management. This does not necessarily mean that the offspring is an incompetent stepping into an easy life. As we have discussed, the role of the relatives is frequently difficult, and they must surmount obstacles other employees do not have. Still, some jealousy must be expected.

Before going into a panic, the manager should first look at the employees who feel resentment and hostility to the family members. Would they exhibit jealousy in any situation? Chances are, the very employees who are jealous or resentful of the family situation are those who work the least and expect the most from a given situation. In large corporations, jealousy is often shown by young managers who are hired in key positions because of their degree of education and their connection with the right college. There is also jealousy among clerical people who view the executive secretary's position as that of a supreme being. Many corporations are trying to eliminate that position for this reason.

There are a number of ways to minimize jealousy. First, in hiring relatives, make sure that they have some highly visible assets that will depress resentment. This may be a management capability, an outgoing personality, or technical skills that can be utilized in the organization. Second, avoid placing relatives under the direct supervision of other close relatives. There is a consensus in family business literature that sons and other relatives perform better and are more accurately judged if they are working in a department or division headed by a nonrelative.

Third, relatives joining the firm should be prepared for some hostility and mistrust from current employees. They must be told that in the course of human relations these resentments do arise and it will be their own personal abilities that can overcome them. Fourth, avoid *salary* discrimination at all cost. Relatives should not make more or less than nonrelatives in comparable positions. Employees tend to be extremely judgmental when it comes to the salaries paid by the company.

2. *Discouragement of outside professionals.* Family businesses may discourage professional executives from seeking employment. The *Wall Street Journal* reported the following:

> OUTSIDER SYNDROME: Nearly a third of 360 corporate executives surveyed by Rene Plessner Associates Inc., New York, said they would be reluctant to join a family-owned company. Another 26% said they would consider such a move only if management showed a fair-minded attitude toward nonfamily executives.

This tends to imply that upward mobility and financial remuneration are lacking in the family organization. Life is usually far more lucrative financially in the large corporation than in the small, closely held company. However, not all people are emotionally equipped to adjust to the corporate hierarchical structure, and their sense of freedom is seriously affected in such positions. People who are desirous of more personal freedom are attracted to small firms where they feel their individual contribution can greatly affect success and growth.

Graduates who step from the door of college into business are idealists. Each one is desirous of becoming president of a large corporation and making a salary in six figures. Unfortunately, the number of these graduates far exceeds the available positions. Many of them will make it to the top of the ladder; others, as they are climbing, will decide that it is not the route for them. Unfortunately, family-owned businesses have not received a favorable press, and their critics are quick to point out the shortcomings and ignore the advantages.

3. *Difficulty in firing.* If relatives are hired as employees, it is more difficult to fire and demote them than nonfamily members. An expression heard in the family-owned business is: "If you fire a relative today, you may dine wth him tonight." Unfortunately, the entrepreneur who is considering termination of a relative must weigh the relative's inadequate performance and the turmoil created by the termination against the problems of leaving him or her in the company. Experience indicates, however, that it is the employee who suffers most. The entrepreneur is harder on the relatives in the company. In the case of offspring, greater effort is expected from them than from other employees in the firm.

4. *Pressure to hire incompetents.* The family-owned business manager may be pressed to hire destitute relatives. Unfortunately, family members tend to take advantage of those who are business owners and assume they can grant employment to any relative in despair. This is a psychological burden for the entrepreneur who may be surrounded by less fortunate relatives. The company cannot afford to become a refuge for all those in despair, and the best way to avoid the situation is never to hire the first one. If they have an educational background that is advantageous to the firm or skills that can be readily put to use, assisting them during a difficult period can be very rewarding. But the born losers should be avoided.

The Social Utility of Nepotism

Unless all the signs are being read wrong, American society is not a happy one. The discontent is not limited to the poor and the near-poor; it is rampant in the middle class as well. People have become cynical about the ability of government to solve problems or even the ability of the political system to produce honest individuals. Government takes billions from the middle class through taxation and spends it for defense and social programs, yet the nation continues to lose credibility internationally and the poor at home are still poor. Giant corporations say they are working to keep your trust, but prices soar and savings are eaten away by inflation. Large unions have become a fixture in the American economy, but millions of people are still unemployed. American family life seems to be feeling these pressures. Divorce rates continue to climb, and generation gaps have not been closed. People of modest incomes can no longer afford hospital care, and the schools for which people pay so dearly produce illiterates while the teachers walk the picket line. Even the millionaire baseball players go on strike. Does nobody give a damn anymore?

The family business—be it firm, farm, or factory—is an island of concern in a who-cares sea. It is, you know, steeped in nepotism. Family members are given first crack at important jobs, and other employees are treated like members of the family. Something more than the profit-and-loss statement goes into decision making. As a result, people can identify with the business, gain satisfaction from doing its work, and enjoy greater security in their jobs.

These businesses have been there all along, but perhaps people are just beginning to appreciate their value. This recognition is part of a general heightening of awareness regarding the importance of the quality of life. The things we have done to ourselves in the name of progress! We virtually destroyed the physical environment before someone decided that perhaps a flowing stream had more value than another labor-saving device. Now people have turned their attention to the social environment. They are choosing no-growth policies, alternative technologies, and small social institutions. They are rediscovering the virtues of strong family ties. They are deciding that they are their brother's keeper. They are resisting being forced into the corporate poker game.

Remember sick jokes? One of them goes like this: "Daddy, I wanta go play." "Be quiet." "But Daddy, I wanta go outside and play." "Knock it off." "Please, Daddy, let me go out and play." "Shut up and deal." Nepotism lets us go out and play.

Notes

[1]From *The Gapes of Wrath,* by John Steinbeck. Copyright 1939, copyright renewed 1967 by John Steinbeck. By permission of Viking Penguin Inc.

2Reprinted by permission of the *Harvard Business Review*. Adapted from "Is Nepotism So Bad?" by David W. Ewing (January-February 1965.) Copyright by the President and Fellows of Harvard Colldge; all rights reserved.

3James C. Abegglen and Hiroshi Mannari, "Leaders of Modern Japan: Social Origins and Mobility," *Economic Development and Cultural Change,* October 1960, Part 2.

4Columbus (Ohio) *Citizen-Journal,* November 20, 1978, p. 26.

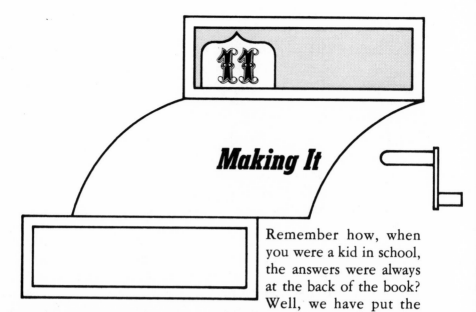

Making It

Remember how, when you were a kid in school, the answers were always at the back of the book? Well, we have put the *questions* at the back. But the questions are not a quiz on what you have read; there are no right or wrong answers. Instead, they are questions that only you can answer for yourself, and they are intended to help you make it in a family-owned business. All you have to do is answer the questions factually and honestly. Before you get your pencil, let us set the stage, or in this case, stages.

Making It in Stages

Making it in the family-owned business means more than establishing a business and operating it profitably; it also means passing the business on to heirs with a minimum of disruption. As we have seen, many business owners would like to forget the last stage; but if they do, their last performance is almost certain to be a poor one. We can never say that someone has made it in a family business until there has been a succession.

The person who makes it thus goes through three stages:

1. *The entrepreneurial stage.* In this period, the business is established and put on a sound financial basis. If rapid growth continues after the business has been set up, the entrepreneurial phase may be protracted. If it does not, the owner moves to the next stages.

217

2. *The sector stage.* During this time, the business achieves a steady state in operations; growth is gradual and the owner is not looking for new worlds to conquer. However, the owner is looking for security in the various sectors into which his or her life is divided.

3. *The retirement stage.* The time comes when an heir, probably an offspring, wants a greater role in the business. The owner must consider first working in "partnership" with the successor, then withdrawing from the business, and finally death. All these can be considered aspects of retirement.

These stages can be plotted in accordance with age to some extent. Exercises in entrepreneurship will occur roughly between the ages of 15 and 35. Only the more precocious are likely to succeed in their teens, of course, and after people have passed age 30, it becomes less and less likely that they will establish a new business when they have not done so already. Thus the twenties are the prime years for the entrepreneur.

Business owners who decide to settle down to running one business will devote virtually all their energies to this between the ages of 35 and 55. The late thirties are likely to be a time when owners are still undergoing some pains from entrepreneurship withdrawal. At age 50, owners who are going to think about it at all note that their time is about two-thirds up, and so they begin to think a little about succession. The managerial prime of life for business owners is thus the forties.

From age 55 to 75, the latter age being a little higher than the average American life expectancy, prudent business owners concentrate more on succession than anything else. Sometimes this does not hit home until a person has reached 60. After 70, those who have not prepared for succession are going to die with their boots on; there is no longer any point in talking to them about preparation for anything.

To summarize very broadly, people concentrate on entrepreneurship in their twenties and early thirties, on management in their forties, and on succession in their sixties. The late thirties and fifties are transition decades.

The reason we have broken this down into stages and age groups is that when people are trying to determine whether they can or are making it in the family-owned business, the questions they ask themselves are different, depending on stage and age.

At age 20, people are probably trying to decide what to do professionally. Should they try to establish a business with a view to leaving it to their children? When people are in their forties and already have a business they should be asking themselves whether they have things well under control. At age 50 or so, they should assess the status of the succession situation. Obviously, the questions they will ask themselves are different in each case.

The best way to make these assessments is to determine the key measure of success at each stage and then ask questions that make it possible for prospects and performance to be rated in terms of those measures. We submit that the following—all hopefully with memorable names—are the core measures:

1. *Entrepreneurial Quotient (EQ)*. A person's potential as an entrepreneur can be evaluated by determining his or her EQ just as we evaluate a person's performance potential in general by measuring his or her intelligence quotient, or IQ.

2. *Sector Security (SS) Score*. The owner of a family-owned business must operate successfully in a number of sectors, as we saw in Chapter 5. The SS Score indicates how well this is done.

3. *Retirement Readiness (RR) Rating*. The RR Rating serves the same function as the SS Score in a later stage of business life.

We hope your pencil is ready now because the questions are about to begin. Here is the drill. We first state the questions and then give a brief explanation as to why the answer is likely to be an appropriate part of the general measuring stick. Then we will put the questions in a compact checklist and tell you how to figure your score.

Before you go to the scoring, we feel compelled to get some caveats on the record. First, the questions and the values assigned to them represent certain propositions about appropriate human behavior in certain situations. What data are there to support these propositions? In some cases there are systematic data that have been gathered, and in some cases there are not. If we waited for all the subjects covered here to be researched thoroughly before we put forth any propositions, the businesspeople we are trying to help would be long dead. We are not waiting. Instead, we are going with what data we have, using experience as possible, and resorting to common sense as necessary. We leave it to the academicians to prove us wrong.

Second, all the propositions assume that the behavior is that of an

American male. Some will resent this seeming chauvinism. Our defense is that we do not have enough data or experience to assert reasonable propositions with regard to female behavior in the business situations we are describing. Gathering such information is a task that remains to be done as women more and more join the business world on equal terms with men.

Third, the scoring values serve only to support relative judgments. The 100s, which indicate that a person has a good chance of making it, could just as well be 90s or 110s. Still, it is useful to have a hard number with which to express a value as long as it is understood that the hard number is derived from soft methodology.

The Entrepreneurial Quotient

In Chapter 4, we looked at some of the sociology and psychology of entrepreneurship, and we hope that material was enlightening. However, the average person trying to decide upon a career wants to make a decision without consulting a bevy of experts about personal matters. You need not see a psychiatrist in order to determine your Entrepreneurial Quotient. Simply look at the way you have handled your life so far. Some people *do* change completely after age 20, but not many. Ponder the following questions.

1.   *Do you reconcile your bank account as soon as the monthly statement comes in?*

Some people are careful about money and some are not. Entrepreneurs are. This is not to say that they will not gamble a bundle on a hot deal, but they always know to the penny how much money is in that bundle. They always know what things cost, whether the costs are going up or down, and whether they are getting a bargain. This is particularly true for small-time entrepreneurs. By the time a person has become a multi-millionaire, it becomes impossible for him to keep track of every penny, although it is surprising how many try. Entrepreneurs appreciate knowing how much money they have at all times so that they can seize opportunities on short notice and not be embarrassed later by a lack of cash.

The way people handle their personal bank accounts is a good tip-off as to how they will handle business funds. Some people never reconcile their bank statements and never know how much money they have until they are overdrawn. The potential entrepreneur is the exact opposite.

2. *Did you earn money on your own from some source other than the family before you were 10 years old?*

Most people who are going to make money in business show an affinity for making money at an early age. This is usually more than the time-honored standards of American industriousness—selling lemonade and delivering papers. The young entrepreneur will develop hustles of various sorts while in elementary school. We once knew a 9 year old who figured out how to turn off the faucets at the local high school and then sold water to the spectators at the semipro baseball games that were played at the high school field on Sundays. There was another kid during World War II, when rubber was in short supply, who organized a scrap collection business. Every kid in the neighborhood scoured the terrain for tires or anything else made of rubber and sold them to the "broker" for a flat fee. He in turn marked up the goods and sold them to the authorities. We recently saw a youngster who was certainly under 10 taking Polaroid pictures of the runners at a local marathon event. A budding sports reporter? Not on your life. He sold the pictures to the runners after they crossed the finish line. Now who would buy pictures of themselves wearing sweat-soaked garb on their bodies and a look of agony on their faces? Well, about two-thirds of these runners did.

The ability to make money at an early age is an especially good indication of entrepreneurial potential today. At an earlier time, families had to scramble to eat and the kids were expected to do their share of scrambling, whether or not they had a knack for it. Youngsters who can find ways to develop an independent income in today's society are likely to be the entrepreneurs of the future.

3. *Did you take part in competitive sports in school and do you continue to do so?*

The great Hall of Fame second baseman Rogers Hornsby once said that any youngster who did not like baseball was un-American. That is undoubtedly going too far, but competitive sports does have quite a hold on the United States. Entrepreneurs obviously have a competitive nature, and a great many of them show this at an early age on the playing field. In school, they quarterback the football team and shortstop the baseball squad. Later on, they will bet dinner over golf and tennis games. Even in pickup backyard basketball games, they will try hard to win.

One should not make too much of the "sports is training for life" litany heard so often from athletic coaches, but the competitive urge that is developed through sports does prepare people to some extent for the business world. A venture analysis is a type of game plan, and it is not a long step from reading a defense to reading the market. However, it is not so much that sports trains people to be entrepreneurs; rather, the same inner drives push people to be athletes and entrepreneurs. And it matters very much to these people whether you won or lost, however you played the game.

4. *Do you remember people's names and faces well?*

Knowledge of names and faces is a tremendous weapon in business competition. All of us like to feel that we are memorable, and we are flattered when someone we met only once can call us by name. Not that we will necessarily buy that person's wares because our names were remembered, mind you, but still . . .

Many youngsters who are good at names also go into politics, where it is a useful trait. However, people are increasingly underwhelmed by name-dropping office seekers. It is well known that politicians are fed people's names on computer printouts and receive up-to-the minute briefings just before they enter the handshake line. Even then, they sometimes blow it. The story is that President Nixon was once shaking hands in a crowd of citizens when a young girl muscled her way to the front and implored him to save Smokey the Bear. The President replied: "Nice to see you, Miss Bear." This kind of mistake costs entrepreneurs money. Forget the names and you can forget the sales.

5. *Were you good in the "hard" subjects—mathematics, biology, engineering, accounting, and so forth—in school?*

Although they can certainly hold jobs in business, people who major in business administration in school are no more likely to be successful entrepreneurs than anyone else. The choice of subject matter can be significant, however. Entrepreneurs are oriented toward results. Take steps 1, 2, and 3 to attain objective X with few ifs, ands, and buts. People like that prefer school subjects in which the answers are not inconclusive. Add a column of figures and you get an exact total, not a mathematical approximation. Design a bridge to cross a stream and it must be at least 300 feet long; 250 feet and you are in the water. Bodies at rest stay at rest until they are put in motion; that's a law, not a guess.

The fact that some people like hard subjects does not necessarily mean that they make good grades in those subjects in school; they simply must like the subject matter. They may, in fact, make poor grades because they are concentrating on how they can use the material to their financial advantage rather than preparing for exams.

This is not to say that an affinity for history, literature, or philosophy bars one from the business world, but if these are a person's primary interests, it is a bad sign for entrepreneurship. In these disciplines, conclusions are festooned with contingencies and questions are answered with other questions. It is hard to gain a competitive advantage in the marketplace with such ammunition.

6. *In school, did you pretty much stay away from such organizations as Scouts and student government?*

Most entrepreneurs are not joiners in their youth. Joining means following the lead of others, being bound by majority votes, and the like. Entrepreneurs tend to be loners who want to go their own way, however others are going. We remember a friend from college who never participated in a single campus activity—no school paper, no band, no student council, not even the business club (and he was a business major). All he did was play poker, an avocation that he insisted taught him more about people than we would ever learn from the social science courses. We were confident that Catfish would never amount to anything. He now runs a sizable hardware business in New Orleans and is taking his son in as a partner. Still plays poker.

Of course, a good deal of joining may be in order after an entrepreneur establishes a business. Chambers of Commerce, Kiwanis clubs, and the like are all places for making contacts and gathering information that may be useful to the business. But at this stage, joining is a tactic, not a character trait as it is during the school years. The ranks of entrepreneurship are not swelled by the big men on campus.

7. *In courting the opposite sex, did you tend to go for one person at a time as opposed to playing the field?*

Entrepreneurs are not ladies men. It is not that they are unappealing to women—quite the opposite—or that they are uninterested in matters of the heart. It is instead that courting takes a certain amount of time. There are preliminaries and buildups and progressions and follow-throughs. Unless one is simply paying for sex (a subject we do not feel qualified to discourse on), these routines must be followed with each new girl being pursued. Playing the field, i.e., dating five or six girls on a random basis, can thus consume a good portion of one's waking hours. The budding entrepreneur always has other things to do.

The most likely thing for an entrepreneur is to settle upon one girl in college, date her as a steady, marry her at graduation, and begin soon after to raise the family that will own the business. With a steady girl, the routines only have to be followed once; missed appointments for pressing reasons will be excused, and energy that might go into courting can go into other types of deal making.

8. *Do you get up early in the morning and find yourself at work before others are out of bed?*

Entrepreneurs are not slugabeds. Although they may stay up late frequently, they always pop out of bed at the crack of dawn ready to put something together. But they are not joggers because jogging is the kind of noncompetitive activity that is foreign to the entrepreneur's nature. More likely, he drinks coffee and plots strategy in the wee hours of the morn.

A large part of the entrepreneur's disinclination to stay in bed is the restless spirit that is a common trait of the breed. Time spent sleeping is almost like time spent eating; human beings must devote a certain amount of time to both, but neither is a productive activity. They are both regenerative in nature. Thus entrepreneurs sleep and eat enough to keep their strength up, but they never tarry at these pursuits. Young people who are prone to tarry at the table or in bed will probably seek a line of work that enables them to continue these habits as they grow older. Entrepreneurship does not.

9.   *Are you either a nonsmoker or a cigarette smoker?*

We expect a world of challenges on this proposition and we may be stretching things a bit, but we will say flatly that pipe and cigar smokers are unlikely to become entrepreneurs. They may take up these habits after they become established businesspeople, but if they smoked cigarettes to begin with, they will go back to them. Pipe smokers tend to be reflective, and the entrepreneur is not given to deep reflection. Cigar smokers tend to rest on their laurels, and the entrepreneur can never afford to do this. Cigarette smokers are harried souls eternally looking for lights and ashtrays. They have bundles of nervous energy to expend, and cigarette smoking is a sign of their impatience to spend them. Pipe and cigar smokers, on the other hand, have the kind of patience that successful entrepreneurs seem to lack.

This is not to say—God forbid—that smoking cigarettes will make one a successful entrepreneur. Nonsmokers can do just as well. They probably have some of the nervousness that is characteristic of cigarette smokers, but they manifest it or placate it in other ways.

10.   *Do you tend to trust your hunches in deciding what to do as opposed to waiting until you have a lot of information on hand?*

A person of entrepreneurial bent is somewhat like the Indian scout who could ride into a green valley where there was no sign of life, rein in the horse, and say, "Indians." No tracks, no smoke signals, no drums—just something in the wind. Those who do not act until all possible objectives have been taken care of and all relevant data have been assembled will rarely make a big mistake, but they will rarely enjoy a big success either. Risk taking is an important part of business success, and acting on hunches certainly involves risks. By hunches, we do not mean visions or dreams or pin-the-tail-on-the-donkey selections. We mean judgments based on factors that cannot be quantified.

We once knew a person who owned a string of movie theaters in a number of medium-sized towns—at least, medium-sized for 1948. All were doing well. The youngsters packed the house for the kiddie matinees and Saturday afternoon westerns; the older kids and adults came in for the Saturday midnight shows and weekly first-run features.

Suddenly, the man sold the entire string—at a good price. Several years later, he opened a television sales and service business. He now has a successful string of *those* in the same towns, and the movie houses that have not been torn down are standing empty. He had not read a single market study, but he had seen some television and was convinced that the time was coming when people would stay home to watch TV rather than venturing out to the Saturday midnight show. His hunch paid off.

11. *Do you keep new ideas in your head instead of writing them down in notebooks?*

Entrepreneurs keep a lot of things in their heads, including their most creative ideas. People who scribble things down on little slips of paper and put them in notebooks or boxes are either writing a novel or preparing a set of cheat notes for an exam. Once an idea is written down, it tends to lie there as a lump of information and become stale. Entrepreneurs like to turn things over in their minds, refine their ideas, and come up with new ideas that are not restricted by pieces of paper in a notebook. This does not mean that note taking in general is a bad idea if the intent is simply to pick up a piece of information to be plugged in somewhere at a later date. But the development of ideas is a process of thought, not research.

We are reminded of a friend who went to a psychiatrist with a problem. Thinking to save time and money, our friend wrote down in five or six single-spaced typewritten sheets the details of his life history so that the psychiatrist would not have to question him about these facts. Of course, the astonished psychiatrist did question him because the process of pulling out the facts was part of the therapy.

12. *Do you close deals with handshakes rather than insisting on written contracts and guarantees?*

Good businesspeople demand contracts; good entrepreneurs find this too confining and are usually prepared to go forth on something less binding in court. The fact is that in the entrepreneurial world, a verbal agreement may be better than a written one. When things are written down, the whole thing becomes a matter for lawyers and judges to interpret. In those circumstances, both parties to the agreement are expected to squeeze everything they can from the other. It is somewhat like the principle of tax avoidance discussed in Chapter 9. When the only bond is a word, it becomes a matter of honor, and no entrepreneur can afford to lose honor. Thus both parties are more likely to try to reach a mutually satisfactory accommodation.

We know a person who cheated shamelessly on his wife for years, had a steady string of mistresses. The couple were finally divorced, and some time later he began living with another woman. They are not married. All cheating ceased. When we asked about his abrupt turnabout, he answered, "Cheating on your wife is okay. After all, she has a marriage contract to protect her interests. But cheating on a girl friend, who has no written protection, is dishonorable. I could never do that." So it goes with entrepreneurs.

13. *Do you bet on long shots rather than favorites?*

Entrepreneurship is a form of gambling, and so one of the clearest tests of anyone's entrepreneurial bent is his or her behavior in an actual gambling situation—betting the horses, playing roulette, or playing cards. Many people, including many successful entrepreneurs, do not gamble in this way at all, of course, but if they do, the betting pattern is a good sign. Caution is the key. The cautious person at the horse tracks bets favorites to show; the entrepreneur bets long shots to win. At five-card stud, the cautious person drops if the first two cards are lousy; the entrepreneur hopes for something better in the next three cards. The cautious roulette player sticks to reds and blacks; the entrepreneur plays number 13.

14. *Do you devote considerably more time and thought to work than to other activities such as hobbies?*

By and large, entrepreneurs are not stamp collectors or beekeepers or bird-watchers. Their principal nighttime and weekend hobby is catching up on work they did not complete during the weekdays. Their pleasure reading is the *Wall Street Journal* and the business section of *Newsweek*. They do engage in some entertainment activities, such as attending plays or concerts or athletic events, but they are apt to make business calls during intermission. All these things, of course, are early signs of workaholism.

Yes	No	
( )	( )	1. Do you reconcile your bank account as soon as the monthly statement comes in?
( )	( )	2. Did you earn money on your own from some source other than the family before you were 10 years old?
( )	( )	3. Did you take part in competitive sports in school and do you continue to do so?
( )	( )	4. Do you remember peoples' names and faces well?
( )	( )	5. Were you good in the "hard" subjects—mathematics, biology, engineering, accounting, and so forth—in school?
( )	( )	6. In school did you pretty much stay away from such organizations as Scouts and student government?
( )	( )	7. In courting the opposite sex, did you tend to go for one person at a time as opposed to playing the field?
( )	( )	8. Do you get up early in the morning and find yourself at work before others are out of bed?
( )	( )	9. Are you either a nonsmoker or a cigarette smoker?
( )	( )	10. Do you tend to trust your hunches in deciding what to do as opposed to waiting until you have a lot of information on hand?
( )	( )	11. Do you keep new ideas in your head instead of writing them down in notebooks?
( )	( )	12. Do you close deals with handshakes rather than insisting on written contracts and guarantees?
( )	( )	13. Do you bet on long shots rather than favorites?
( )	( )	14. Do you devote considerably more time and thought to work than to other activities, such as hobbies?

EQ = Chances of Success as Entrepreneur

130–140	Excellent
100–120	Good
80–90	Fair
70 or below	Poor

Figure 2   Determinants of Entrepreneurial Quotient (EQ).

So much for the explanations, now for the scoring. Figure 2 repeats questions we have just discussed and gives a choice of answers to check. All questions can be answered "yes" or "no." When you have checked your response to all the questions, give yourself 10 points for each "yes" answer. The total of these scores is your Entrepreneurial Quotient (EQ).

What is a good score? If you have an EQ of at least 100, you have a pretty good chance of making it as an entrepreneur. The higher your score (maximum is 140), the better your chances. Conversely, your chances of success worsen as your score sinks below 100. If you do not score higher than 70, forget it and look for another career. The wolves in the entrepreneurial world will eat you alive.

The Sector Security Score

Let us assume that some 20 years have passed since you determined your EQ. You predicted that you would do well in the entrepreneurial world, and you were correct. You now own an established business, and although continued growth is a part of your plans, it is in your management plan, not your entrepreneurial plan. You have settled down to running a business rather than chasing new dreams. You have a family, both nuclear—spouse and children—and extended—assorted relatives on both yours and your spouse's sides—some of whom work in your business. You have some notion of leaving the business to your children, although definite plans along those lines are not even on the drawing board yet. How well are you doing?

Earlier, in a more limited context, we put forth the secure sector theory, the proposition being that the owner of a family business operated in four sectors and that things should be secure in all sectors before another round of major growth could be undertaken successfully. We wish to generalize the concept a bit more here and use it as the basis for devising a measure of making it.

In what sense is a person's life conducted in sectors? It should first be noted that the term "sector" implies a degree of ordering in one's life. Some people do not operate in sectors at all; they do what comes naturally, and things go as they go. To some extent, this style is characteristic of the entrepreneur. However, successful operation of a business demands more order, some notion of goals and of the effort needed to achieve those goals, and some way of structuring the effort. Banging away at targets of opportunity is no longer an appropriate style.

The sector analogy comes from military tactics. When a squad of soldiers is advancing under fire on a target, say the tacticians, they should not wait for heads to pop up and then blast away at random like a bunch of squirrel hunters. Too many shots will be missed, three people will hit the same head, and there will be too many gaps through which fire can be returned. Instead, infantrymen are taught to establish sectors of fire within the area of advance and spend their rounds entirely in this sector, whether they see a specific target or not. By blanketing an entire area in this way, the squad is more likely to overrun the enemy position.

A successful businessperson must proceed in the same way, except that he or she is the entire squad. The entrepreneur has a general objective—a rewarding life consisting of a family and a business—and must expend effort to achieve it, but the area of advance is divided into sectors, and some effort must be channeled.

The sectoring occurs at two levels. First, one's life has both family and business sectors. Second, within these broad sectors there are subsectors. A businessperson is an owner, a manager, a worker, and a human. A family person is a spouse, a parent, a friend, and a person with individual needs. The various sectors overlap, but for purposes of expositional clarity, we can separate them. In an oversimplified graphic, the "field of fire" or "area of advance" might look like Figure 3.

The chances of attaining the goal are maximized when each sector of fire is secure. As in the military, success may still be possible with one or two insecure sectors, but too many of these make success unlikely. With this formulation in mind, we have devised a measure of success that we call the Sector Security Score and have devised a set of questions, the answers to which, when assigned numerical values, go to make up that score. Pencils again, please.

1.   *Are you satisfied that all the relatives employed in the business are qualified for their jobs?*

You are failing as a manager if the place is honeycombed with incompetent relatives. On the other hand, if you employ no relatives at all and consider none of your employees close friends, you do not get high marks as a relative and friend yourself. The family business

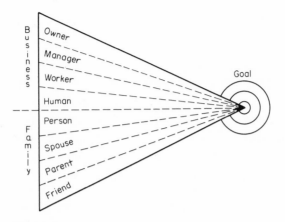

Figure 3

manager, remember, must practice nepotism while still regarding merit as determined by performance. The manager does not enjoy the luxury of simply avoiding the problem, as other businesses do, by making a rule against hiring relatives. Thus, constant vigilance to ease out the unqualified is called for.

"Fitness reports" on relatives should be maintained regularly to make sure they find the proper niche. If Cousin Carmen is not doing well in service, you may give him a shot in sales. Why not simply let him go entirely? We have gone through that already. Remember, it is a family business.

2. *Are employees who are nonrelatives basically satisfied with their jobs?*

Every business has some discontent, of course, but disgruntlement among a significant number of people in key positions is a serious problem for the business. If the sales, service, and financial managers all walk out at the same time, the business will be in trouble.

How do you find out if there is disgruntlement? The best way is to emphasize when you hire nonrelatives that it is a family business but that it is your intention that all employees be suitably rewarded and content with their lot. If an employee believes that is not happening, he or she is to come to you directly with a statement of the case so that an accommodation can be worked out, if possible. Those who fail to do this but who manifest their discontent by slacking off in their work or by backbiting other employees will be shown no mercy. All this will take some of your time, but it is worth it in the long run.

3. *Do you spend at least 20 percent of your time working on something other than a management task?*

In a family business, if you withdraw entirely into a management mode, the employees are likely to regard this as an example of creeping corporatism. When the business started out, in all likelihood, the work force was a group of people trying to make it together and you were regarded primarily as a coworker. It is important that the employees retain this feeling. Besides, doing a job of work as opposed to making decisions keeps the owner in touch with the realities of the business. This does not mean that you should spend your time loading trucks or sweeping floors; the hair-shirt routine will make you look ridiculous, and displaying a willingness to get your hands dirty is not going to increase your employees' sense of job security.

The best way to handle this is to write in a piece of work for yourself when a work plan is being drawn up. If you are in printing and publishing, you may save some of the design work for yourself. If the business involves sales, you may want to serve personally as account executive for some key accounts.

Obviously, the larger the business, the more time you will have to spend on management, and so you may wish to adjust the 20 percent figure recommended for particular circumstances. Even then, however, see if you cannot delegate some of the things that could be called "management," e.g., analyzing the labor distribution, and pick up a few other work tasks.

4. *Does your firm have a written pay and promotion plan that is in fact used to determine pay and promotions?*

Without such a plan, the owner is likely to be badgered constantly for raises by relatives and to hear a lot of complaints from nonrelative employees who feel that they should have gotten promotions. The written plan depersonalizes the employment situation and lets merit rise to the top. Does this not violate the principle that family members are to be given preference? Not at all. You discharge your family obligations by not forcing relatives you are anxious to help go through the same screening process as others in order to get an opportunity to do a job. Once they have been given an opportunity, you apply the same standards in judging their performance as you do for everyone else.

If we may be permitted yet another sports analogy, the preference shown family members is like the preference shown established starters on a pro football team. Theoretically, everyone in training camp has an equal opportunity to make the team. In fact, established players have an edge; they have to play themselves *out* of a job while rookies have to play themselves *in*. The relatives in the business will be in the same spot, and so there is no reason to show additional favoritism in pay and promotions. The written plan will get those who want this added edge off your back.

5. *Has your business operated with no more than one significant cash-flow problem in the last year?*

A cash-flow problem means that you have plenty of assets but not enough cash on hand to meet the payroll. Unless the business is awfully simple, there are sure to be such problems from time to time as you make investments, undergo expansion, add staff, introduce new product lines, and so on. If cash-flow problems occur frequently, however, you are overextended in the business and probably should consider cashing in some assets.

It is not unlike personal finance situations. Anyone may be close to overdrawn at the bank sometimes, but if this occurs every month, one is undoubtedly living beyond one's means. Unfortunately, many of our citizens do not want to face up to this fact and hide behind the cash-flow excuse. Do not make that mistake with your business.

6. *Do you have a relatively small amount of assets in a liquid state?*

This is the other side of the cash-flow coin. One can fail to maximize profits or lose out on growth opportunities if liquidity (i.e., the amount of readily spendable money) is too high. Certainly, the business checking account should always have the bare minimum needed to meet cash-flow needs. But savings accounts should not be allowed to get too fat either. When there is a lot of cash on hand and you are not under pressure to pay dividends to anyone, you should consider business expansion as a way of putting the money to work. Be careful not to get carried away by the entrepreneurial urge, however. One good business, even with high liquidity, is better than four businesses with chronic cash-flow problems.

7. *Do you set aside specific time each week to spend with your spouse and children?*

By now, your family has probably accepted your workaholic habits, but they are not likely to be happy if they never see you at all. The only way to make sure that does not happen is to reserve some time and not let the business intrude on this time. For example, you may decide that Sunday is family day and no amount of pressing business, barring the gravest of emergencies, will take you away from the family. All the problems of the firm, short of its survival, will have to wait until Monday.

Now some will argue that no workaholic can do this any more than an alcoholic can drink in moderation. We think differently. Most alcoholics can get through a full day without drinking as long as they know they can drink the next day. So with workaholics—they do not have to face the future with the spouse and kids wrapped around their necks; they only have to do it one day a week.

"Ever on Sunday" does not guarantee a happy home life, but it is a step in the right direction. If the family is always neglected, you can expect to discover ultimately that the spouse has lovers on the side, the daughter is smoking pot, or the son is one jump ahead of the cops. No amount of argument that "they knew my business came first to start with" will rectify these unpleasant situations. So put aside your financial magazines at least once a week and practice a little better homes and gardens. And take the kids out too.

8. *Have you and your spouse jointly clarified your positions in the company?*

If your business started out with the spouse as the bookkeeper owing to economic necessity, you cannot assume that the role will remain satisfactory indefinitely. Nor can you assume that your spouse is itching to return to domestic life.

When there is no financial reason for your spouse to hold a certain position, both of you should discuss frankly the part each of you wishes to play in the firm. Who knows, you may wind up with a new vice-president for sales whom you did not know was available. The spouse should be given the same opportunity as any other relative to fill a key spot in the company. Nothing is more likely to lead to trouble at home than a failure to let your lifetime partner grow professionally when he or she so desires.

9. *Do you hold regular employee meetings?*

It is important that all the employees in a family business be kept abreast of the things that are happening in the company. They may be asked to make special sacrifices, and they will not be very happy to do so if they have not had the opportunity to prepare themselves or take part in planning that might have avoided the necessity for sacrifices. A monthly meeting at which *all* company affairs are discussed candidly would not be out of order. Again, if the company is very large, it may be necessary to limit the in-group sessions to key workers. If it is a small business, however, all workers should feel that they are members of the in-group.

This does not mean that executive decisions should be subject to majority approval; the sessions should be advisory only. But if you have selected your employees wisely, they are likely to have some good ideas with regard to even the knottiest problems. It is only good business to tap those ideas, and you will never tap them through a suggestion box. Get everyone together to have things out; it will help maintain company spirit and probably lead to better executive decisions.

10. *Does the business have an updated, accurate organization chart?*

The function of an organization chart is to show where everyone fits into the scheme of things. It is a graphic depiction of how decisions are supposed to flow downward and how information is to flow upward. If you have more than one or two employees, you should maintain an organization chart at all times and test it frequently against reality. This is especially important when there are relatives floating around who may try to assume responsibilities that you do not wish them to have.

For example, suppose a nephew comes into the business as an assistant in sales but begins to report directly to the boss, his uncle, rather than reporting through the person in charge of the sales division, who is not a relative. Without a fairly formal statement of the scheme of things, the division head is not sure who the nephew's supervisor is. Perhaps the boss has given the nephew special responsibilities outside the division head's jurisdiction. The organization chart clears all this up. If all the lines in sales still run through the division head, he or she can insist without rancor that either the nephew fall into line or the organization chart be changed. Since changing the company organization is a major matter, the boss cannot simply let the problem slide. More often than not, the problem will be resolved to the division head's satisfaction.

In a way, an organization chart is like a will. Both introduce a degree of formality into situations where, in a perfect world, things could be worked out informally. No way. Operating without an organization chart is like dying without a will; everything is up for grabs, and business suffers.

11.   *Is the family firmly in control of the company, as evidenced by stock ownership?*

As the owner looks around for ways to expand the business and finds a shortage of capital, the siren song of going public is likely to be heard. Although this possibility should not be dismissed out of hand, it should be approached with caution. Not only does going public open the company to government scrutiny—and all the reports that go with it—it makes the family accountable to nonfamily stockholders and increases the possibility that the family may lose control of the company if a disgruntled family member joins forces with nonrelatives.

In order to have the maximum discretion in the operation of a company, the founder should keep all the stock and then will it to some chosen persons. If the stock is divided among individuals, the founder should make sure that all those who have a chunk are loyal to his or her conception of the business. We realize that the management experts will probably deplore this attitude as hopelessly backward and stultifying to the company. In some cases it would be, and we *said* that broadening the base of ownership should not be ruled out irrevocably. But the experts, remember, are likely to be looking at the situation from the viewpoint of some abstract concept of business efficiency. The owner is looking at a life's work and wants to keep it intact.

12.   *Have you taken a vacation within the last year?*

Talking the workaholic into a vacation of even 2 weeks is no small task. However, you who work so hard must keep in mind that you can burn out and not be able to work at all. Force yourself, or let someone else force you. A close friend of ours never took vacations until he remarried. His second wife is a ski nut, and she insisted upon

2 weeks in Vail in early February as virtually a condition of the marriage contract. Now, no matter how hungry the wolf at the company door looks, our friend is off to Vail in early February. His business does as well as it always did.

13.   *Are you engaged in any community activities?*

We noted earlier that entrepreneurs are not joiners. True enough. But those entrepreneurs who have passed to the sector stage will want to change their habits. Participation in community affairs is not only a way for you to cater to your person side, it is also good for business. No matter how successful your business is, you may well need community help at some point. You can hardly expect the local bank to come rushing to your assistance when you have refused repeatedly to help the bank president in his hospital fund-raising drives. And if you decline to work with other businesspeople in improving community services, you may be losing customers and suppliers. Again, reasons of business should not be allowed to crowd out all else. Spending one late afternoon a week with a Little League baseball team can pay big dividends.

14.   *Do you read publications other than your trade journal?*

Owing to the pressures of work, businesspeople tend to become insular. They read their trade journals religiously to pick up practical advice on how to do a better job of cleaning furs, or maintaining inventory, and so on. But they treat matters outside their immediate business needs as extraneous. This is a mistake. Long-range business planning can be done only in the context of a larger economic and social context. The business-people who really want to make it must have some notion of what that context is.

It is stock-taking time again, and we will use the same drill as before. On the Figure 4 checklist, mark either "yes" or "no," then total the numbers to get your Sector Security (SS) Score. With 100 or more, you would seem to be in pretty good shape sectorwise. With 70 or below, you have major problems. If you score in the low range, go back and see where the "nos" popped up; they may all be in one sector. For example, if you never take vacations or spend time with the spouse and kids, it is obvious that the family side of your life is in jeopardy. On the other hand, if you have no organization chart or pay plan, you should brush up on your management techniques.

Yes	No	
( )	( )	1. Are you satisfied that all the relatives employed in your business are qualified for their jobs?
( )	( )	2. Are employees who are nonrelatives basically satisfied with their jobs?
( )	( )	3. Do you spend at least 20 percent of your time working on something other than a management task?
( )	( )	4. Does your firm have a written pay and promotion plan that is in fact used to determine pay and promotions?
( )	( )	5. Has your business operated with no more than one significant cash-flow problem in the last year?
( )	( )	6. Do you have a relatively small amount of assets in a liquid state?
( )	( )	7. Do you set aside specific time each week to spend with your spouse and children?
( )	( )	8. Have you and your spouse jointly clarified your positions in the company?
( )	( )	9. Do you hold regular employee meetings?
( )	( )	10. Does the business have an updated, accurate organization chart?
( )	( )	11. Is the family firmly in control of the company, as evidenced by stock ownership?
( )	( )	12. Have you taken a vacation within the last year?
( )	( )	13. Are you engaged in any community activities?
( )	( )	14. Do you read publications other than your trade journal?

SS Score

130–140	Excellent
100–120	Good
80–90	Fair
70 or below	Poor

Figure 4   Determinants of Sector Security (SS) Score.

The Retirement Readiness Rating

Now you are 60. There is a lot more behind you than there is ahead. The business has expanded and is thriving; you and your spouse have grown old together with only a normal amount of suffering; the kids are all adults. Now comes the biggest test for the family business owner. Are you ready to retire?

Remember that we use retirement broadly to cover several phases of withdrawal from the business. The founder must retire to some extent to make room so that the successor can enter the business. At some point, a formal retirement is called for and the offspring, or someone else, takes over full operation of the business. Finally, the owner retires from life itself and someone inherits what has been built.

The way you have acted in all these withdrawal phases determines your Retirement Readiness (RR) Rating, Figure 5, and once again we have a list of questions for you to answer in order to arrive at that rating. However well you did on EQ and SS scores, it will go for nought if you score poorly on the final rating. The scoring scale is the same: below 70, there is a lot of improving to be done; above 100, you are in good shape.

Now we know this is a painful subject, and so we will not rub salt in your wounds with additional discussion as to why you should be able to answer "yes" to all the Retirement Readiness questions. Chapters 7 through 9 devoted quite a bit of space to the whys and wherefores, and we do not want to remind you of your lack of immortality any more than is necessary. So go right to the checklist with your pencil and hope for a big, fat 140.

Success and Survival

The measures of potential or actual success we have used are largely internal to the family-owned business. Scoring well on all indices does not guarantee success because the business exists as a part of a larger social, economic, and political context over which the business owner has no direct control. Pressures may be exerted within this context that make it difficult for the business to survive.

As we have discussed, the small business in America (and most family businesses are small) has held on as an economic form despite increasing oligopoly in the economy, government regulation that increases costs, and a tax system that many consider punitive. Any of these things may capsize the family-owned business in the long run unless something is done about them. They may put the new entrepreneur to rout, make it difficult for a small business to operate in the black no matter how well managed, and severely hamper the ability of the owner to pass the business on to the family.

Consider, for example, the plight of the entrepreneur in an economic system where the small business lacks access to capital, where

Yes	No	
( )	( )	1. Have you firmly designated someone as your successor as chief executive officer of the business?
( )	( )	2. Did your offspring or whoever you designated as successor have a chance to learn the business by working outside it?
( )	( )	3. Did your successor get good management experience in the company as opposed to doing manual labor?
( )	( )	4. Have all your children grown up with a positive feeling about the business owing to your descriptions of it?
( )	( )	5. Were you able to use company growth, i.e., new divisions, to advantage in training your children?
( )	( )	6. Do you have a firm date set for your formal retirement?
( )	( )	7. Do you have a clear plan for using your time once you have formally retired?
( )	( )	8. Is your "collaborative management" curve on the upswing; i.e., do you and your successor get along well?
( )	( )	9. Are you confident that your successor is as well-equipped to handle the business as you were?
( )	( )	10. Do you have a current will properly drawn up by a lawyer and witnessed by others?
( )	( )	11. Are all your prospective heirs satisfied with the will?
( )	( )	12. Does your spouse know where all the important business documents are?
( )	( )	13. Do you have in place a qualified team for keeping your postmortem business strategy up to date and implementing it when you are gone?
( )	( )	14. Do you and your heirs and experts engage in periodic death drills?

RR Rating

130–140	Excellent
100–120	Good
80–90	Fair
70 or below	Poor

Figure 5 Retirement Readiness (RR) Rating.

there is no graduated corporate income tax based on size as an indication of ability to pay, and where capital-gains taxes are excessive. Arthur Burck, a corporate merger expert, believes that present capital-gains taxes have almost eliminated incentive for entrepreneurs. He puts it this way:

> With respect to present entrepreneurs when they reach the point where they need to "cash out" or achieve liquidity, the tax laws push them into mergers with corporate giants having quality blue-chip stocks for tax-free exchanges that avoid the confiscatory capital gains taxes. In this way, entrepreneurism becomes shackled by the bureaucracy that is inherent in bigness.
>
> The supply of future entrepreneurs is also curbed by the reshuffling of incentives that resulted from tax changes. At one time, ambitious employees of large firms had incentive to leave and start up their own businesses. Income taxes on salaries then reached 70 percent, and even 90 percent in the early postwar years; by contrast, 25 percent was the maximum gains tax on their company's growth. However, in recent years while the Federal gains rate was almost doubled, the maximum rate on salaries was reduced to 50 percent. Consequently, under current tax alternatives, there is little incentive to leave the shelter of large companies where in recent years salaries have skyrocketed—over 1,000 executives are now paid a package exceeding $500,000 a year and many get more. Why leave such security to gamble everything, and then if one succeeds, face a capital gains tax about the same percentage?[1]

Government regulation is one of the biggest managerial problems that small business has, yet it is a sector in which security is hard to obtain. Small business advocates uniformly agree that there is a need for the maintenance of environmental quality, occupational safety, and consumer protection. But regulation forces a burden on small business that large corporations can escape. Large firms have a myriad of resources—lawyers, accountants, and a bureaucratic organization—that enable them to absorb the impact of federal regulation. Small firms have none of these advantages. Notes Professor Galbraith:

> All regulatory policy should have categories. And without retreat on regulatory objectives, there should always be consideration of cost and reporting requirements for the small firm. By treating large and small alike, one treats them differently.[2]

Finally, the popular notion that great wealth should not be amassed has resulted in estate tax laws that have meant the end of many family-owned businesses. Again, little distinction is made between billion dollar corporations and firms with assets of $200,000.

People are certainly aware that small business makes a great contribution to American society and is worth preserving for that reason. Some people even appreciate the special virtues of the small family business as well. Small business is the cutting edge of competition, the nation's job creator, the vanguard of innovation and invention, and a source of civic leadership. Given these advantages, the U.S. Congress has taken steps to provide some relief for small business. Graduated corporate income tax has strong support in Congress and may soon be a reality. Government regulations are undergoing close scrutiny with a view to changes that might help the small firm. And, as discussed in Chapter 9, Congress in 1976 completely revised the antiquated estate tax laws to provide relief to small family farms and businesses.

There is still a long way to go, however, because the two things that probably squeeze small business the most—inflation and continuing concentration of economic power—seem to baffle the nation's lawmakers. No one knows how to control inflation, and although there is much talk of enforcing the antitrust laws against giant corporations, there is not much action.

If it is to succeed and survive, family-owned business must be recognized for the strong balancing force that it is in American society, and it must be allowed to continue to provide the country with the positive benefits that have made individual entrepreneurs national legends. Perhaps what we really need is a Family Business Facilitation Index to apply to government. But that is another story.

Notes

[1] *Future of Small Business in America.* A report of the Subcommittee on Antitrust, Consumers, and Employment of the Committee on Small Business, 2d Sess., 1978, pp. 25–26.
[2] Ibid., p. 32.

Index